JOURNEY
TO
NOWHERE

Keith Quinn

JOURNEY TO NOWHERE

**A Personal Diary of the
Rugby World Cup Year**

TRIO
BOOKS

For Maggie and James

"The farther one travels,
the less one knows."

"The Inner Light".
Written and Sung by George Harrison
The Beatles, 1968.

COVER PHOTO: Carlos Spencer and Richie McCaw in despair as the All Blacks bow out of the 2003 Rugby World Cup.   PHOTOSPORT

National Library of New Zealand Cataloguing-in-Publication Data

Quinn, Keith.
Journey to Nowhere: A Personal Diary of the Rugby World Cup Year / Keith Quinn.

ISBN 0-9582455-2-5

1. Quinn, Keith. 2. All Blacks (Rugby team)
3. World Cup (Rugby football)—(2003—Australia)
4. Rugby Union football—New Zealand. I. Title.

796.33365092—dc 22

First published in 2004 by Trio Books Ltd
PO Box 17 021, Karori, Wellington, New Zealand.

Printed by Printlink, Petone, Wellington.

CONTENTS

INTRODUCTION

The idea for a diary of the 2003 Rugby World Cup year came late in 2002 after a meeting I had with Joseph Romanos, the Wellington sports journalist and publisher. We have enjoyed working together on several books in recent years.

We decided on a day-to-day diary of events leading up to and during the World Cup in Australia.

I wrote most days on my laptop, at the various hotels and motels I stayed in during the year, or at airports, or at home, under the working headline "One Man's Rugby World Cup Diary". At the end of the year we added the book's title, "Journey to Nowhere", since the first word was one used most regularly, most notably by coach John Mitchell, when discussing the All Blacks' campaign. I had hoped the book would be called "All Black Triumph" or some such, but it was not to be.

Some of the people I write of are not rugby people at all, but are folks I met during my own journey through the year. It is a personal diary, representing my views of an intriguing rugby year.

While I wrote the book with the approval of my employer, TVNZ, the book does not represent the opinions of TVNZ or anyone else associated with the Rugby World Cup.

I thank TVNZ for allowing me to write the diary in my free time and put it into print.

Each month I submitted, by email, my text to the book's editors, Joseph Romanos and Phil Murray. Even though I sometimes changed my mind over various issues, no alterations were made to the substance of the text once I had submitted my script. Because of this, the book shows how my views on issues evolved during the year. For example, readers will see that I changed my mind greatly on some All Black selections.

Stories came and went during the year; like the Doug Howlett threat to play overseas, the campaign to make Rupeni Caucaunibuca an All Black, the Jonah Lomu saga, in all its twists and turns, and the player World Cup bonuses dispute. That's the way the year was. Some stories arose at the World Cup itself, while others surfaced after the team had arrived home. I have tried to be straight with my opinions and not "beat up" any stories.

Sometimes I have commented about opinions expressed by my media colleagues. I listened to, read and watched programmes about the World Cup from as many sources as I could, because I felt those stories were part of the opinion-making process. Bearing in mind that I have often been on the receiving end of other people's views of my work, I hope my colleagues will not take my comments of their work in bad odour. It's just the old maxim: "I, too, have an opinion."

The 2003 year was a fascinating time for me. I travelled and worked extensively overseas and throughout New Zealand. I was away from home for nearly half of the year. At one point I worked through the SARS virus scare; on another matter I was sent to hospital three times. I became a grandfather again, and a wonderful, close friend passed away. On occasions I stood in the midst of huge crowds, at other times I spent hours on my own behind the closed doors of hotels and motels. I worked with fantastic people, and met some particularly dull people too. But, above all, I travelled to, and worked at, my fifth Rugby World Cup. What a fantastic experience it was. Totally challenging, totally enjoyable.

I have been watching international rugby for close on half a century(!) and broadcasting since the 1960s. During that time I have seen great coaches and players, and some not so great. We saw a bit of both in New Zealand rugby in 2003. In my last diary entry of the year, I have made some personal judgements – what went wrong and why, how things could be improved, what to avoid ... I've given my personal evaluation of some of the key New Zealand rugby figures of 2003, trying to place them in an historical perspective.

There are people I must thank concerning the publication of this book. First, to Trio Books of Wellington, for the courage they showed and the opportunity they gave me to write this book (especially Gael Woods, Joseph Romanos and Phil Murray, for their patience and guidance). Then to the good people at Printlink, especially Lisa Wright, so full of commonsense, who designed the book and made so many helpful suggestions. To my many friends and colleagues at TVNZ, especially the fantastic staff of 50 or so, led by producer Stu Dennison, who worked so diligently and professionally at the World Cup. Also, thanks to Steve Jamieson and Graeme Patrick, who were the "tourism" film crew who travelled to Australia with me in July.

I would also like to thank cartoonists Tom Scott and Jim Hubbard for their excellent and appropriate contributions. Also the various newspapers which provided the dramatic backdrop of headlines throughout the year. A number of photographs were supplied by that outstanding New Zealand agency, *Photosport*, but others which are labelled *Keith Quinn Collection* were taken by myself, as well as Steve Jamieson, Graeme Patrick, John Robertson, Maree Simpson, John McBeth, Alan Barnes, Anne Quinn, Mark Jefferson and Bernadine Oliver-Kerby. The photo of John Davies was kindly supplied by Charles Callis, curator of the museum, The New Zealand Olympic Committee.

Big thanks go to John McBeth, for his local "Wellington" support, and to Peter Marriott, also of Wellington, for his World Cup statistics. Also to Peter Sellers, in Dunedin, who wrote me such newsy letters while I was in Sydney. They were much appreciated. Also to my old friends who have helped, backed up and been on hand this year: Frankie Deges, Chris Thau, Wyn Gruffydd, John Hart, Grant Fox, Willie Lose, Jeff Wilson, Alan Trotter, Cyril Delaney, Mort Thomson, Shirley Waru, Doc Williams, Blair Wingfield, Garry Ward, and Carol and Evan Johnson. And our personal local friends at home from 30 years: the McGuinnesses, Christies, Camerons and Shennans.

A special thought and love goes here too, to Patsy and Ely Davies, of Auckland. They will know what I mean.

Last, but not least, I must pay tribute to my ever-patient family: my wife Anne and our adult kids Rowan, Shelley and Bennett, and Ben's wife Claire; plus grandkids Maggie and James. Without their understanding of my many absences, this diary would never have seen the light of day.

Keith Quinn
January 2004

JANUARY

"The door is always open for others ..."

JANUARY 1

For me, the Rugby World Cup year 2003 starts with a bag packed at home, a 7am rushed taxi ride to the airport, and a flight from Wellington to Auckland. The trip isn't for rugby business, it's to broadcast the ASB Women's Tennis Classic. Nothing wrong with that, I love the tennis. But as the plane takes off I can't help but think of the people like me, all over New Zealand, who will be saying to themselves that, with the arrival of 2003, at last *it* has arrived – the year of the fifth Rugby World Cup.

For most New Zealanders, first thoughts on New Year's Day are not about rugby. In fact, in my copy of today's *The Dominion Post*, the only mention of rugby is a column reflecting on the sad death, three days earlier, of the All Black great of the 1950s and 60s, Don "The Boot" Clarke.

The newspapers today are generally filled with holiday pictures. The majority of Kiwis on New Year's Day will be recovering from a hangover after the previous evening's celebrations, or heading to the beach or the races, getting home in time to watch the Auckland Cup or New Zealand

I've known John Mitchell since well before he became a noted rugby player and coach. Here we're pictured during his time as England's assistant coach.

A lot can change in 11 months, but this is my long-range selection of the All Black team for the World Cup final.

play India in a day-night one-day cricket international. That's the way we are at this time of the year.

As the plane lifts into the sky, my thoughts drift forward to the Rugby World Cup that will begin in just 10 months' time. I suppose I'm different. Call me a committed winter person if you like. You won't catch me spreading out a beach towel anywhere on this planet. My first thoughts in the New Year are about – yes, you guessed it – the once-beautiful game of rugby union.

I reflect first about how close the World Cup is. Only 10 months till kick-off in Sydney. A few months less than that till the announcement of the 30-man All Black team. I start the year with a key question: As of today, who would I like to see run out for the All Blacks when they play in the World Cup final in Sydney on November 22?

Here is my ideal team, assuming everyone will be fit, written on my Air New Zealand boarding pass: Leon MacDonald, Jonah Lomu, Tana Umaga (vice-captain), Doug Howlett, Aaron Mauger, Andrew Merhtens, Danny Lee, Scott Robertson, Marty Holah, Chris Jack, Ali Williams, Reuben Thorne, Greg Somerville, Anton Oliver (captain), Dave Hewett.

Naturally, I reserve the right to change this team depending on the goings-on in 2003.

I think about how the Cup will affect me. That's only natural – a lot of work lies ahead. I'll be directly involved with the commentaries of the World Cup again, as I have been in the other four, from 1987–1999. This year, the World Cup is to be brought to New Zealand viewers via Television New Zealand's coverage. No Sky or TV3 on this one.

There are already a number of World Cup issues to consider. For a start, after excited early planning for 20 or 21 games to be played within our shores, the sub-hosting (or sharing) of the games between New Zealand and Australia collapsed in 2002. Now no games will be played in New Zealand. This is a massive blow. The public perception, and probably most of the media's as well, is that the New Zealand Rugby Union members were a bunch of dunderheads who had little idea about how a major world tournament should be managed.

For 15 years New Zealanders had dreamed of hosting more World Cup games. Let's face it: our country hugely enjoyed the 1987 confirmation that we were the best rugby team in the world. In that year the first World Cup was staged in New Zealand and Australia and the All Blacks beat France by 20 points in the final at Eden Park. We New Zealanders told each other haughtily that we had known for decades that the All Blacks were the best at playing the last great amateur game. It was confirmation of what we had been telling the world for years.

However, since 1987 life had not been as rosy for All Black supporters. In 1991 there was defeat in the semi-finals of the second World Cup, in 1995 the All Blacks lost cruelly in the final after extra time against the Springboks, and in 1999 our team was again beaten in the semi-finals. The realists among us had to face the fact that we were not the best in the world any more.

Of course, not many New Zealanders were heard saying that. To most Kiwis, we are still the world's best. If it hadn't been for several bad bounces, a bout of food-poisoning, and lack of leadership from a coach we loved one year but turned on the next, plus any amount of dodgy refereeing and testicle-grabbing, we would have won all four World Cups played so far!

Instead, Heaven forbid, other countries have greater claims to being the best. There's Australia, our trans-Tasman buddies (with their two Cup wins, in 1991 and 1999), South Africa (who squeaked past our team in 1995), and even England, with their powerful forwards. Could they all start the 2003 World Cup more favoured than the All Blacks?

Then there is the matter of the All Black team itself. In 2002 the test XV, under the new captain, (the very silent) Reuben Thorne, won the Tri

Nations Championship, and that should not be overlooked. Overall in 2002 the All Blacks won eight tests, drew one and lost two.

Though those results looked okay, the New Zealand public fretted about the losses, even though they were both last-minute affairs, to Australia in Sydney and to England at Twickenham. There was also nervousness about the make-up of the All Black team, and at the outward comportment of All Black coach John Mitchell.

He had been swung into power late in 2001, after the collapse in confidence of the previous man in charge, Wayne Smith. Everything started so promisingly for Mitchell that year, as he took his first All Black team on an unbeaten world tour (well, they beat Ireland, Scotland and Argentina). A year later, though, many in the public and the media believed he was doing strange things to the composition of the All Blacks team.

And the way he was speaking, with a Mitchell-rugby-non-speak all his own, became of concern and amusement to many. Martin Devlin's impersonation of Mitchell on Radio Sport was so cruelly funny that I saw several letters in the papers asking Devlin to stop, because it was too real.

As 2002 ended, Mitchell's media interviews were becoming fewer, and a story appeared in several papers saying that in 2003 the All Black coach would not be talking to those in the media he judged to be "negative". Curious behaviour indeed, and worth watching this year.

It seemed to me – and this was from a distance, because I wasn't there – that on the All Blacks' November tour to France, England and Wales, Mitchell was only intermittently available to the media. Robbie Deans, his assistant, undertook much more of the public interviewing tasks.

Having said that, I was requested by two magazines, *Australian Rugby Review* and *Rugby World (UK)*, to preview that All Black tour. I made the usual request to interview Mitchell via the NZRU media office – cap-in-hand is the approach the media must take these days. My first call requesting an interview with Mitchell was on a Wednesday. On the following Tuesday my phone rang at home and it was Mitchell calling me back (apparently I was not to have any of his phone numbers). He chatted from his cellphone while he drove from Dunedin to Invercargill. At least twice we were cut off because he had driven into a dead-zone, but it was an interview in which he gave me some considerable substance. I mention it to indicate how difficult it is these days to gain access to those in power in the All Blacks.

Mitchell's plan, stated several times to me and in other public utterances around that time, was to "widen the base" of those challenging for World Cup selection. To that end he used 45 players in the 11 tests during 2002. This created spirited debate among those who believed that the All Black jersey should still be sacrosanct and awarded only to the best players for each test. "Remember 1966 against the British Lions," said one mate of mine. "We used only 16 players in the whole four-test series."

I've had mixed feelings about Mitchell's long-term thinking on this matter, and that has led to heated debate with friends and colleagues, who accuse me of sitting on the fence. Mitchell believes that if a player goes down hurt at any stage this year, right up till departure for Australia, he will be more easily able to call on a replacement to step into the test arena than if that player had been given no test experience.

So here I am, flying into Auckland, and for my first positive rugby thought of the year I will come off the fence – I think Mitchell is on the right track with his policy. He might be strange, paranoid even, but in the modern world of big-hits rugby, with playing careers being much shorter (another Mitchell theory expounded to me), and the action and pressure more cut-throat, the team that will run on to the field for New Zealand at the World Cup is bound to contain only those survivors of a number of injury crises along the way. As a result of Mitchell's forward thinking, he should have plenty of back-up players.

A final thought from today: in the obituaries for the much-loved D B Clarke, I've read several mentions of Big Don in his time being "like Jonah Lomu is today" in terms of his public profile and the way he was admired. That leads me to wonder how Jonah will be perceived by the New Zealand public in the roller-coaster world that his rugby life has become. At the very least, I hope that, as Don Clarke was, Lomu is treated decently by everyone in the country. And that includes John Mitchell.

JANUARY 5

Big Jonah Lomu has his first public outing in World Cup year today. There he is, sitting under a large umbrella, staying out of the sun at the women's pro tennis tournament in Auckland.

Life doesn't change much for this remarkable New Zealand personality. As he walks into the stadium and takes his seat, a buzz of pointing and whispering and grabbing for binoculars goes around the crowd. And, in the first weekend editions of the papers for the year, there are only three major Jonah stories. There is a front page item in the *Sunday News* about him hitting speeds of 200 kmh at the Meremere drag strip in his Nissan Skyline drag racer. In *The Sunday Star-Times* there is comment about him choosing not to sign his autograph in Tribute. This is the book written by Aucklander Paul Verdon, which is modestly being billed as "the greatest book, of the greatest game, of the greatest team of all". There is also a mention of a multi-million-dollar contract that will apparently be coming Lomu's way from Bristol immediately after the World Cup. More news, more angles, more Lomu speculation. It sells papers. Life does not change for him.

At the tennis, he seems anything but hurried or uncooperative or worried about his rugby future. Looking relaxed and affable, he is readily available to be interviewed by our TV people almost as soon as he sits down. When our young reporter asks him what he hopes to achieve this year, Jonah doesn't mention the World Cup at all, expressing interest in being ready for Hurricanes training, which is to begin next week.

Nothing has changed concerning the public demands and scrutiny on Jonah's life. For him, every day is a day in the public eye. At a women's tennis tournament you might have expected a chance for him to relax. He is dressed in the outfit of an American baseball team, behind sunglasses and with a cap perched precariously on his head. But as he leaves the stands late in the day and heads towards a waiting car, he is spotted instantly. Two young players rush to put aside their rackets and grasp their cameras. When Jonah obliges with a friendly pose, other players from different countries approach and soon it is a scramble of flashing lights and flashing teeth.

Earlier today, I showed my imaginary All Black World Cup final team to a mate. Naturally, being Kiwi blokes we disagreed in a few places. Like, for instance, my preference for Marty Holah over Richie McCaw in the openside flank position. This was preposterous to my friend. I told him that my view was based purely on late-season form – Holah was great in Britain and France, whereas McCaw had looked tired at the end of the domestic season.

Using the same logic, my friend offered Carlos Spencer as first five-eighth over Andrew Mehrtens. I had to partially go along with that thinking. And I said my preference for Anton Oliver as captain depended on his recovery from achilles tendon injury. Otherwise I might even favour Tana Umaga to take the All Blacks into this critical year. Reuben Thorne as captain looks too quiet for me, I said.

We also talked about Taine Randell, who so generously came in at John Mitchell's behest to lead the All Blacks on the late-season tour. For his troubles, Randell was sternly criticised by Mitchell for being "let down by a lack of fitness" on the tour. That was in the Christmas edition of *New Zealand Rugby World*. With candour that would have landed John Hart in a whole heap of trouble, Mitchell also said: 'In 2003 ... Jonah Lomu needs (again) to earn his place on merit. If he can get himself fit, then he is good enough to be in contention for selection."

Does that mean that, despite Lomu having scored two tries and played well against England only weeks earlier, Mitchell is doing again what he did before the 2002 tour, when he said that all the team was selected on merit, "except for Lomu". I always thought it was sound business and sports management technique not to discipline anyone in front of his peers. Not to mention doing it several times in front of the whole country.

JANUARY 6

The first All Black crisis of the year.

I can't believe the stories in the papers today, that star All Black wing Doug Howlett, in a World Cup year, is in serious contract difficulties with the NZRU. Pay talks have apparently stalled at $200,000 per year for the flying Aucklander. Agreement will be reached on this any day. Surely.

Howlett is, quite simply, the All Blacks' best back at the moment, having risen quickly to be a world force. On the surface, and based on his 2002 form, he merits a rise into the top bracket of New Zealand rugby contractees, alongside the likes of Lomu, Mehrtens, and Umaga. On the other hand, if Howlett gets paid super-bucks, no doubt the braying will begin from the knockers over the generosity of the union.

The bottom line is: this problem must be sorted out. In a World Cup year there would be no sadder example of professionalism going awry than if a prominent New Zealand player disappeared from the scene, claiming he wasn't being paid enough.

My first thought is to tell Howlett's agents that if he prefers to shiver for a Scottish or English club on a Wednesday night in November, instead of playing in the Rugby World Cup for his country in Australia, under the sun, in rugby's greatest showpiece, then let him go.

But in my New Year's dream I saw Howlett sprinting in to score a try in the World Cup final and then pictured him standing, as he does, with eyes flashing, with his Hollywood smile, to take the embraces of his team-mates. So I want this sorted out, desperately.

JANUARY 8

Well, the Howlett story does go away. It takes exactly three days. The NZRU and Howlett agree to terms today for a three-year extension to his playing time in New Zealand. Until the end of 2005.

After the discussions end there is "no further comment" by both parties. *The New Zealand Herald* reports today that the agreement will put Howlett into the "lower end" of the top-bracket of pay. That sounds like about $400,000 a year for our Dougie.

Union gets Howlett's signature

Auckland and Blues wing Doug Howlett has signed a new contract with the NZRFU, keeping him in this country until the end of the 2005 season.

Two days of meetings have resolved a long-running dispute which led H...w... ...ntest

Crisis averted.

JANUARY 10

The sponsorship officer at the Heineken Open tennis tournament, Peter Wills, a most genial chap, laments tonight that the loss of the sub-hosting rights to the World Cup means that his New Zealand-based arm of the worldwide Heineken company will lose millions of dollars in revenue from beer sales. Mind you, Heineken will now be supplying four million litres of the stuff to Australia to cope with the thirsty crowds over there during the Cup.

JANUARY 12

A man stops me at the Stanley Street tennis stadium today and offers the first good rugby joke of the year: What's the difference between the modern All Blacks set-up and the Indian rail system? Answer: There are more hangers-on in the All Blacks.

I'm heading home after the two professional tennis tournaments in Auckland. My Wellington cab driver – "Jamesey 1" is his taxi name – says he's worried about the rugby year ahead. "These teams, these coaches, why don't they just give the bloody ball to Jonah?" he asks plaintively.

After what's gone on over the past couple of years, it seems a fair question. I tell Jamesey 1 that the night before in my Auckland hotel I was watching an ESPN Sports programme on the thinking of some great American football coaches. One of them, Marty Schottenheimer, of the Kansas City Chiefs, had a theory. "When a tough touchdown is needed or a key move is required, I always say: 'Let's use our best player and let's use our best move.'"

Jamesey 1 agrees with that logic. We both hope the big man will be used more in every game he plays in this important year.

JANUARY 13

Home again on yet another scorching Wellington summer's day and it's straight back to work on my morning radio piece for Martin Devlin's Radio Sport Breakfast show. It's up at 6am and on to the air, chatting, arguing, and discussing sports events of the day with Devlin after the 7.30am news. It's fun, and challenging, and I've been doing it for five years now.

I mention to Martin that both TV1 and TV3 news last night showed shots of what were called "44 All Black World Cup hopefuls" sweating and straining their way through the first of five fitness sessions John Mitchell has called for top players during the year. The sessions are in addition to whatever practice and training players are doing for their Super 12 teams.

All this and there's still 274 days, or 6576 hours, or 394,560 minutes, or more than 23 million seconds, until the World Cup kicks off on October 10. I'm able to tell Martin the exact timing from a countdown website I have discovered called www.klitch.net. In his usual maniacal manner, Devlin devours the news and shouts about the website all week. I'm almost sorry I gave away my little secret to him.

The location for the All Black hopefuls' training is the Millennium Institute in Mairangi Bay, north of Auckland. The cameras capture a selection of the stars belting their way through 40m sprints. One TV shot shows Tony Woodcock pulling up with what looks like a hamstring twinge. Hopefully it's not the first of many injuries seen this year. And *The New Zealand Herald* runs a 10 x 8 photo of Anton Oliver striving hard in his run, with head back and face distorted. It's great to see "Hatchet" back to full fitness again. Will he get the All Black captaincy back?

Afterwards, Mitchell is interviewed briefly. He seems unsmiling and in no mood for media intrusions. I jot down a couple of his quotes. One: "There are 44 contenders here, but the door is always open for others outside this group [to make the All Blacks this year]."

I'm pleased to hear him say that. Remember Michael Jones coming in from nowhere and being the star of the 1987 World Cup? And Jonah Lomu going to South Africa in 1995 as virtually the last All Black on to the plane?

Mitchell also says that for this year's World Cup he rates England, Australia, France and South Africa as Cup-winning contenders. He never mentions New Zealand. I guess that's taken as read. In my first sighting of him for the year, Mitch has that old-fashioned steely look in his eye.

JANUARY 24

My mate Alan Trotter calls today from Durban. "Trotts" is a great guy. He's an old boy of Hutt Valley High School and a former Rotorua lawyer, international water polo player and coach (for South Africa and New Zealand), and an excellent raconteur. He went to live in South Africa 12 years ago. He's now in the travel business and his company, Touchdown Travel, is a subsidiary company to the Natal Rugby Union, and has secured rights to organise tour groups to the World Cup.

Trotts tells me down the phone: "You think it will be expensive for Kiwis to travel to the World Cup in Australia? How about for South Africans? The way the rand is over here it's a nightmare for the ordinary man to go. As of today, we need 5.23 rand just to get one Aussie dollar to spend over there. In all the recent travel groups I've done, to Britain, Europe and New Zealand, it used to be mainly mum and dad who could travel, but now 80 per cent of our business to the World Cup will come from corporate groups. They're the only ones left who can afford to pay up and send their best clients."

Trotts has an amusing spin on the Springboks' recent on-field woes: "Concerning the Springbok team's hopes of winning, and the value of the rand, we've even had to bring in a travel plan called 'Come Home and Watch the Final'. In this one you pay to go to Australia and watch a couple of South Africa's games, and *maybe* the team will make a semi-final. But after the 53–3 loss to England at Twickenham a few months ago, the fans here are saying the Springboks are unlikely to make the final. Hence our promotion. Our people won't be able to afford to pay to stay and watch two *other* teams battle it out."

Sensational news today. Russia are banned from further involvement in this year's World Cup, which rules out their chance of taking one of the last two places in the finals. The IRB says three South Africans who played for the Russians were not eligible to represent Russia.

To ban Russia from playing in the qualifier against Tunisia in a few days will be devastating to the future of rugby over there. I saw their best players at the Sevens World Cup in 2001 and they have a real flair for the game. In addition, the fine of £75,000 imposed by the IRB might be the death-knell of the game in Russia.

On the face of it, Russia may have a reasonable defence. They say the three players had played in all six previous qualifying games, starting eight months ago, and that they had approval to play them. One British paper is already dubbing the scandal "Babushka-gate".

JANUARY 27

Another sensation – this time a drugs scandal. All this and we haven't reached the end of January! My reaction on hearing that Otago prop Joe McDonnell had returned a positive test for the banned drug salbutamol after a drug test taken before the All Black-France game in Paris last November is: how foolish can one man be? Not only do I wonder at his foolhardiness, but I also wonder at the systems in place within the New Zealand Rugby Union. Did he not know that salbutamol is banned unless players inform officialdom that they have an asthma condition? McDonnell surely must have known it was on the banned list. And as for using another person's inhaler (as was reported), that too is dummage (my newly-invented word) of the highest level.

Apparently the player in question is a nice bloke, but I fear the International Rugby Board might hammer him on this issue. The smear of a drug ban might even cost him a place in the World Cup team. First the Russians, now McDonnell.

JANUARY 28

Patsy Clarke, widow of much-missed All Black fullback Don Clarke, gets it just right in *The New Zealand Herald's* Weekend edition today. Big Don died on December 29, 2002, and there have been several remembrance services for him in New Zealand.

Patsy wrote to the *Herald* to thank all the people around the country who had sent messages of condolence to the family. In her letter she says: "The generous contribution made to the Hamilton Service by Bishop Muru Walters, Sir Howard Morrison and Sir Colin Meads was a wonderful tribute ..."

Sir Colin Meads? It looks good on paper to me. Well said, Mrs Clarke.

It's just a pity the New Zealand Government can't open its strict hold on the laws governing knighthoods and award three more. Sir Colin Means would be one. Sir Peter Snell and Sir John Walker would be the others. Then, in my opinion, the Government could close the law again.

JANUARY 29

I get a fresh insight into All Black selection today. Not of the current era, but of the days of the mighty coach, Fred Allen, in the 1960s. I was chosen as one of five people to form a selection panel for an Australian book publication, *Hard Fought and Fair,* concerning the greatest All Blacks of all time. The selection panel is Sir Terry McLean, David Kirk, Andy Haden, Fred Allen and myself.

We select via a telephone hook-up from Andy's office in Auckland and have a lively hour of to-and-fro. We have to pick a team. We all have strong ideas and express them. The ideas from each of us are all soundly based. I try to hold my own in such august company.

But (and this is a big but) when it comes to the *final* decision as to which great All Black from a span of a century is best suited for each position, Fred Allen, aged 83, has the boomingest presence, the loudest logic, and yes, Fred always has the final say. It is unwritten and unsaid, but to the rest of the panel, Fred is our boss.

I can't help reflecting that, in the All Black selection rooms of the 1960s, when Fred hunkered down in darkened rooms with Les George, Ivan Vodanovich and co, he would have eventually got his way. Over the phone he puts me in my place nicely a few times.

Incidentally, here is our all-time New Zealand team: Bob Scott, John Kirwan, Bryan Williams, Johnny Smith, Bert Cooke, Andrew Mehrtens, Des Connor, Zinzan Brooke, Ian Kirkpatrick, Michael Jones, Colin Meads, Tiny White, Ken Gray, Sean Fitzpatrick and Kevin Skinner. Reserves: Jeff Wilson, Mark Nicholls, Sid Going, Wilson Whineray, Maurice Brownlie, Bruce McLeod.

Detect a Fred influence?

FEBRUARY

"Things Have Changed."

FEBRUARY 9

I enjoy reading Phil Gifford's columns in *The Sunday Star-Times*. They're always lively reading, with plenty of quotes (attributed and otherwise), and there is, 99 per cent of the time, a heavy leaning towards anything to do with red and black. Phil's emphasis on promoting Canterbury rugby people (and, to a lesser extent, Otago's) might be fair enough on the grounds that:

1. Canterbury have been the principal supplier of All Blacks in recent years.
2. The radio station Phil works for, More FM, just happens to go into Canterbury (and Otago), taking his and Simon Barnett's morning radio show.

Nevertheless, as Phil blithely taps away for each Sunday's column, I have a vision of him thinking: "What good things can I say about Canterbury this week?" My image of him is strange, considering all the years Phil lived in Auckland and heavily promoted anything to do with Auckland. I recall interviewing him on television one time when he wore a blue and white scarf.

Don't get me wrong: Phil and I are mates, old sparring partners. We had a drink together at Christmas time and his wife Jan gave me my favourite tie, a stylistic representation in silk of the Beatles.

In his first column of the year, on January 26, Phil tried hard to write about the America's Cup yachting, but gave up halfway through to instead launch into criticism of one "sneering" (but unnamed) commentator who had dared to be scornful of Brad Thorn's decision, 15 months earlier, in November 2001, to turn down playing for the All Blacks after John Mitchell had picked him to tour Ireland, Scotland and Argentina. Thorn just happens to be a transplanted lad to Canterbury, of course.

In column two, on February 2, Phil was heavily committed to promoting Canterbury's All Black players who had been rested from the 2002 end-of-year tour of England, Wales and France. He seemed most irritated about an (unnamed) New Zealand rugby official, who sat next to

That's it, Phil. Start as you mean to go on. Aren't the Crusaders great!

Canterbury flanker Richie McCaw while Richie was resting from the All Blacks but was on holiday in Paris. The official had shouted loudly "11 or 12 times", wrote Phil in indignation, about the brilliance of Marty Holah as the openside flanker in the 20–20 draw against France.

In column three, today, Phil grits his teeth and hammers the keyboards at the rising tide of nationwide discussion about who will be the All Black captain for the World Cup. He seems equally comfortable with Anton Oliver, of Otago, or Reuben Thorne, from Canterbury. (Both are in his radio audience regions.) But Phil then tells a story that I, for one, have never heard, about a great (but, you guessed it, unnamed) All Black of the 1950s rejecting the captaincy because, while being "scared of nothing on the field, he was terrified of making the after-match speeches".

I wish I knew who that great captain was. From Canterbury, perhaps?

I like to read widely. I'll monitor writings this year from all over the place. So I'll look forward to the week when Phil writes a column that leaves out any mention of Crusaders, Cantabs, lambs, Toddy, Rubes, Mehrts, Richie, Justin, Grizz, Fergie, Robbie, Jade Stadium, or Colombo Street. When that happens the rest of us should declare a national holiday, as well as stop being paranoid about how bloody good they are down there at playing rugby. (And having writers – unnamed – who delight in promoting it each week.)

The All Black captaincy is going to be a stimulating discussion point this year. Sitting next to Gifford's column in the February 9 issue of *The Sunday Star-Times* is the result of a poll taken by the Internet website *Planet Rugby,* in which worldwide surfers responded to a question as to who should lead New Zealand at the World Cup. The poll declares Taine Randell the most popular choice. Randell polls 38 per cent, Reuben Thorne secures 25 per cent, and Anton Oliver just 1 per cent.

My preference is still for Oliver to return as captain, after that horrendous achilles tendon tear. I have been impressed by his openness

FINAL FOUR

Thorne back in frame for All Blacks captain

THE race for the All Black captaincy is down to the last four. **By JAMES BELFIELD** England, Wales and France. "Those four have been the ones who have captained place on playing just leadership

Keep Randell as All Black captain say fans

MEMO TO coach John Mitchell: Kiwi rugby fans want Otago and Highlanders' loose forward Taine Randell retained as an All Black captain.

A poll of 750 New Zealanders conducted for the Sunday Star-Times by UMR Research showed 32% wanted the man who led the team to the skipper's job last year to keep the skipper's job.

In a surprising result, only 9% opted for Canterbury's Reuben Thorne, the captain before Randell, but who was rested for the northern tour. It is understood Thorne is still Mitchell's pick for the captaincy.

The public's second pick was the Hurricanes' inspirational midfield back Tana Umaga, who has been having a blinder of a season in the Super 12. Umaga got 25% of the votes, while ex-captain Anton Oliver, an Otago Highlander colleague of Randell's, received 14%.

Randell edges out Umaga as most popular choice mainly because of his support from female fans.

Women favoured him by a 35-23 % margin over Umaga, while among men, Randell was preferred by a much narrower 28-27% margin.

In the 60-plus age group, Randell was the No 1 pick by 36-19% over Umaga.

UMR managing director Stephen Mills said the only chink in Randell's polling numbers was among those who called themselves "very interested" in the game.

They accounted for 30% of those surveyed and 38% of them picked Umaga as number one, compared with 31% for Randell, 19% for Oliver and 11% for Thorne. Of those polled, 19% were unsure of who should be captain, while 1% nominated no one.

Let Tana lead All Blacks

Dwyer backs brilliant Umaga as doubts linger over recent captains

By DUNCAN JOHNSTONE

WORLD CUP winning coach Bob Dwyer believes Tana Umaga has was be All Black captain.

Dwyer reckons Umaga has the att to step up the play

All Black coach John Mitchell has already used option on Ol **A BIT** backs Nic **GRAND MATCH** the Walla- centre Dwyer inside Jones and Allure to comple Hurricanes develop who has respect back and A attack

Oliver the only option for captain

IT'S impossible to know what John Mitchell is thinking while moments of truth in the Super 12 are starting to come thick and — but a les thin

There's the form, or lack of it, by most of his chosen ones of the past year, the Crusaders, and there's the golden run being enjoyed by the Hurricanes — a run that should be extended further against the Waratahs on Friday night.

There's the Blues who are still top of the table even though the Highlanders, in the gutsiest manner possible, showed last Friday night how their playmakers, especially Carlos Spencer, can be closed down.

Everyone has thoughts on who should lead the All Blacks, but few agree.

and authoritative manner, not to mention his aggression as a hooker. Outwardly he is not of the stoic, gruff, Colin Meads way. The players seem to want to play for him. Even though I don't think Anton particularly relishes the media attention, he does give something of quality to the scribblers and scrabblers of the Fourth Estate. That is unlike a recent (but unnamed) Canterbury captain I can think of.

Doing a piece to camera with my good mate John McBeth outside the Wellington Stadium. It's good to be able to report on New Zealand finally winning the Wellington leg of the world sevens circuit.

Wellington wakes slowly today and peeks a bleary eye from under its covers. The party at Westpac Stadium over the past two days watching the IRB World Sevens series was amazing to be part of. Music blaring, hoopla in the grandstands, crazy costumes in the crowds, men and women of a certain age blissfully dancing outrageously, and partying of the wildest kind built up and finally greeted a New Zealand win. It was two days of the best that sevens rugby can offer. Yet there are still those who say: "Sevens does nothing for New Zealand rugby." To me, they are conservatives who can see only heavy-footed forwards, endless scrums, rucks and mauls, and the need for 15-a-side as rugby's only expression. They do not see sevens as a stand-alone sport worthy of respect.

While it was wonderful to see New Zealand win the Wellington leg of the series for the first time, the tournament didn't appear to uncover a new Jonah Lomu or Christian Cullen to star at the World Cup later this year.

FEBRUARY **10**

The Cricket World Cup begins in Cape Town. The opening ceremony is lavish and profligate. It makes me wonder why the first game doesn't just start and allow the South African organisers to save the staging budget of more than 20 million rand. However, there's talk, too, of a spectacular opening ceremony in Sydney before the Rugby World Cup. It takes me back to the late Lew Pryme, when he was chief executive of Auckland Rugby, coming up with an opening ceremony before the first World Cup in New Zealand. Some kids shuffled in carrying flags. There were, of course, marching girls, the puckish John Kendall-Carpenter, of the organising committee, who made the first of several far-too-long speeches, and poor Waka Nathan, the much-loved local ex-All Black, was persuaded to do a lap of honour. As he trudged around in a slightly too-tight All Black jersey, a freezing shower of rain came down. He looked decidedly uncomfortable.

Because Waka worked for Steinlager, the beer sponsors of the Cup, no doubt he would have made his run for free. The marching girls would probably have been given free tickets to the Italy versus New Zealand game that followed, the same would have applied for the flag-bearing children. And Kendall-Carpenter would have leaned back in smugness in the best seat in the grandstand, knowing that the budget for the whole ceremony would have been not millions, but peanuts.

At the Cricket World Cup opener I look for Rudi van Vuuren in the Namibian team's march-past. He is in the unique position of probably playing in two World Cups in the same year. He is a robust fast bowler and has been a more than useful five-eighths and goal-kicker in Namibia's rugby team.

FEBRUARY **12**

Today, the biggest shock story of the year so far blasts across our cosy Down Under sports world. Pushing George W Bush's posturing over Iraq and the tragedy of the crashed Columbia space capsule off the front page of *The New Zealand Herald* is a story of superstar Australian cricketer Shane Warne leaving cricket's World Cup after having tested positive to a banned diuretic drug.

While the *Herald* and *The Press* go big on Warne's plight, *The Dominion Post* surprisingly gives Warne's problems only a smallish sidebar on the back page. This is the cricket equivalent of Jonah Lomu testing positive for a banned substance before the Rugby World Cup. If that happened – and bearing in mind that Jonah's recent break-up with his girlfriend constituted major news – there would not be headlines big enough to cope with the story.

Speaking of which, during the week All Black Joe McDonnell got off his charge of taking a prohibited drug. It, too, made only a small story. Curiously, Peter de Villiers of France, having been dropped from his team after testing positive for cocaine and ecstasy, made a bigger story.

Here's a positive story: Joe Rokocoko, the 20-year-old Fijian wing, has cracked selection in the Blues for the Super 12, having already been a New Zealand Schoolboy, Under-19, Under-21 and sevens representative.

Given what I saw of Joe on the sevens world tour in 2002, I think he should be a "must" selection for John Mitchell's All Blacks this year. It might be a fixation with me, but I believe that New Zealand's team for the Cup must have elements of freshness about it, otherwise it will be the "same old, same old" from our blokes. Mind you, the same principle applies to all countries. Any team, in this video age, that sends an unchanged squad from their previous season's work runs the risk of their previous plays having been well and truly analysed by their rivals' technical therapists.

I present Rokocoko as an infusion of a new-look player – unknown and unseen at the top level. He is very quick and offers very unusual things to rugby, like a unique stop-and-roll running turn. Could he do to the World Cup this year for the All Blacks what Jonah Lomu did in 1995?

FEBRUARY 16

I get up this morning at some ungodly hour and stagger through a quiet house to turn on The Rugby Channel for what I suppose is the unofficial beginning of the run-up to this year's World Cup.

It is the start of the Six Nations Championship in Europe and I watch two matches in a row – England versus France and Wales versus Italy.

Conclusions? The England team is boring – oops, they're a winning team. And the French backs have forgotten how to play with their previous joie de vivre. New Zealand referee Paul Honiss plays a significant role, coming down hard on the French play, but not so strictly on the Poms, so Jonny Wilkinson is able to kick 19 points (including four first-half penalties), the difference between the teams in the end.

The Wales-Italy game is a battle of two New Zealand coaches, and John Kirwan's Italians score a great 29–17 win over Steve Hansen's Welsh. *The New Zealand Herald* spelt "Kirwin's" name wrong in its Monday headline (how soon they forget), although one of its staff said it was an attempt at a play on words. Anyway, there is no doubt which team deserves to win.

The Italians play with great excitement, while the Welsh look stuttering and anxious. Two of the best players for Italy are young Kiwis Matt Phillips, from Northland, and Aaron Persico, from Lower Hutt. Persico was a young lad kicking around the edges of senior play for the famous Petone club before his Italian roots called him overseas. The last time I saw him he was standing at the Hutt Recreation Ground in Lower Hutt, wearing a beanie hat pulled low like hundreds of other kids there, home on holiday and watching the 2002 All Blacks practising. Now, a few months later, he plays a game of sufficient quality to suggest he will make the Italian team that hopes to give New Zealand a tough World Cup opener in Melbourne in October.

Though life looks great for Kirwan at the end of the game, as the TV shows him standing and cheering Italy's win, the local coverage then goes where no TV cameras have gone before. They sneak a lingering look into the defeated Welsh team's dressing room. There the players sit, still and silent. Those who do move can only pick at their bootlaces. In the centre of the room, head down, but stroking his chin deep in thought, is Hansen, gazing intently at the ends of his shoes. His head does not come up in the time the camera stays on the shot. It is probably the first TV insight into the pain of any country's rugby test team in defeat.

After watching the two games, I grab my copy of *The Sunday Star-Times* from the letterbox. In my usual style, I dash to get it in my jarmies. Phil Gifford begins his column today by talking about money issues surrounding the upcoming Super 12 series, but, you guessed it, by the end he had returned to a heavy promotion of his beloved (Canterbury) Crusaders. "Super 12 for the Crusaders has been a dream walking since 1998, building the careers of everybody from players, coaches and officials, to security men and women, flag makers and hot dog vendors." What Phil, no mention of breakfast radio rating hopefuls?

FEBRUARY 17

I can't possibly watch another Six Nations match this weekend, not when all afternoon I watch the thrilling second race of the America's Cup – with Alinghi beating Team New Zealand by just seven seconds – and then most of the night I watch the New Zealand cricket team beat South Africa in the World Cup in Johannesburg. Stephen Fleming, that well-known Wellingtonian, bats like a prince to score 134 not out.

Apparently, while the cricket is on, over at Murrayfield in Edinburgh, the Irish storm all over the park to beat Scotland 36–6. It is the first win by the Irish at Murrayfield for 18 years. The Rugby World Cup signs don't seem too good for the Scots and their Six Nations match with Wales might be a cracker.

FEBRUARY 18

The (Auckland) Blues have announced their first team for the Super 12 series and have named Joe Rokocoko to play on one wing, with Doug Howlett moving to fullback. Rupeni Caucaunibuca will be on the other wing. A top chance for my boy Joe.

I'm in Auckland this week, getting ready for the Halberg Awards on Thursday, and I reckon the news about Joe "Roko" is particularly good. I'm giving him a plug to a lot of my colleagues here, saying: "Joe must be in the All Blacks team for the World Cup." A lot of the Aucks are still saying: "Joe Who?"

FEBRUARY 19

I see Ric Salizzo in the TVNZ offices today. His show, *Sports Café*, has switched from Sky to TV2 this year. I wish him well for the show, which is to start tonight. Ric tells me he has been on the phone to John Kirwan about Italy's weekend game. Says Ric: "I asked JK what he said beforehand to fire up the Italian team. He said he told them, 'Boys, this is the biggest game of your life, but there's bad news. Our bus hasn't arrived at the hotel to take us to the ground'." Apparently the team travelled by urgently-hired mini-buses and even had difficulty getting into Rome's Stadio Flaminio. None of the usual soccer staffers manning the gates recognised the rugby players.

FEBRUARY 20

The Halberg Awards show at the Auckland Showgrounds, a live telecast with 1200 people present, is not exactly a night of triumph for rugby. The only finalists in any category come from The (Canterbury) Crusaders. Their 2002 winning Super 12 team made the final four in the Team category, and coach Robbie Deans was nominated for Coach of the Year.

It is traditional for those nominated to appear in some shape or form at the prestigious show. Like at the Oscars announcements in Hollywood, the TV cameras pan across the nervous faces of the nominees just before the winners are announced. The Crusaders, however, chose not to accept an offer by the organisers to fly Deans or any players from the 2002 team to the dinner. Only team manager Darren Shand and Canterbury Rugby chief executive Hamish Riach attend.

TVNZ offered Deans the opportunity to sit in a studio in Christchurch and be live on screen, waiting for the coaching category result to be announced. Deans, talking to TVNZ via the Crusaders media people, because that's the way it works these days, chose not to take that option. As a final fallback option, TVNZ then offered the Crusaders media people the option of having Deans go into the studio any time during the afternoon before the dinner to have a recorded shot of Robbie taken, which would look as though he was in the studio waiting for the

Always working, even while grabbing a quick bite to eat!

announcement. But the Crusaders wouldn't even go with that.

All other nominees in every category make the effort to be present at the dinner, the exceptions being those who are overseas, or unavailable owing to a clash of functions. Barbara Kendall, for example, is committed to an America's Cup event, but comes out on to the deck of a yacht on a chilly evening to wait for her announcement.

The Crusaders' reasons for their no-show in their two nominated categories are that they have a match coming up two days after the dinner and cannot come out of their "camp".

Make of that what you will.

For me, the rugby highlight of the night is Bronwyn Fitzpatrick accepting induction into the New Zealand Sports Hall of Fame on behalf of her husband, Sean. Bronwyn delivers a speech of thanks for Sean, who is in Sydney as the Blues team manager, and does a great job. It shouldn't be a surprise – Bronwyn is a highly-accomplished person, and her speech is the kind of response that is rarely heard from male rugby types. Genuine and appropriate in every way, it is a lesson to the "gee-whizz, aw shucks, our-fellas-your-fellas" stuff heard so often from rugby men.

The Super 12 rugby series begins tonight, with two games involving New Zealand teams. It is ridiculously early to begin, but there is a lot to get through this year.

In keeping with a slow build-up to the season (well, this is my excuse), I do not watch the opening games live. Instead, with our friends Spencer and Diane Logan, the Quinns attend a concert at Victoria University for a Kiwi-Irish band, Grada. It is a great show, and enjoying it three rows in front of me is none other than former All Black captain Graham Mourie and his family. I speak to him during the concert's half-time break and he looks relaxed and free from the hassle of coaching the frustrating Hurricanes, or the Wellington representative team. Although he is an NZRU board member, Mourie says the past six months have been marvellous, a real chance to catch up with family matters. (He also says his interest in Irish music dates from his visit to Cork in the days before the famous match against Munster in 1978.)

Getting home about midnight, Anne slips off to bed and I spin the video back and start replaying the Chiefs versus Highlanders fixture in

The find of the Super 12.

Hamilton. I mean, a bloke has to do what a bloke has to do. Rugby comes before a cuddle, right?

One player to catch my eye is (current) All Black captain Taine Randell. He is sharp and aggressive, and, playing in front of John Mitchell, is surely making some kind of statement.

Then it is the Blues against the Waratahs. Despite the terribly wet and treacherous conditions, this is a better game, but only just. The ball is extremely slippery and many passes go to the floor. Through the mire, three Blues players shine – stand-in first five-eighth Orene Ai'i, who shows some superb touches and is named Man of the Match, and the two wings, Rupeni Caucaunibuca and – you guessed it – Joe Rokocoko, who scores a memorable try. There is a reverse pass from Ai'i and Joe cuts through the flailing Waratahs defenders to swallow-dive in under the posts.

Rupeni is a Fijian international and joins a wonderful list of potential World Cup wings who will be available for that country's coach, Mac McCallion, to choose from. How's this for a list of Fijian wing hopefuls: Rupeni, Filimoni Delasau (playing in France), Norman Ligairi (ex-Southland, then Harlequins in London), Aisea Tuilevu (Highlanders), Iliesa Tanivula and Fero Lasagavibau (both in the Blues second XV) and Marika Vunibaka (Crusaders). How does Fiji grow these guys?

FEBRUARY 22

Tonight the Hurricanes debut against the champion Crusaders. The Crusaders are far from their best but win 37–21. Their first five-eighth for the game is Daniel Carter, who looks an excellent prospect. Andrew Mehrtens is in the reserves. Is there any reason for this? It is hard to gauge, given that one has to go through various media levels to find out anything about any team these days.

Still, Mehrts does come into the game quite early, as Nathan Mauger limps off. The formerly baby-faced Mehrtens, now looking well into rugby midlife, is sporting an impressive summer growth of side-burns. He plays well enough and kicks some significant goals, but I reckon this is a season when he might be under pressure. Maybe he'll play better under the rising demands of being a key points-gatherer and tactical dictator. In recent tests, he has made too many mistakes to be considered the old

Nice side-burns ... but what about his form?

Mehrts of total dependability. Still, he kicks the critical goals and we know that goal-kicking will be vital to win the Super 12 and the World Cup.

The Hurricanes' best players are the two young locks, Kristian Ormsby and Luke Andrews. They more than hold their own against their highly-respected opponent Chris Jack, who is paired with the returned-from-the-wilderness Brad Thorn. Crusaders flanker and captain Reuben Thorne is hardly seen.

I hope my feelings about the Crusaders' no-show for the Halberg Awards does not affect my view that their players look a trifle too spiffy against the Hurricanes. Mehrtens has the long side-burns, Justin Marshall has a pair of Mr Spock *Star Trek* needle-side-burns, the forwards have more tape around their legs than you would see at a Gulf War hospital, and players like Scott Robertson and Aaron Mauger can often be seen looking up at the giant TV screen to check their appearance. Mark Hammett's superior attitude allows the opposition a try. At a Hurricanes lineout throw-in, he is so busy complaining to the touch judge about something that he misses his young opposite, Joe Ward, crashing past him for a try.

FEBRUARY 23

In the nicely revamped *Sunday Star-Times* today, it takes Phil Gifford three paragraphs (of 14) to mention the Crusaders.

FEBRUARY 24

Another weekend of Six Nations play. Scotland are awful, losing to France in Paris, and Italy cannot continue their good form, losing to Ireland at home. In the 5.30am game the Cardiff crowd give their team a rousing welcome home. Half-an-hour before kick-off against England, a Welsh male-voice choir is assembled on the middle of the field. As they launch into rousing Welsh songs, "Cwm Rhondda", "We'll Keep a Welcome", "Sospan Fach" and even "Delilah", the new Welsh captain, David Humphreys, runs the Welsh team round and round the field in a tight huddle. You can see the 34-year-old recalled skipper exhorting his team to use the cheers and passion from the 75,000 fans to raise their game against the auld enemy.

In my days as a touring TV commentator, I had been in that throng many times, but repetition never dulls the experience. Wonderful, wonderful Cardiff, where the singing can bring tears to your eyes. The pre-game plan to use the singing as motivation works. Wales are a different team from a week earlier. Sure, England beat them 26–9, but what a change – Wales are a competitive outfit. Again one is left wondering if England are as good as their headline writers claim. They are not totally convincing.

Bob Dylan is in town tonight and plays a great concert at Queens Wharf Events Centre. As a tribute to the local Super 12 team, I thought he might have considered playing "This is the Story of the Hurricanes", but alas, he doesn't. However, when he launches into one song that I feel is appropriate, I look along the row of seats I'm in, trying to catch the eye of the new chairman of the New Zealand Rugby Union, Jock Hobbs. The song is a kind of anthem by which New Zealand rugby might live in the Hobbs era. "Things Have Changed" is the noisy, boisterous message that Dylan belts out.

FEBRUARY **26**

Eroni Clarke signals today that he is going to Japan to continue his professional rugby career. Sad, but inevitable, I guess. Eroni won't be a candidate for the World Cup this year and a lucrative offshore contract for a couple of years is a nice way for him to wind down his playing days. He'll be remembered as one of the game's nicest blokes.

My favourite memory of him is on that terrible day when he snapped his achilles tendon while playing at Carisbrook. We in the media rushed around the ground after the game to check on his condition. It was a significant news story. Officials at Carisbrook frowned on our approach to the First Aid room door. But it was part-open and through it we could see Eroni lying there, leg in the air, already heavily encased in bandages. His season was over, and in that moment – who could tell? – maybe his career. But he motioned the officials away and signalled for us to come in. So John McBeth and I entered the tiny room. Before we could find appropriate words for what must have been a devastating situation for him, Eroni sat up, and said: "G'day boys. How are you? Keith, how's your family?" I still shake my head about that moment. What a splendid person Eroni Clarke is. Good luck to him.

MARCH

MARCH 1

There is a wonderful blur this weekend. For 24 hours from Friday night a man (like me) is "forced" to watch four Super 12 matches in a row ("You don't understand, darling. Watching these games is *research* for the World Cup.").

After two rounds of the competition, there have been notable aspects that might have a bearing on the selection of the All Blacks.

First, to see Troy Flavell's foot come squashing down on the face of Greg Smith six minutes into the Blues versus Chiefs game in Hamilton brings a holler from me, to no-one in particular, of: "He's got to go!"

Smith is bloodied and concussed by the flying boot and is led to the sideline, looking bewildered. The referee, Paddy O'Brien, thankfully does not refer the matter to the television referee upstairs. Instead, he goes to his closest touch judge, Kevin Rowe, who informs him of the horror of what he has seen. O'Brien, who had been obscured from the incident, is heard to say: "What you're telling me is a red card offence?" "Yes," Rowe replies emphatically. At that, Paddy turns on his heel and summons Flavell and Blues captain Xavier Rush. A brief word and then O'Brien's hand dips into his pocket and a red card is pulled out. Flavell is dispatched.

It is the correct decision for a horror foul. The image of blood dripping down Smith's face is not one rugby needs this year. It crosses my mind that the incident took place at almost the same place on the same field where Richard Loe delivered his never-to-be-forgotten eye-gouge on Greg Cooper in the 1992 NPC final. Flavell will have a blemish against him for life. That's the way it is in New Zealand.

That the Blues still win, 30–27, with 14 against 15 for most of the match, will leave the Chiefs deeply embarrassed.

The next day at Napier the Hurricanes have their moments, scoring four tries, but are well-beaten, 46–34, by the Bulls, who thus record their first win in New Zealand.

Several aspects give food for thought. The Bulls forwards are so monstrous, and have such scrummaging power, that their tactical approach could be used by the Springboks later in the year. Why not? It's simple and suits Springbok thinking. Two superb inside backs, Joost van der Westhuizen and Louis Koen, backed up by the big pack. Between them, they thump the ball downfield or between the posts with great regularity (Koen now has 55 points from two Super 12 games). I'm left wondering what Rudolph Straeuli, the Springbok coach, would have been thinking.

Another disturbing thing about the Hurricanes game is the sight of Christian Cullen being outrun a number of times. He seems well short of the speed he once had. Maybe the knee problems he had will prevent him from regaining the pace and elusiveness that once dazzled the rugby world.

Then, with my TV attention span fading, I attempt to sit through the Crusaders ruthlessly casting aside a challenge from the Reds of Queensland. Brad Thorn's play catches my eye. He looks good, playing at lock against his old Aussie mates. It could be that the controversy of 2001, when he turned down touring with the All Blacks, will be forgotten and he will make the New Zealand team for the World Cup. With Flavell blotting his copybook and Thorn playing superbly, maybe this weekend marks the changing of the guard with regard to selection of a utility second rower.

MARCH 2

No need to tell you which Super 12 team is mentioned in the headline for Phil Gifford's column today in *The Sunday Star-Times*.

Later today, the Swiss crew Alinghi sails away to victory in race five of the America's Cup and Team New Zealand's hopes of retaining the ornate piece of Victorian silverware, which has been bolted to the floor of the Royal New Zealand Yacht Squadron's clubhouse, are gone. The Cup is to be presented to Russell Coutts. For those who live in Auckland, the holding of the Cup for eight years has been a fabulous era.

When I see Dean Barker, a downcast figure sitting on the deck of his beaten boat as it sails past sympathetic crowds cheering and waving "Loyal" flags, I have a vision of the 1999 All Blacks arriving home in dribs and drabs from their unsuccessful World Cup campaign in Britain.

No-one cheered the All Blacks. They were abused, especially coach John Hart. But four years later, the yachting campaign brought sympathy from the New Zealand public. How did that happen?

I predict that if the All Blacks don't win the World Cup they, and their coaching staff especially, will be rubbished from pillar to post when they return home.

MARCH 3

Troy Flavell goes to the NZRU judiciary tonight in Wellington and is suspended for three months. He is shown on TV3's News being driven away in a fast car, with newspaper cameras flashing. His hurried departure looks like a scene from an Old Bailey trial.

The decision is about right. It's corny to say, but "if you do the crime you do the time". Flavell's World Cup hopes will probably be dashed as a result. I can't understand Auckland chief executive David White, Blues manager Sean Fitzpatrick, and coach Peter Sloane – three sensible blokes – almost defending Flavell's actions. Why wouldn't someone in charge of the Auckland team, at a time like this, clearly say: "Yep, we know he's done wrong for himself and the game. We agree he had to be suspended and we apologise to Greg Smith." Instead, at times like this, and I've heard it a hundred times before, team officials seem duty-bound to defend their man.

MARCH 4

A big planning day for TVNZ's World Cup coverage. Schedules are released from producer Stu Dennison's office showing which commentators will be doing each game across the four broadcasting organisations that have the Down Under TV rights. The list of broadcasts has to be released with eight separate listings of time differences, between Greenwich Mean Time, daylight saving, summer time, the various Australian States and good old New Zealand. Most games will be in a perfect medium-to-late time zone in the evenings in New Zealand. Those of us involved in the rugby planning in the TVNZ sports office are secretly hoping the World Cup ratings will blow away the ratings the America's Cup contests recently delivered.

For me, there is a list of 23 games to be broadcast over the six weeks of the tournament. It's going to be tough on the tonsils but extremely exciting. John McBeth will front all the programmes from our Sydney Studio. Secret negotiations for commentary assistance have begun with people like Grant Fox and Jeff Wilson. We're hoping both will come on board. It was surprising that one of Sky TV's highest-profile New Zealand commentators rang one day to offer himself for the World Cup as an expert co-commentator. His interest was politely declined. As I said to him: "With no disrespect, we want to make this World Cup look like a TVNZ show."

Having said that I'm delighted to hear today from my old touring production colleague, Gavin Service. We did many a mile together in the old days before he went to Sky to continue his career as a rugby and cricket director. Now he tells me he has been offered a contract to direct a number of telecasts from the World Cup. Well done, Gav, a feather in your cap.

MARCH 5

At last there are signs of contrition from the Blues over the Flavell incident. On Radio Sport this morning, Peter Sloane has the grace to describe Flavell's actions as "silly". There is also distance created by David White. Says White: "If Troy wants to appeal, he'll be doing it on his own." Fair enough. But why not an apology even before Troy went to the judiciary? It might have helped.

MARCH 6

A curious remark by Murray Deaker on his Newstalk ZB radio show tonight. I can't quote him precisely, but it is along the lines of: "I don't entirely go along with the belief that when Auckland rugby is strong, New Zealand rugby is strong. I prefer to say that when Auckland rugby *and* Canterbury rugby is strong, New Zealand rugby is strong."

Well, that is a deep, reflective observation about our national game, Murray. With 27 of the 55 All Blacks so far used by John Mitchell in his time as coach coming from those two provinces, I'd say you've summed up New Zealand rugby pretty soundly.

And a late announcement today: Flavell has decided not to appeal his suspension.

MARCH 7

Off to a family wedding on Waiheke Island, there is an early crisis. As the Quinn and Kearney families gather to celebrate the nuptials of Heath Quinn to Stephanie Haugh, there is the grim discovery that there is no Sky TV in our motel unit. Nice view, nice beach and all that, but no capacity to watch the Hurricanes play the Stormers in Wellington.

No worries, though ... somebody discovers there is a big-screen TV available at the Waiheke RSA. What better place than an RSA for the arriving families to congregate before a wedding? Perfect, I'd say.

But at my first trip to the bar, an old bloke steps up, hauls back and gives me a solid punch on the arm. "Why did you do that to me, sir?" I ask him, taken aback.

"Because," he says through a wrinkly squint, "I don't like you and never have." He hobbles back to his mates, no doubt to regale them with the story of how he dropped that bloke who has been talking rubbish on TV for years.

Things get better. The rest of the greeting on the island, and at the RSA, is warm. The Hurricanes win well, the fish and chips served from the RSA canteen are world class and the wedding weekend is great. As I fly home a few days later, a young woman I've never met before, wearing a red jacket, taps me on the arm at Wellington Airport and congratulates me for all the good work I've done on TV over the years. I decide to remember her name – Tanya Saunders – and put it in these pages to remind me that not all New Zealanders are like the squinty old digger on Waiheke Island.

The disturbing feature of the weekend is Jonah Lomu's performance. He has his first start this season for the Hurricanes, but, playing against modest Stormers opposition, looks lethargic and out of sorts. Coach Colin

Cooper subs him off after 52 minutes. The rumblings about Jonah's All Black future are growing louder.

MARCH 10

Because of marital goings-on, it's not possible to see coverage of any of the other Super 12 games. So I try to catch up with the highlights on TV newscasts over the next few days. The result of the Blues' win, 39–5 over the Crusaders at Albany, had been whispered around the wedding reception. Seeing the game on TV a few days later, it certainly was an awesome victory for the Aucklanders. The game included more brilliance from the flying Rupeni Caucaunibuca. Another try to him from a searing run.

Rupeni Caucaunibuca ... he's going to the World Cup, but who will he play for?

As well, Carlos Spencer's control and virtuosity in the first five-eighth jersey was a joy to watch. Now the pundits and talkback callers are proclaiming him as the front-runner for the All Black test spot. On current form, stretching back to last season, this is hard to argue against. But under the heading of fairness, the talent of Andrew Mehrtens has not been sighted to any extent this season, because Daniel Carter has been preferred so far by Crusaders coach Robbie Deans. And Mehrts has been injured, too. Or so they say. There is a whisper doing the rounds, and it was touched on a few days ago in *The New Zealand Herald*, that there is conflict between Mehrtens and Deans.

MARCH 11

On the Sky TV show *Reunion* tonight, panellist Murray Mexted announces, in a semi-light-hearted way, that he'd "like to see the NZRU change the rules somehow to get Rupeni Caucaunibuca into the All Blacks for the World Cup".

No chance, Murray. Rules are rules. Steve Devine's appearance in an Australian sevens team a few years ago was deemed to be not official enough to warrant his expulsion from the 2002 All Blacks, but Rupeni has played over parts of two seasons with the Fiji team on the sevens world circuit. So there is no loophole to use. And anyway, we are New Zealand, Fiji is Fiji. There's no need for New Zealand to bully the Fijians. Rupeni is their jewel. Fiji need all the players they can get for the World Cup.

MARCH 12

I wake this morning to news that Australia have thumped New Zealand in the Cricket World Cup. Not a good start to the day.

At lunchtime it's more interesting. I go to the new waterfront offices of the NZRU to meet new chief executive Chris Moller. My presence there is part of his plan to touch base with "significant" people in New Zealand rugby. Kind of a personal induction course he is running for himself. As a man new to the high echelons of rugby politics, he is seeking opinions on how the game is run in New Zealand.

We chat over coffee in his office, and an image flits through my mind of the many photographs you see of visitors to the White House chatting with the President. Alas, there is no camera there to capture the moment for me.

Chris seems personable and is expressive about his hopes for the game in New Zealand. He seems to listen with interest when I talk of my personal fascination over the IRB's global expansion policy in the past few years and how it has been good for the game. I wander over my approval of the work done in that regard by Vernon Pugh as the board's chairman. I take the opportunity to stand on another of my soapboxes and declare it is "a disgrace" that the All Blacks have never played a test match in Apia, Samoa. I express concern that expectations of the All Blacks winning every test they play is out of control with the New Zealand public. And I declare that I cannot abide those New Zealanders who view Polynesians as the weakness of our rugby game. "They are *not* Chris," I say. "They are our bloody strength." We agree on that point.

As the discussion winds up, I add: "How're you going to feel when people like me in the media have to get stuck into you blokes in the NZRU for things we believe you've done wrong?"

"No problem," he replies with an upward spreading of the hands. "As long as you play the ball, not the man, I'll be okay with it."

MARCH 13

Stu Dennison, TVNZ's rugby producer for the World Cup, continues to be hard at it with his colleagues in Channel 7 in Sydney and MNet in South Africa. Today they add the exact commentary schedules from seven separate commentary groups from three countries. I now know exactly which games I'm to do. Among my broadcasts will be All Black games, plus the Wallabies and Springboks. But the World Cup is all about being thoroughly prepared for every team, like Georgia versus Uruguay, which I will call on the world feed out of Sydney on October 28, and Romania versus Namibia 48 hours later. Already some of my files for each of the 20 competing countries are starting to bulge impressively.

With nearly four games per week to do, I must make sure my fitness is okay. My sleeping patterns in Australia must be established early. I will arrange to make a little sign to dangle around key places in my hotel room with the words: "Go to bed early, you are *not* the spring chicken you once were."

MARCH 14

A curious reaction today to the announcement from *The Daily Telegraph* in London that the IRB is planning to have bonus points awarded for World Cup pool matches. (An extra competition point for a winning or losing team scoring four tries in any game, or a losing team securing a point for being within sevens points of the winner's total.)

The announcement hits the news at 7am in New Zealand, just as I am wondering what to say to Martin Devlin in my morning Radio Sport comment slot. I'm able then to opine that the bonus points idea is a good one and will more clearly identify the top two teams in any group of the pool competition. Good point, Keith, I think.

Then I have to hold my telephone back from my ear as dear old Marty launches into a total condemnation of the idea. I chip back that: "I never heard you complain about the bonus points system in the eight years of Super 12 series or NPC, Martin."

Devlin thunders, as only he can, that he's never been in favour of bonus points. "It's a namby-pamby way of losing teams being honoured."

Later, another of his correspondents, "Councillor" John Morrison, the former test cricketer, claims that any more of losing teams getting bonuses and "soon the losers will be getting more than the winners".

Morrison's is a funny comment, but I stick by my original point. Bonus points in the various competitions in the SANZAR countries have made for many a thrilling contest. Interest is maintained throughout, and sometimes at the end of a game *both* teams are striving for bonus points. Why not carry this into the World Cup? And let me say this: bonus points are not as silly as finishing the final of the soccer World Cup with a penalty shoot-out.

MARCH 15

Bernie Fraser rings up today seeking Peter Bush's phone number. It's good to hear from such an excellent rugby bloke. I ask the 1979–85 All

Black wing if he is happy with the way things are looking with the boys.

"Look mate," he replies, "that Sam Tuitupou (Blues second five-eighth) has got to be the toughest midfield tackler I've ever seen. And, by the way, I reckon we'll win the bloody Cup."

MARCH 16

Another weekend of Super 12 competition is over and the Blues, who had a bye this weekend, are still on the top of the table. Funny that. All the other teams seem to be able to beat each other at the moment. For those of us who live in the lower half of the North Island, the return to a "sequence" of wins by the Hurricanes is pleasing. Sequence of wins? Well, two wins in a row.

But the best part of the Hurricanes' 35–20 win over the Sharks in Durban is the return to form of Christian Cullen. He scores two tries, makes another for his wing Lome Fa'atau, and pulls off two stunning try-saving tackles. His pace still looks short of what it once was. And his face still looks taciturn, to the point of unease, in the TV close-ups, but overall he seems to have adopted a different playing persona.

Jonah Lomu was dropped by coach Colin Cooper from the starting line-up for this game. But Jonah, labelled simply "the big fella" by the South African TV commentators, comes on with 20 minutes left. Nothing, in terms of a running chance, comes his way, so once more he is left languishing on the edge of the game. Once more talkback callers cruelly pinpoint his decline, with rising resentment.

In the Hurricanes everyone raves about Tana Umaga's role in the midfield play, and many favourable comments are made about the rise of Ma'a Nonu at centre. Nonu has certainly been impressive, but, to my mind, the two midfielders cut back inside far too often. Admittedly things are awfully crowded by the time the ball gets to them, but too often the Hurricanes wings do not receive any running chances. Compare that to the headlines Rupeni Caucaunibuca and Joe Rokocoko are getting for Auckland. They are getting many scoring opportunities in every game.

MARCH 17

The results are through from two more World Cup qualifying matches. In Seoul, Tonga travel well and beat the home team 75–0. One shudders to think what the result might be in Nuku'alofa in the return match next week. And in Valence d'Agen, France, Spain beat Tunisia 33–16 in a one-off qualifier. The Spanish Lions will next play a home and away series against the United States in April. My pick is Spain to beat US, which means Tonga will go into New Zealand's pool at the World Cup, while Spain (or the US) will be in the pool headed by France and Scotland.

John Mitchell makes a rare public appearance tonight, on *Deaker on Sport* on Sky TV. I don't see it, but apparently he outlines his hopes for the future and looks calm and composed. A scoop for Deaks.

MARCH 18

Look what you started, Murray Mexted.

This push to have Rupeni Caucaunibuca included in the All Black squad for the Cup is bringing dishonour to New Zealand rugby thinkers who should know better. Rupeni didn't even play last weekend, yet the papers and media are full of it, calling for the New Zealand union to push for a change in the rules.

MARCH 19

Up and back to Auckland for the day to appear on *The Press Box* on Sky TV. Sure enough, one of the subjects for debate among the eminent panel of Tony Smith *(The Press)*, Wynne Gray *(The New Zealand Herald)*, Duncan Johnstone (*The Sunday Star-Times*) and yours truly (strangely captioned on the show as *TVNZ Guru*) is the availability of Rupeni Caucaunibuca for the All Blacks.

This is based on Murray Mexted's *Reunion* show comment the previous week. Then we had Peter Sloane, the Blues coach, quoted in the *Sunday News* saying: "I'm sure the New Zealand public would be very happy if Rupeni was available to play on one wing for the All Blacks this year." Following that we had Monday's *The Dominion Post* in Wellington including this line: "The New Zealand Rugby Union has to do something to make sure this lad is wearing black for the World Cup."

Everyone on the panel agrees the discussion is going nowhere, as rules are rules. Yet this rugby niggle still has legs, as they say. For the public, and some of the media, it will not go away.

MARCH 20

A very sad day. Not merely because I have an appointment to see Earle Kirton, the former All Black, who is my dentist, but because American George W Bush declares war on Iraq this afternoon.

I travel into town by rail and as the train sweeps out from the motorway underpass at Petone and the glorious harbour comes into view, I can't help thinking: why would people want to drop bombs on each other? The harbour is like a millpond. The world is such a beautiful place. In the train are a couple of schoolgirls giggling, a baby cradled in her mother's arms and a serious bloke reading a book. We are ordinary travellers going about our business. How are ordinary travellers going to cope in Baghdad in the coming weeks?

George Bush appears on TV at 1pm and, watching in the TVNZ newsroom, I see him, looking like a possum with his eyes caught in the headlights, declare that his troops will attack on land, sea and air as of now. Having Earle drill the living shite out of one of my teeth today is a way better feeling than the one I have watching Bush have his say.

I lie in "Ernie's" dentist chair, giving him a damned good listening to on the much more interesting subject of rugby. He speaks of the confidence he, too, has, from a distance of six months, in the All Blacks winning the World Cup. "At last," he says from behind his mask, but with eyes flashing, "Auckland are spinning the ball [in the Super 12] and we're no longer winning by playing 'Canberra rugby'."

This tough, defensive way of playing – as adopted by the Canberra Raiders rugby league team and the Brumbies, and bettered by the Crusaders in winning their consecutive Super 12 titles, does not go down well with a committed backline coach like Kirton. Hence his delight that the Blues outer backs, men like (whoops, his name again) Rupeni Caucaunibuca, are getting deep running ball in space this season.

"If Mitch gets our guys to play like that, with 'gas' [Earle's favourite expression], we'll win the bloody thing."

Coming up for air, I ask Earle about Mehrtens and Lomu. Then I settle back while "The Mask" launches into another dissertation of his private rugby theory. His young nurse looks patiently into the middle distance. I get the impression she has heard this many times before.

"By God, someone in the Hurricanes and the All Blacks should be looking after Jonah better. His coaches – they all rubbish him in public now – giving all the quotes about how unfit Jonah is. Why don't they look after the lad? Inside big Jonah there's a soft, quiet, shy, Polynesian boy, you know.

"As for Mehrts, he ran the blind when I coached him in the All Blacks. He bloody well had to. Otherwise Laurie and I would give him a kick up the arse. Now he's lost confidence in doing it and Carlos has got the jump on him this season. Mind you, Mehrts'll be back. He so bright, you know."

I leave the surgery with a throbbing jaw, and a head full of wisdom (none of it having come from the White House) and stagger home. It helps when men who *do* know about rugby confirm what you feel.

MARCH 21

A sobering day. TVNZ has put me on stand-down from flying to Hong Kong and Beijing for the big sevens events over the next fortnight. Because of the war, and the outbreak of an untreatable strain of pneumonia, there is an edict out from upstairs along the lines of: "Only for essential work are staff members permitted to fly overseas."

"Gee, I'm no hero," I tell TVNZ Sport boss Denis Harvey when he rings me with the news.

If I don't go it will be disappointing for one significant reason. Our daughter, Shelley, an English-language teacher in Seoul these days, was going to meet me in Beijing in the second week of the fortnight trip. If we don't get that quality time together we'll both be grumpy. (That's a family joke. My nickname at home is Grumpy. Can't imagine why.)

MARCH 22

Settling into a weekend of sports watching (and war watching on the amazing TV coverage from Iraq). My first game is Blues versus Reds in Whangarei. The score, 62–20, reflects another sparkling effort by the Blues. The next night I'm up at 1am to nervously watch a couple of games. The Hurricanes against the Cats in Bloemfontein is controversial, with several incidents overshadowing a game of a much higher standard of running and skill than the Ireland-Wales game earlier.

Ireland beat the Welsh 25–24 to continue a sequence of winning every away game in Cardiff (or once at Wembley) since 1983, 10 in all. Several times the TV coverage cuts to the Welsh coach Steve Hansen sitting in the stands, and one time he put up his thumb as if a win was coming. Alas for Hansen, the New Zealander, it did not and his record with Wales since taking over from Graham Henry in the equivalent match last year now reads: played 14, won four, lost 10.

MARCH 23

An amazing day. After having written as usual about the Crusaders in his last two columns, "Crusader Phil Gifford" devotes his entire *Sunday Star-Times* column to Taine Randell's outburst against the South African judiciary. His column is good, strong stuff, but then again, his radio station does get heard in Dunedin, doesn't it?

The significant World Cup news today is that Tonga made it as the 19th qualifying nation for the finals. At home, in familiar conditions in Nuku'alofa, they beat Korea in the return match 119–0, for a two-game winning margin of 194–0.

Tuilevu penalty a disgrace – Randell

Much as I admire Taine Randell, I feel he's out of line with his comments.

MARCH 24

Another visit to the dentist. This time Earle Kirton tells me that the best halfback in the country this season is currently David Gibson of the Blues. "But Earle, he isn't even the Auckland No 1," I say through a mouth full of dental equipment. "Well, he should be," replies the man from behind the mask. "He's the best passer of the ball in the country, and if we're going to win the World Cup, we've got to spin it." Again, the pretty nurse gazes with serenity and amusement.

The day peaks at 5.15pm with a call from Denis Harvey from the TVNZ office in Auckland. "Keith, keep your bags packed," he says. "You're cleared to fly to the Hong Kong Sevens."

MARCH 25

Up early and off to Hong Kong for the IRB sevens tournament. Arrive late in the afternoon to meet fellow tournament commentators and production crew – Steve Jamieson (New Zealand), Max Heddy and Nigel Starmer-Smith (England) and Wyn Gruffydd (Wales).

Our optimism for a typically great weekend is immediately thrown into doubt by the sight of Gordon Tietjens greeting us with his hand across his mouth. That kind of lighthearted reaction belies the seriousness of concern about the mystery SARS (Severe Acute Respiratory Syndrome) virus racing across Asia. As we arrive at the Marco Polo Hotel, 316 cases of the virus have been detected in Hong Kong and 10 people have died. There is no known cure.

MARCH 27

The situation is now very serious. With all 24 sevens teams present, the day begins with the story that a huge International Banking Conference in the city has been cancelled because of health concerns. More serious to the many tourists who were going to combine a weekend of rock and roll and rugby is the cancellation of two Rolling Stones concerts.

Our large group of international media rushes to the Hong Kong Stadium for an important announcement. The betting is that the sevens will be called off. However, the tournament officials file in and, though sober-faced, announce that despite the cancellation of other events in the city, the rugby will go ahead. We shamelessly grab our media packs and free T-shirts and head back to town.

The health scare overshadows thoughts of the war in the Middle East, except that over the weekend it gives me the chance to chat with the World Cup tournament director, Fraser Neill. He is a friendly Australian who formerly worked for the NZRU and is now is based in Dublin working for the IRB.

Fraser joins the increasingly large group of people I'm running into wherever I go who are saying: "Your New Zealand team looks favourite to win the Cup". I note Fraser's comment. He watches a lot of rugby around the world.

I ask Fraser about the bonus points scoring system for the World Cup. Is the system in place for the World Cup? "Yes, it is," he replies. "It has been approved at the board level." Can it be altered before the competition starts? "Well, yes it could. You never know what the IRB board can do."

Fraser announces that the 20 World Cup teams will each be allowed 12 people in their management teams. Thirty players with 12 management personnel seems too high a percentage of officials to me. I suppose they'll all have jobs to do.

Mind you, excessive control of rugby seems to be catching on – each of the 57 games of the Hong Kong sevens is controlled by 11 people. I kid you not – 11 people. They are the referee, two sideline touch judges, two in-goal touch judges, one man sitting on the sideline keeping official time, two men with clipboards writing things down (about what I know not), one man holding up the numbers boards for the interchange of players, another ushering those players on and off the field and yet another

We joke about it, but the SARS virus is a real threat during the Hong Kong Sevens.

with the job of not only directing punished yellow-carded players to sit on a sideline chair, but also of talking into a sideline microphone that only the referee can hear. Something to do with the ref hearing of changes above the crowd noise.

MARCH 30

Three days of glorious sevens finish on a top note for the England team, coached by the ex-rugby league star Joe Lydon and captained by little Simon Amor. Their team races away from New Zealand in the final to win 22–17. It's a thriller all the way and the tournament is a huge success. In Ugo Monye and Richard Haughton, the English team have way too much pace for the battered and bruised Kiwis. Eric Rush and Antony Tuitavake miss the final because of injury.

The seriousness of the SARS situation is hammered home when the Beijing sevens event, scheduled to be the next stop on the sevens tour, is cancelled. While this is a personal disappointment for me, because I will miss meeting my daughter, Shelley, and her partner, Mike Barrett, who were coming to Beijing from Seoul for the event, the decision is common sense. Instead, we reporters all scramble for the first available flights out of Hong Kong.

"Those English fellas don't like tackling our big black fellas."

APRIL **2**

Back from the Hong Kong sevens, TVNZ has "stood down" Steve Jamieson and me for up to 10 days because of concerns among the staff that we might have been in contact with the SARS virus. So here I sit at home, reading newspapers, clipping stories and catching up on emails.

The rest period is interrupted today by a call from Stu Dennison, with further news about the World Cup planning. Dammit Stu, go away – can't you see I'm sick!

APRIL **3**

Anne and I celebrate our 33rd wedding anniversary at home with a bottle of Moet and Chandon and Chinese takeaways. Ah, how perfect life is.

The Singapore sevens in a fortnight has been postponed because of SARS fears. This threat is becoming more worrying to New Zealanders. It has pushed the Middle East war story off the front pages. A member of the Fijian sevens team, Kini Salabogi, has been taken to hospital in Suva for rest and checks. While in Hong Kong, he had the flu so badly that he didn't play in any games.

Should we ask even now: will this virus be out of control in October and affect the staging of the World Cup?

APRIL **4**

Mr Hobbs and Mr Moller head to Dublin to attend an IRB meeting. Delegates from 85 countries will be there, but only 13 countries can vote on any big changes. Those old funny ways still exist. On departure, Mr Moller states that the New Zealand union hopes there will be discussion about change to the IRB's eligibility laws. The New Zealand union wants

The diary, the diary ... always working on the blessed diary!

international sevens representation to have no effect on players wanting to play for another country at the 15-a-side game.

Unbelievably, this story continues to get space in all the media. I reckon the New Zealand union's attitude is almost a case of "bringing the game into disrepute". We know that the union's record of assisting rugby in the Pacific is modest at best. The All Blacks, for example, have never played in Samoa or Tonga. Now, with the arrival of the brilliant Rupeni Caucaunibuca, New Zealand officials are braying about how much they have supported rugby in the Pacific. Yet they want to discuss changes that would mean a claim on Rupeni could be made to make him one of ours. All this, conveniently, in a World Cup year.

It would be very sad if an All Black team were to run out at the World Cup with Rupeni in the side. In *The Listener,* Joseph Romanos urged New Zealand to "try to win the World Cup fairly, not by some shonky sleight of hand by which we rob Fiji of an outstanding player". Fair comment. And a good word too – "shonky".

APRIL **5**

I sneak out of home today (against my SARS banning) to watch the beginning of the club rugby season. I go to watch my son Ben play for Petone. With shouts of support, disappointment, despair and "aw c'mon, ref" echoing from all directions across the five playing fields, it's great to be there. Ben's team, the Petone Police XV, have a disappointment with their goal-kicker. He misses a handy conversion attempt in the last minute, so they win only 98–0.

At one point, Ben crashes over for a try. He tells me later that he stood up and glanced over proudly to see what reaction there was from his dear father. "But," he says, with a heavy sigh, "you weren't bloody looking Dad, you were watching another game."

As I stand there at the Petone Rec, along comes that faithful servant of Wellington and New Zealand rugby, former All Black captain Andy Leslie. He is resplendent in his Wellington rep blazer and new tie, befitting his first day in office as president of the Wellington Rugby Union.

Together, in 10 minutes flat, we sort out the world of rugby and its ills. Andy is delighted, as I am, to note the gradual return to form this year of Christian Cullen for the Hurricanes. We agree he is not as quick as before, but his timing and understanding of the fullback role seem better. Jerry Collins' play is admired by both of us and we reflect that more than one or two whispers are being heard that Tana Umaga might be considered for All Black captaincy.

Andy says: "The All Blacks will have to get Andrew Mehrtens back soon. I reckon we'll need his steadiness and control at first-five for the World Cup. Have you heard how bad his injury is?"

That question nags me. This weekend is yet another when Mehrtens has been a no-show for the Crusaders. I phone a mate close to the rugby action in Christchurch and ask him what's wrong with Mehrts.

My mate won't reply unless I assure him the conversation is going to be off the record. Puzzled, I agree. What he then tells me about Mehrtens' concentration makes surprising news. "And everybody in Christchurch knows about it too," he adds pointedly.

Will Mehrtens finally get a start for the Crusaders? Or will they continue to show faith in the burgeoning talent of young Daniel Carter?

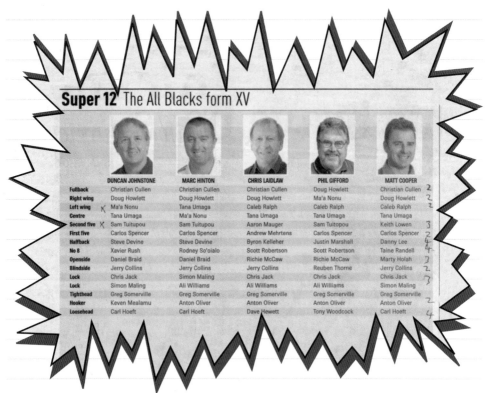

Super 12 The All Blacks form XV

	DUNCAN JOHNSTONE	MARC HINTON	CHRIS LAIDLAW	PHIL GIFFORD	MATT COOPER	
Fullback	Christian Cullen	Christian Cullen	Christian Cullen	Doug Howlett	Christian Cullen	2
Right wing	Doug Howlett	Doug Howlett	Doug Howlett	Ma'a Nonu	Doug Howlett	2
Left wing	Ma'a Nonu ✗	Tana Umaga	Caleb Ralph	Caleb Ralph	Caleb Ralph	2
Centre	Tana Umaga	Ma'a Nonu	Tana Umaga	Tana Umaga	Tana Umaga	
Second five	Sam Tuitupou ✗	Sam Tuitupou	Aaron Mauger	Sam Tuitupou	Keith Lowen	3
First five	Carlos Spencer	Carlos Spencer	Andrew Mehrtens	Carlos Spencer	Carlos Spencer	2
Halfback	Steve Devine	Steve Devine	Byron Kelleher	Justin Marshall	Danny Lee	4
No 8	Xavier Rush	Rodney So'oialo	Scott Robertson	Scott Robertson	Taine Randell	4
Openside	Daniel Braid	Daniel Braid	Richie McCaw	Richie McCaw	Marty Holah	3
Blindside	Jerry Collins	Jerry Collins	Jerry Collins	Reuben Thorne	Jerry Collins	2
Lock	Chris Jack	Simon Maling	Chris Jack	Chris Jack	Chris Jack	3
Lock	Simon Maling	Ali Williams	Ali Williams	Ali Williams	Simon Maling	
Tighthead	Greg Somerville	Greg Somerville	Greg Somerville	Greg Somerville	Greg Somerville	
Hooker	Keven Mealamu	Anton Oliver	Anton Oliver	Anton Oliver	Anton Oliver	2
Loosehead	Carl Hoeft	Carl Hoeft	Dave Hewett	Tony Woodcock	Carl Hoeft	4

*Even **The Sunday Star-Times** panel of experts can't agree.*

APRIL 6

I cannot make my usual playful observations about Phil Gifford's columns after his appropriate and supportive piece in *The Sunday Star-Times* today. His subject is Jonah Lomu's withdrawal from play because of kidney failure and is headed: "Savour the Gift of Jonah". Phil observes that many New Zealanders have not given Jonah the respect he richly deserves, as a player and a person. He concludes with this thought: "Jonah Lomu has been a special gift to the game in this country. It's a melancholy thought that he may have to be lost to rugby before everyone realises how lucky we were to have him."

It seems the whole country wishes Lomu the best and there is a strong desire that he will be okay to live a full and fruitful life. If that includes getting back on to the footy field, well, even better.

The Sunday Star-Times asks a panel of five writers and columnists to select an All Black team from the in-form Super 12 players so far. There is little consensus. Only tighthead prop Greg Somerville gains five votes in his favoured position. Tana Umaga gains five votes also, but across both midfield positions. Four votes go to Christian Cullen, Doug Howlett, Carlos Spencer, Chris Jack, Anton Oliver and the ever-impressive Jerry Collins. It's staggering to think that 33 players make the team lists submitted by the five writers. Having such a spread of talent must make John Mitchell smile. His idea of widening the base seems to have caught on.

APRIL 7

With England having swept aside the Irish to win the Six Nation Grand Slam last weekend, an intriguing story comes out of Britain today. Clive Woodward, the smooth, urbane England coach now has the World Cup more sharply in his vision. But he faces a dilemma. His kingpin is clearly flyhalf Jonny Wilkinson. Does Woodward send him Down Under on England's pre-Cup tour of Australasia? If he does, he might be the target of determined hit-men? Or does he leave Wilkinson at home in cotton wool? A tough question for Woodie, considering his flyhalf back-up is so meagre in talent by comparison.

APRIL 9

Sad news from France today. Former New Zealand resident Tony Marsh has cancer and is undergoing chemotherapy. Tony has risen to become a vital part of coach Bernard Laporte's backline planning since he headed to France in 1999. They are saying from Paris that the French selectors hope Tony will have shaken off his illness by World Cup time, but that is surely doubtful.

I often reflect on the tiny role I played in Marsh becoming eligible to play for France. He had left New Zealand after being included in a New Zealand A team that toured Tonga and Samoa. Under IRB rules, that would have made Marsh ineligible to play for any other country. In essence, he was to be a New Zealand rugby player for life.

But in Paris, France-based New Zealand rugby writer Ian Borthwick heard a whisper that the French selectors had been so impressed with

Marsh's form in Montferrand club play that they wanted to check his eligibility. According to Ian, calls to NZRU headquarters could not throw definitive light on the Marsh case. The French federation was told that Marsh had made the A tour and therefore would not be cleared to play for his adopted country.

That's when Ian rang me and asked if I would make a final check. I pulled out the appropriate *Rugby Almanack,* while Ian waited on the line. Sure enough, there was T Marsh's name listed in the team that toured Tonga and Samoa.

But he did not play in either of the "tests". His only appearance was against the Samoan President's XV, a game deemed second class, because the President's team used more than seven replacements. Therefore it could be argued that Marsh had not played for New Zealand A at all. Ian hung up, and later told me the case for Marsh to become a French rugby man was being re-argued. He passed muster. I felt good about my role in getting a bloke to play in the white-hot atmosphere of international rugby. How sad that his career is now curtailed. As with Jonah Lomu, we hope Tony can get back to his best.

APRIL 10

A day of celebration and poignancy. Being April 10, it is the 35th anniversary of the 1968 ferry disaster in Wellington Harbour. A massive storm drove the *Wahine* on to rocks at the harbour entrance and 52 people drowned. I was a young reporter who got up and went to work as usual that day. I did my eight hours, then caught my regular bus home. Yes, I noted it was extremely windy, but nothing untoward happened to me. I followed the unfolding grim events on the black-and-white TV set in our front room.

I do not subscribe to the theory that Wellington is a particularly windy city, though that day there were gales of truly ghastly proportions. The other example of comparable wind was on the day of the second test between New Zealand and France in 1961. That day a man sitting in the towering Millard Stand had his hat whipped away in the gale. That evening he received a phone call from a woman in Karori saying she had read his name in the lining of a hat bowling along the street. Karori is nearly 20 kilometres from Athletic Park.

But back to the present time. Exactly 35 years after 1968, another thing happened of note in our city on April 10. At about 8.30pm today a baby is born to Ben and Claire Quinn. Their second child and the second grandchild for "Grannie-Annie and Grumpy" (that's us folks). We are delighted of course, as is wee Maggie, their first-born. Along with Claire's parents, Carol and Evan Johnson, from West Kilbride in Scotland, who came out for the birth, we drink a wee dram to mark James' arrival.

Also, the Iraqi city of Baghdad falls today to the invading forces from the US and Britain. I mention it only because it is a day of shame for the world to mark. This age does not need massive loss of life from invasions and takeovers of nations.

APRIL 11

In Dublin delegates from 85 rugby nations meet with plenty to talk about. Principal on the agenda is the vote to decide the venue for the 2007 Rugby World Cup. France wins the day over England by 18 votes to three. While there is wide approval of the outcome (and I'm among those who applaud and break into bad broken French all day), it's interesting to note that a number of publications and columnists suddenly voted for Britain as the best choice. Fair enough, but God willing I might be around in 2007 to savour the delights of the south of France, a place I have loved since I first went there in 1977.

Tonight John McBeth and I warm up our vocal chords on *The Breeze*, a local radio station, by commentating on the Waratahs versus Hurricanes at the Westpac Stadium. The Hurricanes race away to a 42–26 win, their sixth successive victory. Afterwards we stagger away, drunk with the optimism that all the Hurricanes' leading players will make the World Cup XV. We do that with an extra cheer in our hearts, because the win has put the fabulous, beautiful Hurricanes top of the Super 12 table. (Okay, okay, we know that the Blues are unbeaten and have *two* games in hand.) The Hurricanes top of the table? It's too much to believe.

APRIL 12

Top of the table

Semifinal on the horizon

I don't mind waking up to this heading.

The Dominion Post this morning gives the excitement of last night's rise to the top of the table the most modest headline possible in the paper's short history. Not an exclamation mark in sight!!!!!

TVNZ starts today a new programme on Saturday afternoons. It's called *Gillette Sportsfix*. It's a snappy-looking presentation, fronted by Eric Young and produced by Richard Becht. My first job is to present a piece on why the Canterbury Crusaders are not doing well this season. So I do and an hour after my piece goes to air the red-and-blacks thrash the Cats of Johannesburg 65–34. Did the power of TV bring about the change of form?

APRIL 13

Overnight the Blues are fantastic in Pretoria and crush the Bulls 56–28. So the Hurricanes' time at the top is only 36 hours. Still, never mind – we loved it while it lasted. Can we hope for a seventh consecutive win next week?

Another story of note in *The Sunday Star-Times* is from Phil Gifford announcing he is going north to work for Radio Sport in Auckland. I say, good on you mate, now we'll get some balance in your reporting. (Phil's column today begins by quoting an unnamed Crusaders rugby player saying: "Things are 'sweet as'. We just have to be patient. We know the good times will come.")

I keep mentioning these Super 12 scores and stories because increasingly the form of the leading New Zealand, South African and Australian players is likely to take them to the World Cup.

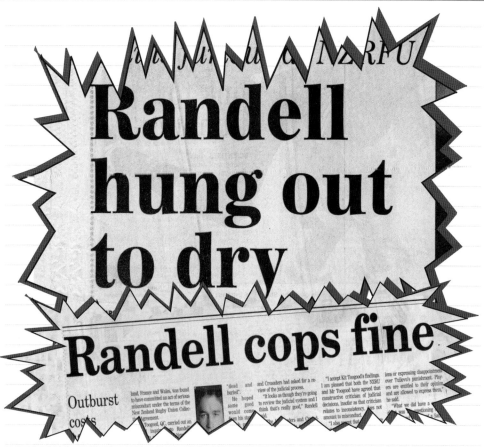

Randell hung out to dry

Randell cops fine

Outburst costs

land, France and Wales, was found to have committed an act of serious misconduct under the terms of the New Zealand Rugby Union Collective Agreement.

Toogood, QC, carried out an inquiry... Randell

"dead and buried".
He hoped some good would come from his statement

and Crusaders had asked for a review of the judicial process.
"It looks as though they're going to review the judicial system and I think that's really good," Randell said.

"I accept Kit Toogood's findings. I am pleased that both the NZRU and Mr Toogood have agreed that constructive criticism of judicial decisions, insofar as that criticism relates to inconsistency, does not amount to misconduct.
"I also accept that

ions or expressing disappointment over Tullevu's punishment. Players are entitled to their opinions and are allowed to express them," he said.
"What we did have a... was questioning...

But honestly, Taine, what did you expect?

The Sunday Star-Times headlines its sports pages today by shouting "Let Tana lead the All Blacks", but such resounding confidence is muted by the fact that the message comes from an Australian, Bob Dwyer. However, Bob's not on his own. Ever more people are swinging in behind the dreadlocked Wellingtonian as the man needed to lead the All Blacks into battle this season.

What does John Mitchell think about this issue? We don't know. Mitch hasn't been sighted or quoted for weeks now.

APRIL 14

Taine Randell is punished by the New Zealand Rugby Union today for his outburst against the South African arm of the Super 12 judiciary.

Taine is fined $3000. It's not an unexpected decision, as he didn't publicly seem to offer any qualification to the remarks he made a month ago in Durban, when he called the South African Super 12 judiciary "a disgrace, and lacking credibility and integrity". Remember, Taine is the current All Black captain. I don't feel Taine should be speaking like this against the judiciary, the people who are essentially the guardians of fair play, regardless of which country they are from. Taine's been playing well this year, and must still be a contender for the Cup team.

APRIL 15

A most rewarding day. I fly to New Plymouth to watch the Hurricanes train before their next Super 12 game. A more composed, restrained and confident team you couldn't wish to meet. And their work is under the quiet guidance of two understated coaches, Colin Cooper and Murray Roulston.

While doing separate TV interviews with them, I discovered both coaches had spent 20 years as freezing workers. "That gives us an understanding of people and systems, and a real earthy concept of 'team'," they both said.

No hotshot city coaches these two. Instead they're men who have valued their rise through coaching in small areas (the Clifton club in Waitara for Cooper, and Ashburton and Wanganui for Roulston) and then through the NZRU's Regional Development Officer coaching scheme. Both swear by it. It's made them men who can coach and put the rugby message across to young blokes. They also don't hold back from admitting they can learn from the experience of players like "Tana, Cully, Jonah and them".

Cooper and Roulston: it's a pleasure to be around them and their team.

And guess who's also there, lurking under a tree to keep out of the way of our cameras and the blazing Taranaki sun? John Mitchell. He isn't giving interviews, but is cheery and bright and looking confident as we exchange greetings. Is it possible that he, too, is learning from some of the Hurricanes' methods?

Mitchell's men down to last five

■ RUGBY
JIM KAYES

ONLY five places remain open in the 26-man All Blacks squad to be named next month for tests against England, Wales and France in June.
The Hurricanes will be under the microscope as the All Blacks selectors will ... with their three ... ng the move to ...

'We are very close to finalising the team. There are probably only five positions left but players can still play their way out. ...ing our tenure there have been ...es ...new playing his way out d... th... a...' — John

This story, a good interview of John Mitchell by **The Dominion Post's** *Jim Kayes, pricked my professional pride.*

APRIL 16

Dammit! There in *The Dominion Post* this morning is John Mitchell quoted all over the back page, saying he has virtually selected 21 of the 26 players he will be calling on in his first All Black squad of the season. So he spoke to one paper, but not to other members of the media. Fair enough, I guess. I'm only jealous.

I suppose I could have phoned from New Plymouth to Wellington and spoken to the NZRU All Black media officer Matt McIlraith at his office, and arranged an interview with John Mitchell, who stood metres away from me all day in New Plymouth. But I didn't. So I missed out. That's how interviews are arranged these days.

The Dominion Post story, by Jim Kayes, contains some intriguing quotes. For example, Mitchell says he has already decided on a high percentage of his first All Black squad, but surely he'll wait to see what happens as the Super 12 gets to its business end? Or does he not feel the toughest matches of the tournament are those he should be using to gauge his top players?

APRIL 17

More advance planning by TVNZ re the Rugby World Cup. This time it's a plan to send Keith Quinn throughout Australia. An itinerary is being mapped out. It looks like fun – and hard work.

APRIL 18

Super 12 features on every day of the four-day Easter weekend. On Friday night, the Crusaders struggle yet again, this time against the Sharks, winning only 23–18. They definitely aren't the team of yesteryear. Yet again there is no sign of Mehrts, even in the reserves. They say his knee is keeping him out. Or are there other reasons? Coming home in the car from New Plymouth the other night, I heard Murray Deaker on Newstalk ZB allude to "other rumours I'm hearing about Mehrtens". So it's not just me who has heard them.

APRIL 19

The proud grandparents of the new Quinn/Johnson offspring gather at our place and, drinks in hand, settle to watch the Saturday night game, the Hurricanes against the Highlanders. The TV cameras capture a glimpse of Billy Connolly sitting in the crowd.

Carol Johnson (baby James Quinn's maternal grandmother from Scotland) seems a little bewildered at our excitement at the start of the game, but by midway through the second half, she is shouting as loud the rest of us. (Well, *nearly* as loud.) The Hurricanes are outstanding in the second spell and outplay the "Mains-landers", transforming the half-time 9–15 half-time deficit to 37–15 in their favour. We celebrate the excellence of their seventh consecutive win, not to mention the fine play again of Ma'a Nonu in combination with Tana Umaga. Could it *really* be possible that Nonu will play in the World Cup? The drums have been beating ever louder these past few months.

One late-night radio listener thinks so. He blurts out that "the Poms would hate it if Nonu and Umaga are running at them in the midfield, 'coz we all know those English fellas don't like tackling our big black fellas".

APRIL 20

This morning *The Sunday Star-Times* yelps a story at us from Marc Hinton, saying: "All Black coach John Mitchell is preparing to stack his test squad with Crusaders and recall Reuben Thorne as captain."

The only foundation for the story is a quote from "sources close to the All Blacks", who are apparently indicating that Mitchell is looking to return to the strong Crusaders influence he had in his All Black teams last year. Adds the paper: "Mitchell's faith in his 2002 Tri Nations players has remained firm despite their scratchy Super 12 form." Scratchy? The Crusaders have looked awful compared to last year.

So maybe we're going to get again the Canterblacks, as some papers called the All Blacks last year, or Red Blacks, as *The Sunday Star-Times* labels them today. It's a lot of supposition, though, based on unnamed sources.

APRIL 21

Wynne Gray, of *The New Zealand Herald,* has come bounding out from behind his keyboard with a counter to the previous day's discussion. Writes Gray: "If Mitchell was keen to use Reuben Thorne as captain again, how could that be justified on his moderate impact this season, compared with the regular dynamism shown by Jerry Collins or even the consistency of Justin Collins?"

Gray also calls the Umaga-Nonu midfield combination the Twin Terrors. I hope his description catches on.

Gray does not go with the thinking that John Mitchell will revert to the Crusaders' style of last year. "Mitchell Must Go For Form" is the

Herald's headline for this story.

I continue to gain encouragement from the strong public and media push for a change of All Blacks style. While it's good for Mitchell to be able to pick his World Cup squad from a wider base of experienced internationals, he told the first squad of All Black hopefuls in January that the door was open for others and that he would probably go outside the first squad of 44 players and bring in new talent. That sentiment is being talked up more every day as the World Cup draws closer. The powerful Ma'a Nonu is being spoken of most in that new category at the moment.

APRIL 22

170 days till World Cup kick-off.

APRIL 23

I fly to Dunedin to do more filming for *Gillette Sportsfix*. The welcome is warm from the Highlanders and I speak at length to Carl Hoeft, Simon Maling and Anton Oliver. They are to be edited for the "Contenders"

KEITH QUINN COLLECTION

With Anton Oliver, who I'd have leading the All Blacks this year.

segment of the show. Oliver is different from so many other young rugby players. He has powers of expression and a breadth of vocabulary that is somewhat disconcerting when heard for the first time. None of this "We'll take it one game at a time" stuff or "our fellas" and "their fellas". Anton speaks to me of the "abyss that there will be for Highlanders players if they don't make the Super 12 semi-finals". By abyss, he means there will be less chance of the Highlanders players catching the selectors' eyes if their team doesn't make the top four.

I come away from the interview thinking Anton *must* be the All Black captain this year.

On the way home at Christchurch airport I sneak a look at *The Press's* back page, where Bob Schumacher has taken the unusual step of writing an All Black teaser story, naming two All Black teams, one based on the

All Blacks teaser

MITCHELL'S XV			FORM XV		
15	Leon MacDonald	(Canterbury)	15	Christian Cullen	(Wellington)
14	Doug Howlett	(Auckland)	14	Doug Howlett	(Auckland)
13	Tana Umaga	(Wellington)	13	Tana Umaga	(Wellington)
12	Aaron Mauger	(Canterbury)	12	Ma'a Nonu	(Wellington)
11	Caleb Ralph	(Canterbury)	11	Joe Rokocoko	(Auckland)
10	Andrew Mehrtens	(Canterbury)	10	Carlos Spencer	(Auckland)
9	Justin Marshall	(Canterbury)	9	Steve Devine	(Auckland)
8	Taine Randell	(Otago)	8	Taine Randell	(Otago)
7	Richard McCaw	(Canterbury)	7	Richard McCaw	(Canterbury)
6	Reuben Thorne (c)	(Canterbury)	6	Jerry Collins	(Wellington)
5	Chris Jack	(Canterbury)	5	Chris Jack	(Canterbury)
4	Simon Maling	(Otago)	4	Ali Williams	(Auckland)
3	Greg Somerville	(Canterbury)	3	Greg Somerville	(Canterbury)
2	Anton Oliver	(Otago)	2	Anton Oliver (c)	(Otago)
1	David Hewett	(Canterbury)	1	Carl Hoeft	(Otago)

Provincial representation:
Canterbury 10, Otago 3, Auckland 1, Wellington 1

Provincial representation:
Auckland 5, Wellington 4, Canterbury 3, Otago 3

HAVE YOUR SAY – Send us your All Black team: **EMAIL:** sport@press.co.nz **FAX:** 364 8483 **POST:** Sports Dept, Private Bag 4722, Cathedral Square, Christchurch

Bob Schumacher's thought-provoking piece in **The Press.**

successes of 2002 and another that Bob calls the Form XV of 2003. Canterbury readers would have sighed with satisfaction at the former team, which has 10 Crusaders players in the XV, but not admired Bob's form team of 2003. Only Greg Somerville, Chris Jack and Richard McCaw make the grade in the updated selection. Reuben Thorne is captain of Mitchell's XV (the 2002 team), and Anton Oliver captain of the 2003 Form XV.

APRIL 24

Other names go into the captaincy frame today. Already we have Anton Oliver back to full fitness and looking a good prospect, Reuben Thorne still getting his share of leadership mentions, Tana Umaga's support growing, and some backing for Taine Randell to continue as leader. Then along comes the newest monthly sports magazine to hit our shelves. *International Rugby New Zealand* it's called, though it looks like a British-based publication with pages inserted for New Zealand readership. It boldly names Richie McCaw and Aaron Mauger as possible captaincy contenders for the All Blacks this year.

APRIL 25

Anne and I are up early and go into town to stand in the rain at the Cenotaph and watch the old soldiers parade at the Anzac Day Dawn Parade. Beautiful they are, the old blokes who march proudly in the half-light, though their numbers are dwindling each year. Conversely, the number of kids who go to watch is increasing. It's great to be there and see it all.

With New Zealand this year celebrating 100 years of test rugby and with the expectation of doing well later at the World Cup, is there a message in the line of the last hymn at the Memorial Service? "O God our help in ages past, our hope for years to come."

Back home over breakfast, two newspaper stories catch my eye. First, Chris Laidlaw makes a strong plea for Anton Oliver to be made captain. Good column, Chris, I say.

Then there is the distressing news that Vernon Pugh, chairman of the International Rugby Board, has died in Cardiff at the age of only 57.

It's a moment of reflection for me, as just 12 months earlier in a dusty, drafty grandstand in Beijing, Pugh gave me the interview of my life, giving his view on why it was the New Zealand Rugby Union and not the IRB that had messed up the details of the sub-hosting arrangements for the World Cup.

I'd sat and listened to Vernon as he quietly and methodically dismissed the strong words of criticism that had been publicly uttered in New Zealand by Mr Rutherford and Mr McCaw. I had no doubt that Pugh was furious with the New Zealanders and from that point was sure the 2003 Cup matches were gone from our country. A fortnight later that was confirmed by the official IRB rejection vote in Dublin.

As we sat in Beijing, Pugh said he would scribble out a few notes that summarised our conversation and leave them at the hotel for me. I wondered if this would actually happen, as he was a busy man and it might have been a convenient way for him to move on from our conversation.

Sure enough though, a day later, an envelope was slid under my hotel room door. In Pugh's handwriting was a summary of his irritation at the way he had been spoken about in the media in New Zealand by NZRU officials, with rebuttal of all the New Zealand arguments.

On my return, I mentioned these notes in various media outlets and was condemned by some as a "Pugh fan". However, my belief in his integrity was supported when delegates from all New Zealand's provincial rugby unions met later in the winter and threw out all of the major decision-makers involved in that massive cock-up.

Vernon Pugh was a great man for the world game of rugby, taking it to places it had been unheard of previously. Too often New Zealanders dismissed the work he undertook to expand rugby into a more global game with comments like: "That country! Their national team wouldn't win a game in our NPC Division Three." It was such a shame that New Zealanders did not better understand Pugh's work.

Anzac Day ends for me with a viewing of a stirring Super 12 game from Dunedin, as the Highlanders come back from their disappointments of New Plymouth last week and roundly thrash the Brumbies. Skipper Taine Randell leads the way with his most powerful display in years, including a 40-metre dash to score under the posts.

Somebody points out that the half-time and full-time scores were very appropriate for the Anzac atmosphere. It was 19–14 at half-time and 19–45 at the end.

APRIL 26

Is it me, or is the weekend's round of Super 12 matches not so exciting without the Hurricanes, who have the bye? The Blues are unimpressive in Auckland, but still have too much for the Sharks and remain unbeaten. The Crusaders stumble in Pretoria, going down 31–32 to the Bulls, admittedly to a last-minute dropped goal by Louis Koen. The Chiefs also lose narrowly, to the Stormers in Cape Town.

There is one notable aspect of hope. In Pretoria, Andrew Mehrtens is given the starting role at first five-eighth for the Crusaders. He makes a commanding return to top football, scoring a nippy try, landing all manner of place kicks and snapping over a dropped goal that at the time looked like the match-winner. Mehrts isn't just impressive because of his 21-point haul, he kicks deftly and with great judgment, guides his outside backs well and generally looks like the Mehrts of old. In fact, the only real change from the 2002 version of Mehrtens is a healthy growth of sideburns, which might be hiding his slightly rounder face. It looks as if he might be carrying the odd extra kilo or two. It's great to see him back.

APRIL 27

Only one item of note in today's Sunday papers. The *Sunday News* goes big with a story that Jonah Lomu is back training. Apparently he's doing light jogging, with Eric Rush as his training partner. Good news for the Big Fella.

APRIL 29

At last the Rupeni Caucaunibuca eligibility situation is sorted out. It emerges today that the brilliant wing – who some say is the best in the world – will play for Fiji, if selected, this year. This is surely no surprise. It was always obvious that, as Rupeni had played for Fiji in sevens, he had made a lifetime's rugby commitment to that country. It seems unbelievable that the story has rumbled along for eight weeks since Murray Mexted made that first jocular reference to Rupeni perhaps shifting his allegiance to the All Blacks.

Today I go to the NZRU's annual meeting, at their flash new headquarters on Wellington's waterfront. More than 100 delegates don't exactly sit there dumbly as proceedings unfold, but certainly sit there numbly through the two-hour formalities. Hardly a question is asked. There's not even the tiniest smatter of applause when chairman Jock Hobbs finishes his first speech as boss. Surely he rates a burst of encouragement to keep up the good work?

I have a camera crew there and, feeling mischievous, go around and ask a number of delegates to explain the almost eerie calmness and serenity. None can explain it. But everyone seems to feel rugby is in good heart again. I also ask which two teams will meet in the World Cup final. All 12 have New Zealand as one of the finalists. About half favoured England as the other.

MAY

"You can't pick players on what they used to be."

MAY 1

Mayday! Mayday! The word is being trumpeted. John Mitchell is to speak to the nation via an exclusive interview on Sky TV's *Reunion* show.

"'Bout time, too," says an anxious nation.

So there we are tonight, perhaps hundreds of thousands of us, perched on our sofas waiting for words to drop down from the great man, words we can interpret to help us understand Mitch's thinking ahead of the World Cup.

Overall, his performance is impressive. He looks calm and relaxed, his head newly-shaven (and polished?). His ears look great. He answers Tony Johnson's earnest questions with the usual composure and there are some morsels in there for us to nibble on.

For instance, the coach says, "In New Zealand rugby we tend to live in the past. What's on offer *now* is more important to me." Hearing that, we jump up and down and think: "Wow, he's gonna pick Nonu, Rokocoko, Muliaina and Tuitupou. Good on you, Mitch, old mate!" Well, that's my spin on the comment.

Later, the coach reiterates that he'll be picking three sets of All Black teams this season. One group of 26 will play against England, Wales and France. Then he'll review things and announce another squad to play the Tri Nations series. Finally, in late August, the World Cup squad of 30 will be announced.

The interview potters along until Tony asks about Reuben Thorne's form this year. Mitchell's face does not flicker. With his normal wide-eyed and steady stare, he compliments Thorne as having been "great last year, and did a great job as captain, with a huge work rate". But then, in the revelation of the night, Mitch declares that Thorne hasn't offered a big work rate yet this season. "This is a crucial time for him. He is a quality man, a quality individual, and we expect him to raise his standards in the remaining games."

For Mitchell to be that blunt about one of the main contenders for World Cup leadership is a sensation.

MAY 2

Today we discover that Mitchell's chat on Sky wasn't as exclusive as was made out. The coach features, full-face, on the cover of *Rugby News* today. His question-and-answer interview with editor Dave Campbell ranges over a number of issues. The cover headline is: "I know exactly what we're up for."

In the discussion with Campbell, the method of judging the favoured All Black contenders week by week is outlined. It is a curious method of exactness and detail. Each of the selectors makes judgments on each game based on "subjective live viewing", backed up by "objective viewing via videotape and statistical data".

Players are judged on skills and the "quality of the actions they make". A maximum of 10 points can go for each player based on physical qualities, current form and past form. "Special qualities", like leadership, or a "gift to play rugby", are also considered. Detail is also attended to regarding set play, second-phase play, defensive skills, flexibility, versatility, focus, "team fit", reaction under pressure and mental strength.

A form team is named privately by selectors Mitchell, Mark Shaw and Kieran Crowley after each Super 12 round, and differences selectors have with each other are debated before next week's play.

Their system is certainly more extensive than mine. I simply put a tick next to a player who shines, then have a cup of tea.

On a personal level, I'm not feeling so good today. Tonight I visit my doctor, Stewart Reid, at Lower Hutt's Ropata Clinic. With his sound knowledge of rugby and outstanding ability at golf, sometimes our discussions on my health last only a few minutes. Discussions on sport with this gentle Scotsman can last much longer. He's a good man and has greatly helped me through a few health crises over the years.

You see, doc, I've got this delicate problem. Not to go into too many details (I suggest readers might not be too interested in looking up peri-anal abscess), but it's a little gory, I'm afraid. Put it this way, it's very difficult to sit down at the moment. Basically, I haven't felt well since returning from Hong Kong a month ago. I'm slightly nervous of having a Lower Hutt version of SARS.

"You haven't anything like that," says Dr Reid, writing a prescription.

"I want to be right for the World Cup, doc," I say.

MAY 3

Of more relevance, with New Zealand's World Cup hopes in mind, is the form of the Blues in the Super 12. Our front-running team, unbeaten so far, have looked like they're also suffering from a mystery ailment these last few weeks. While they're still winning, their 25–16 victory over the Sharks last week was "ugly", according to coach Peter Sloane. This weekend they look far from a champion team in beating the Cats 33–9. Only Carlos Spencer looks at his best at the moment. Ali Williams, Joe Rokocoko, Doug Howlett, and Sam Tuitupou aren't far off either. But as a team they will be disappointed by their recent form.

Tonight, with the aid of a soft cushion to sit on, I go to the Westpac Stadium and broadcast the Hurricanes versus Brumbies match for *The Breeze*. It's a clinical performance from the Aussies, who end the Hurricanes' winning sequence of seven. Led by George Gregan, the Brumbies are excellent. The winning score is 35–27. Certainly, the Hurricanes miss Rodney So'oialo, who's out with an injured knee. A packed house enjoys a thrilling game, nonetheless.

As I pack up and head for home, I reflect that I have become the world's first rugby commentator to do a match while sitting on a smuggled-in rubber ring. My word, my backside is sore!

Home tonight after the rugby, I slump down on the couch (oh, the relief) to watch as the Crusaders continue their return to form. This time, they demolish the home team 51–13 in Cape Town, a record 38-point margin against the Stormers at home. Andrew Mehrtens suffers some bad luck that prevents him pushing further claims to regain his All Black spot. He suffers a badly gashed hand and leaves the field. It looks nasty.

MAY 4

The captaincy debate rages. *The Sunday Star-Times* publishes a UMR Research poll covering 750 New Zealanders. The result shows the people want Taine Randell retained as captain. He polls 32 per cent, while Reuben Thorne scores only 9 per cent. In fact, Tana Umaga is second with 25 per cent. My favourite, Anton Oliver, gathers 14 per cent. The rumours say

Randell is people's choice to lead All Blacks

Preferred All Black captain (by region)

By MARC HINTON

Which of the following would you prefer to be the All Black captain?

Auckland (200) | Provincial (371) | Christchurch (95) | Wellington (85)

TAINE RANDELL is the man New Zealanders want leading the All Blacks at the World Cup.

skipper has such a poor endorsement from the people.

Conversely Randell's rating

Highlander, is almost certain the starting hooker and is a strong leader, if somewhat a reluctant one. Umaga, by contrast, is revelling in the responsibility of

The fans want Taine, but will it matter?

John Mitchell favours Thorne. Can't see it myself yet, but I'm a fair man, open to change.

Thorne did play his best game of the season in Cape Town. Coming just days after Mitchell's TV utterances about needing to improve his work-rate, was this a coincidence?

Also today, Norm Hewitt, in his *Sunday News* column, says the Aussies are faking it in the Super 12, not giving the tournament their full concentration. Norm feels that's the reason the Australian teams are down the table. It's Norm's opinion, of course. I've been employed to watch and talk about rugby for 35 years and have yet to see a major team tank a game.

Still, Norm might dismiss my opinions as those coming from a "pain in the arse". The way I'm feeling at the moment, he'd be right!

MAY 5

Today I have to admit the rubber ring hasn't helped. Another visit to Dr Reid. This time he is not talking golf. He is serious and dispatches me to the Accident and Emergency Department of Lower Hutt Hospital. At the hospital, one quick look and a nice man wheels me away to have overnight surgery.

MAY 6

I wake with all manner of caring people asking how I am. I was operated on overnight. Only a short operation, but a full surgical blackout for me. The abscess has been fixed. I immediately feel better than a day or so ago. But boy, my backside still hurts. Right now, I couldn't give a monkey's about the World Cup. I'd just like to walk without pain and sit with freedom again.

Anne drives me home after a 24-hour hospital stay, with me sitting precariously on the ubiquitous rubber ring. Thank goodness we live close by. I stagger to bed. I've been told I'll be there for up to two weeks.

I cancel my daily morning broadcast on Radio Sport for a fortnight. My friends ring to ask what the problem is. I'm reluctant to say anything. I'm scared of my newspaper mates making a headline out of a broken-down commentator whose bum is sore. Imagine how they would phrase it. "Pain in the Arse" leaps to mind again.

MAY 7

The community nurses' daily visits begin. They are lovely people, kind and considerate to old blokes like me with old bloke's problems.

MAY 8

I'm stuck in bed, so dear Anne has called the Sky serviceman, and soon I have their coverage in my bedroom, while my radio catches Phil Gifford's first day on Radio Sport. He has the 4pm–6pm slot and I reckon he'll be good for the station. He opens his first show with an hour-long tribute to Laurie Mains, who has announced his retirement from the Highlanders today. Or did the news just slip out? Phil doesn't seem even slightly taken aback when Colin Weatherall, chairman of the Otago Rugby Union, says: "Everyone down here, at some time or another, has been on the end of one of Laurie's bursts while he's been coach." Or when Phil rings Eric Rush for a comment on how he found Laurie when Eric was in the All Blacks. "I was as scared as hell of him," says Eric.

There is definitely more to Laurie's early retirement announcement. Why would a coach do that with up to three matches left in the Super 12? Will there be a confirmation of the unhappiness in the Highlanders camp that was alluded to by Wynne Gray in *The New Zealand Herald* last month?

MAY 9

Today talkback radio is swamped with another issue. Every Tom, Dick and Harry has been whipped into a frenzy over the IRB announcement that World Cup matches undecided after extra time and sudden death will be decided by five players from each team being asked to take part in a sudden death drop-kicking contest. To me, the frenzy is all about a nervousness, a paranoia even, creeping into our country over the World Cup. Every issue involved with the event is seen as a conspiracy, either Aussie-driven or IRB-plotted, against the All Blacks marching to victory on November 22.

A couple of months ago, New Zealanders were also suspicious about the IRB's motives for introducing bonus points for round-robin games at the Cup.

On both issues, my reaction is that neither will affect the outcome of the tournament in a big way. See if I'm right.

And then there's the issue of the International Rugby Union Players Association. They want members of their union not to sign contracts to compete at the tournament, because they feel players will be denied the opportunity to promote themselves in a commercial sense during the competition. The association people have worked the media and the follow-dog public into believing they are the good guys fighting for the rights of the poor, much-maligned and underpaid professional players, who, in turn, are battling away against the IRB monolith, which is taking all the money.

All of this cleverly overlooks the fact that the same professional body scuttled the proposed Northern versus Southern Hemisphere game by demanding outrageous sums of money for its members before they would play. The Vernon Pugh idea for the game, controversial though it might have been, was worthily-based, seeking to provide funds to rugby's poorer nations, like Romania, Tonga, Samoa and Fiji.

Later today, when I am settling in for a quiet night of Super 12, an email comes through from Stu Dennison in Auckland. It's 59 pages long! Haven't you heard I'm sick, Stu?

It is, however, a fascinating plan, set out by the Australian Tourist Commission, with a multitude of ideas for filming by a TVNZ crew over three weeks in July-August. All designed to promote the best Aussie tourists spots and rugby history. The finished items are to be shown on TVNZ during the World Cup. It looks like it'll be fun to do, but hard work, with much planning. Stu is setting up a meeting within the next 10 days. I might suggest the meeting be at my place. I'm still supine, unable to spend much time sitting up. I hope my backside will heal by lying on the couch or on the bed.

The Hurricanes give it everything tonight on Eden Park against the Blues in the last of the round-robin play, but the home team wins well, 29–17. Loyal Hurricanes fans might say the difference between the two teams is the play of Carlos Spencer and Ali Williams. But the Blues are clearly better. Some Blues tries are breathtaking. Joe Rokocoko combines with Spencer in a thrilling 90-metre dash after which little Sam Tuitupou scores. Spencer scores a try after an outside break from flyhalf, the like of which only 1950s Welsh and Lions wizard Cliff Morgan might have matched. And finally Doug Howlett sprints in to score after a "banana kick" by Spencer. Only rugby league's Andrew Johns has done these regularly. I've never seen such a kick in rugby union.

The quality of play is way ahead of anything else seen recently, and both teams will be worthy semi-finalists. The match that follows in Canberra, with the much-maligned Crusaders shaping up against the always hard-to-beat-at-home Brumbies, is also a cracker.

The Crusaders win 28–21 with another admirable performance. Mehrtens does not play, his gashed hand keeping him out. Norm Maxwell is also absent. He's another Crusader looking for big-match form. Reuben Thorne has an excellent game, so is he timing his run to perfection?

At the end of the weekend, we find that the semi-finals pit the Hurricanes against the Crusaders at Jade Stadium and the Blues, now scorching favourites, at home to the Brumbies.

MAY 10

It could have been all four New Zealand teams in the semis, but the Highlanders stumble against the Reds at Ballymore. It's 28–23 at the end, but I'm jumping off my couch screaming at referee Andre Watson to go upstairs to check with the video official concerning the last-minute try attempt by Aisea Tuilevu. He doesn't, so the match is over. Curiously, none of the TV commentators seem to notice that Tuilevu has scored. I'm so incensed I immediately ring Wayne Graham in Dunedin and tell him his beloved Highlanders were robbed. He agrees.

Mind you, nothing has been going right for the Highlanders lately. The Mains resignation has created a lot of talk. The TV cameras show him sitting in the stands at Ballymore, looking rather forlorn. His wife, Anne-Marie, is sitting with him. She is entitled to be, as she is, after all, the Highlanders media officer. On the other side of Laurie are several empty seats. Is he really *that* far distanced from his team?

MAY 11

A quiet day. I have a column to write for *Rugby News*. I mention the Tuilevu thing and Andre Watson's non-action. I'm glad I do. The magazine doesn't hit the stands till Tuesday, but no-one's talking about the incident today. I reckon I got it right from the couch. No-one else seems to want to know.

MAY 12

Today – Monday – is the start of my second week on sick leave. With no morning Radio Sport to do, life is a bit of a luxury except for this damned pain in the backside. Still, I'll battle on.

And oh, how everyone wants to climb on the bandwagon today to rubbish poor old Andre Watson. It seems at last that second, third and fourth viewing of the video confirms the that the Highlanders should have been awarded a try by Tuilevu and perhaps won the game (if the conversion had been successful).

Who knows what might have followed? The Highlanders winning their semi-final? Well, it could have happened. And, charging into the final, a number of the Highlanders, performing well, might have played themselves into John Mitchell's thinking.

Andre Watson is taking a hammering from all quarters. He's a nice man and loves the game to bits. I recall a long conversation with him in Singapore at the sevens last year, when he proudly revealed how few players he had sent off. Only three or four, I think it was, in all his years of reffing. He *loves* the game. But, like a halfback dropping a pass, a midfielder getting offside or a first five-eighth missing a kick from in front, people *do* make mistakes. I reckon that on this occasion Andre was too hasty in dismissing the try and immediately signalling the end of the game.

MAY 13

On *Reunion* tonight Tony Johnson seems to be leading the charge in criticising Andre Watson. Replay after replay is shown of the Tuilevu try-scoring incident, with resulting analysis. In trumpeting that he has some kind of scoop, Tony seems to forget that he – at the ground in Brisbane, with the advantage of all the video replays – did not see the possibilities of a try. Watson did *not* have same advantages.

MAY 14

Suddenly the Andre Watson story has disappeared from discussion and debate. Gone, just like that. Now, scandal of a different type erupts. On the *Holmes* TV show, there is Laurie Mains tonight, interviewed by Hamish Clark in Dunedin. Mains lays into all manner of things over his retirement. He names one of the players he's had "issues" with this year.

It's compelling viewing. Clark, asking the questions, seems stunned by what Mains is offering. The interview is all about the undercurrent of difficulties and dissension in recent weeks within the Highlanders. Chris Laidlaw, on Sky TV, calls Laurie a tragic figure, on the basis of this latest Mains outburst. I agree.

Mains says he's had ongoing issues with Anton Oliver since returning from South Africa to coach Oliver at the Highlanders. This is akin to condemnation in the modern New Zealand rugby world, where what comes out of TV can influence many people's thinking. Is this an attempt by Mains to alert those who believe in him that Oliver is not suitable to be the All Black captain this year, or even be an All Black?

Mains, strangely, also takes the opportunity to hark back to two of his hoary old chestnuts: his rivalry with John Hart; and his belief that somebody called Suzy was involved in poisoning his All Black team before the 1995 World Cup final in Johannesburg.

Of Hart, Mains tells Clark that he recalls a meeting between the two at Carisbrook late in 1995, after Hart had taken over as All Black coach. "He came down to pick my brains ... he asked me about everything I knew," Mains scoffs.

I cannot understand why Mains would raise that meeting in an interview nearly eight years later. And, to offer a different viewpoint, I recall the meeting as being a reasonable thing for Hart, the new coach, to do. After all, Mains had just retired as coach, so surely Hart would want to understand who had gone well in the previous regime.

I have a recollection today that I've kept notes about that meeting. So I stumble off the couch and in my study I find the notebook detailing their meeting. I had started to keep notes, as I had thoughts of writing a book about the whole Alex Wyllie-Mains-Hart rivalry.

Of their meeting on December 20, 1995, I took the following quotes from the interviews each offered on *One News*. Hart: "It was an information-sharing opportunity." Mains: "There never was any problem between John and I. The rivalry was largely built up by the news media."

Why didn't Laurie say *then* that the meeting was all about "Hart picking my brains"?

And as for the Suzy story, Mains has raised this periodically over the years, as if he is trying to create fact out of personal conjecture that this woman was involved in the alleged deliberate food poisoning of his team. He has never produced evidence that a woman called Suzy worked at the hotel where the team stayed.

Laurie has always been weird when his theories about the incident have been questioned. Once, at Johannesburg in 1999, I interviewed him on film. He denied then that Suzy existed and said, in fact, that reference to her should never gone into his biography as a fact.

Another time, on the day the Springboks played New Zealand in Christchurch in 1996, I was asked on radio's *National Programme* about the whole poisoning issue. I raised doubts about how the illness of the team had come about. Laurie was doing Sky commentaries that day and he and I met at the bottom of the ladder leading to the two commentary boxes. He was agitated about what I'd said and asked me for my fax number. "Why?" I asked. "Because I'm going to sue you ," said Laurie.

His wife, standing nearby, looked embarrassed and Stu Dennison, the TVNZ producer with me, said: "What the hell was that all about?" I couldn't say anything other than: "I think Laurie disagrees with me." Nothing ever did come through on my fax from him on that subject.

MAY 15

There is further fallout on the Mains-Highlanders break-up. Whether much of this has anything to do with the World Cup remains to be seen, except that all hell has now broken loose. This morning, Highlanders chief executive John Hornbrook goes on Radio Sport with Brendan Telfer and speaks of the "climate of fear" in which the players have operated under the coaching regime this year of Mains. Because Anton Oliver's name has been put out into the public domain (by Mains on the *Holmes* show) as one who did not like the Mains methods, his image and style as an All Black contender is now being debated widely. Oliver is saying nothing.

To change the subject completely, there is a personal anniversary for me today. It is that of my first broadcast on air. I remember it for several reasons. I was very nervous, but at the same time very proud. It was on my mother's birthday – May 15, 1967 – and I was a lad of 20. That makes it 36 years ago. I have the tape of the young voice reading a radio sports news bulletin that day. If I may say so, it was a fair effort by the young lad, but the stumble on the last story has come down 36 years to haunt me!

I was reading the last story, about a world middleweight boxing champion, but it came out as "world widdlemeight"! And, just so my faux pas is not forgotten, the horror word widdlemeight is replayed every day these days as part of Martin Devlin's Radio Sport breakfast show intro to my daily comment piece.

MAY 16

John McBeth, of TVNZ's *Gillette SportsFix*, is dispatched to Dunedin to chase the Mains-Hornbrook-Highlanders story and is getting right in among it. But everyone is ducking for cover now that the discomfit of Otago rugby is in the open. John reports one interesting comment to me. At one point during the day, Mains asks him: "Why is Keith Quinn always getting into me?" As I haven't commentated at any rugby involving any of Mains' teams since 1999, this is another intriguing comment from the man.

Flashback to a pleasant lunch at Johannesburg with Laurie Mains and his wife Anne-Marie. This was the day Laurie told me the famed Suzy never existed.

While it is true we don't see eye to eye on a number of issues, the last time we were together for any length of time, we had a nice lunch and a chat at Ellis Park, Johannesburg. But fast-forward to May 2003, and I wonder if Mains may be upset at what I wrote in last week's *Quinnt-Essential* column in *Rugby News*?

Here is what I wrote:

A lot of nice things were said about Laurie Mains during last week, once his departure from the Highlanders coaching job was made public. But after the nice things came the questions about disharmony within the Highlanders team during the year. Makes you wonder about Wynne Gray's story in The New Zealand Herald *a month ago. Wynne wrote then of southern discord but his story was roundly rubbished by Highlanders officials. Now, maybe, can we think Wynne got it pretty well correct? Controversial man that Laurie! Always has been.*

Also today comes the first Super 12 semi-final. The Hurricanes travel to Jade Stadium to meet the Crusaders. Running his new Radio Sport show, Phil Gifford phones me at home and tries to bait me into declaring blind parochialism for the Hurricanes. I must admit I simply can't go along with his red and black taunts. We tussle away and he seems surprised when I pick the Crusaders to win.

And so it proves, quite comprehensively in the end, 39–16. The Crusaders are "ruthlessly efficient", as coach Bill Freeman used to say in the 1960s. Aaron Mauger at first five-eighth controls the tactical switches with great authority, while Daniel Carter, improving in every game, is dynamic one place further out. One of Carter's chase-down tackles of Christian Cullen is so good that Carter could be earning himself a shot at World Cup status. Impressive also for the Crusaders are loose forwards Richard McCaw, Sam Broomhall and Reuben Thorne.

Thorne continues to surprise me. He was lacking in forward thrust in earlier rounds, downright sluggish you might say, but in the past few weeks has led much more from the front. With that has come a rise in the Crusaders' fortunes. They are worthy finalists.

The Hurricanes give it a good shot, and by winning seven games in a row at one point of the season they came out way ahead in the critics' eyes. Maybe the best thing for them, in terms of individual assessments, is the way Ma'a Nonu and Jerry Collins played their way into the All Black frame. The way the team played, urged on by coaches Colin Cooper and Murray Roulston and skipper Tana Umaga, was a joy for locals to watch.

MAY 17

Saturday night and second semi-final time. After the excellence of the Crusaders in Christchurch 24 hours ago, it is almost a case of "match it", as the Blues take on the Brumbies at Eden Park. Again, this is an excellent performance by the Blues, who win 42–21. They score six tries, and some of them are thrillers. Joe Rokocoko goes over twice and of the others, Steve Devine's is the best. The little Blues No 9 has a great battle with George Gregan until Devine clashes head-on with his teammate Justin Collins and is carried off. It looks serious.

The final shapes as a classic – the Crusaders' style of efficiency and hard forward drive against the brilliance of the Blues.

MAY 18

For a magazine interview I am hoping to do for a British publication, I try again today to obtain an interview with John Mitchell. "No chance, I think," says Matt McIlraith, of the NZRU. I also try to get an interview with Doug Howlett. "Okay," says Sean Fitzpatrick, the Blues manager. "Send me an email and I'll put it in his pigeon hole."

MAY 19

At the start of my third week off work and feeling frustrated at not being involved, I am tuning in to radio stations galore and trying to read as widely as I can. It's all to do with the World Cup.

One interesting question is posed on Martin Devlin's Radio Sport morning: "Is it better for the All Blacks' World Cup chances if the Blues win the Super 12 final this weekend? Or does the Crusaders' style better suit our All Black team?" The debate goes on about the composition of the team, and the style they will play on the (presumably) rock-hard fields of Australia in October and November.

A TVNZ World Cup planning meeting is scheduled for today. I have to apologise to Stu Dennison, who is coming from Auckland to meet Quinn, McBeth and our statistician Peter Marriott.

"Stu," I lament, "I'm still lying here, cast on the couch. I can't move." So the meeting is held at my place. I sit precariously on the soft cushions, trying to balance on my good buttock.

MAY 20

I may be an old crock, but I'm on the front page of *The New Zealand Herald* today. A reporter rang to ask what I thought of the appointment of Andre Watson to referee the Super 12 final. I say: "He is an excellent choice." I don't go along with the myriads of radio talkback callers calling him a fool of a whistler.

No Mitchell interview, no Howlett interview, and they're emailing with more urgency from London asking for a story from me. I ring the Crusaders. "What's Mehrts doing?" I ask, ever so politely, of Jo Malcolm, their media officer. She replies: "Mehrts is not doing media these days."

So Jo offers Sam Broomhall. He and I talk over the phone, of his hopes and dreams. What a nice young bloke. It turns out that he, Marty Holah, Chris Jack and Byron Kelleher were on tour in Britain in 1997 and sat in the stands at Twickenham as members of the New Zealand Youth Team. They watched the All Blacks draw 26–26 with England. Within four seasons, all were All Blacks and now all are in with a chance of playing at the World Cup.

MAY 21

Steve Devine is ruled out of the Super 12 final by a combination of concussion and neck injury. For his sake, it's a good decision. Tough for the little bloke, though, as many are calling the final a kind of All Black trial. Devine is such a feisty little scrumhalf. We have to hope he comes right quickly for the bigger things that lie ahead. His replacement is David Gibson, who is rated highly by a few, including my dentist, Earle Kirton, and also Chris Laidlaw.

Anne brings home a bunch of rugby magazines today. It's always good to read the opinions of my old mates in the press. (Is it my imagination, or has Phil Gifford started to write more of his columns with a rising mention of the Blues, now that he's back living in Auckland? I'll continue to monitor.)

Among today's magazines, there is one slightly strange article that I don't understand. It's in *NZ Rugby World* and is headlined "The Age of Paradox". It's penned by Kevin Roberts, who was once a New Zealand Rugby Union councillor. Roberts has impressive business credentials: he is chief executive of Saatchi and Saatchi worldwide; and is a personal friend to the stars, if you get my drift.

His article seems to be about the word "paradox" being vital to the planning of the All Blacks for the World Cup.

"Okay," I think, "I'll read this."

So I do. Several times. But I'm blowed if I know what it is all about. Cop these selected quotes:

Unlocking the power of paradox will be the secret of All Blacks success in 2003. England have backed off paradox and chosen rigour, power, process and Jonny Wilkinson's left boot. They will be formidable.

Paradox is about working with two contradictory ideas, embracing them and building them together to the highest level of performance. This is the Japanese dynamic of Kaizen ... the essence of paradox is to refuse to make a choice. Every time you choose you lose.

The Northern Hemisphere are terrified of paradox. They are locked in the old paradigm of either/or. We (the All Blacks), on the other hand, have the richness of resource to confront and embrace paradox.

And if you need further convincing that we do indeed live in the Age of Paradox, then consider this. The best rapper in the world is white, the best golfer in the world is black, the French think America is arrogant, the Germans don't want to go to war and Switzerland holds the America's Cup!

Forgive me. There is much more to this column, and, to be fair, I repeat that I have quoted randomly. Maybe I'm missing something. Did I not have a decent enough education to grasp this kind of writing?

Paradox? Paradox? What happened to the old: "Okay boys, let's give it to them up the guts today"? That's what real rugby blokes understand. To me, such writing is show-off nonsense.

I have a pleasant task to do today. From our World Cup meeting the other day, it is my job to ring Colin Hawke, the esteemed former New Zealand international rugby referee, to ask him if he will consider coming to the Cup with TVNZ and being a part of our rugby panel coverage. We would love to have Colin on board. It is our belief, and I hope this is not seen too much as a criticism of Sky's weekly coverage (which I happen to think is excellent), that they have a tendency to over-commentate on refereeing matters.

We at TVNZ would like to have a point of difference at the World Cup. And Colin will be, we think, an excellent man to do that. Imagine a controversial decision, not just left hanging by commentators and panellists, who have no credentials for understanding rugby's complicated laws. Instead, we have a sage judge explaining about how and why a referee made such a call.

Colin is very keen and we leave the conversation with him hoping to have a chat with his employer for clearance.

MAY 22

Anne flies to my brother's son's wedding in Sydney today. I can't go, so I'm left alone for the weekend with my daily visits from the community nurses and a stack of beautifully home-cooked meals in the freezer.

I listen to Earle Kirton, who is on with Brendan Telfer on Radio Sport this morning, and am almost cheering at the logic of Earnie's pronouncements. They are talking about the upcoming All Black squad announcement, only five days away.

"We won't win the World Cup with the Brumbies/Crusaders style of attacking defence. We're not big enough. We got muscled and munched last time we played the Poms. We must move the ball," he says.

Great stuff Earle. Go boy. You *are* the greatest dentist in the world.

He carries on: "Our team must play more towards the Blues' style. Our backs are superior to most in the world. We must go faster, wider. England and France are too big for us. We can't go one-off without being muscled."

By now really steamed up, Earle adds: "Maybe we should play two number sevens – McCaw and Holah. I'm not sure about Reuben Thorne. Sure his relationship with Mitch seems good, but he has no X-factor. We need a No 6 forward who will run and take chances. Has Reuben got that? I haven't seen it.

"And at No 8, why not give Troy Flavell a go? We don't seem to have a tall one there at the moment. When Flavell comes back [from suspension], try him there.

"At halfback, I favour Devine, with Gibson in the squad. Not Marshall. He doesn't get it out quick any more. And half-a-second through the air in a scrumhalf's pass is worth two metres to our running backs."

Earle wraps up his on-air explosion of logic with: "Listen, we can't win the Cup playing Canterbury's rugby style. I hate those Rangitoto Yanks (a favourite Kirton description of Aucklanders), but for the style our All Blacks have to take to the World Cup, we just have to go the Auckland way this time."

Well said, Earle. For about the first time, the great Telfer could offer none of his famous argumentative rebuttal during the 20-minute tirade.

Today is also a time for reflection. On May 22, 1987 – 16 years ago today – the first Rugby World Cup kicked off at Eden Park. New Zealand played Italy. The 70–6 win was a record test score by the All Blacks. I was the TV commentator with Earle Kirton. Poor Italy, we thought. How hopeless they were. And what a try was scored by John Kirwan. It was a bursting, swerving, weaving 70-metre run, charging through the whole Italian team. What an irony that in 2003 Kirwan is coach of the Italian team.

What of the others who played that day – where are they now?

John Gallagher – after a career in British rugby league, he is a schoolmaster and part-time TV pundit in London.

Craig Green – he left New Zealand for Italy shortly after the World Cup and essentially has never been home since. He is a successful club coach in Italy.

John Kirwan – after playing rugby league for the Warriors and club rugby union in Italy and Japan, he is the coach of the Italian World Cup team.

Joe Stanley – works in sports promotion in Auckland.

Warwick Taylor – a long-standing schoolmaster and part-time rugby commentator in Christchurch.

Grant Fox – prominent in sports promotion of events in New Zealand. Also a coach (of the Auckland NPC team) and TV commentator.

David Kirk – successful businessman now resident in Sydney.

Wayne Shelford – professional rugby coach with the Saracens club in London, now back in New Zealand.

Michael Jones – businessman in Auckland. Also assistant coach of the Manu Samoa rugby team.

Gary Whetton – financial advisor in his own company in Auckland.

Alan Whetton – in partnership with former World Cup teammate Andy Dalton in sports promotion and marketing in Auckland.

Murray Pierce – a former Wellington policeman who has switched to personal financial management.

John Drake – a financial consultant in Tauranga and rugby commentator.

Steve McDowell – manages a gymnasium in Auckland.

Sean Fitzpatrick – manager of the Blues rugby team, the Auckland NPC rugby team and also involved in business and personal promotion in Auckland.

MAY 23

One day to the Super 12 final. It is strangely quiet in a rugby sense today. One of the rare Fridays when there is a Warriors rugby league game to watch. Also the National Bank Cup netball final from Invercargill and the New Zealand cricketers winning a one-day triangular series in Dambulla, Sri Lanka. The cricket isn't great, but a bunch of Kiwi lads from New Zealand turn up at the ground, wearing the one-day uniform from the early 1980s. They sit all day in the searing sun, taking turns at holding up a sign that says: "Bring Back Beige!" That is all very well, but every New Zealander with red blood knows that what they are really saying is "Bring Back Buck"!

MAY 24

The Super 12 final is worth waiting for. A chanting, cheering packed house at Eden Park, making the kind of noise that hasn't been heard in that city for decades, sees the Blues get home 21–17. It's a superb tussle and it crosses my mind that both sides would easily qualify for at least the quarter-final stage at the World Cup.

The Blues however, will have surprised many, including good judges like Earle Kirton, by playing only a modest percentage of the high-speed game. Instead, the tactic is for Carlos Spencer to send high up-and-under kicks towards the Crusaders' defences, giving the Blues opportunities to disrupt and bustle.

The plan works. But only just. It is a tight game, and a superb showcase of our current talent for John Mitchell to peruse. Some players play way above their previous best, like darting little Dave Gibson, Rico Gear on one wing, burly Blues props Kees Meeuws and Deacan Manu, and Crusaders hooker Mark Hammett, who scores two tries and goes great guns. Some players disappoint slightly, such as Crusaders lock Brad Thorn and the under-pressure fullback Leon MacDonald. It is said later that Thorn played with a heavy dose of the flu. Daniel Carter misses some significant early kicks at goal, too.

The battle between the locks Ali Williams and Chris Jack is monumentally tough. They both look All Black quality to me. Justin

Marshall is robust in the tight/loose play, but his passing provides confirmation of the Kirton comments relating to lack of speed of delivery. Andrew Mehrtens comes into the game from the bench before half-time. His ginger sideboards show up well in the TV close-ups and he gives it everything, but he still doesn't look at his best. He's not sharp enough. Will the All Black selectors name him?

The battle of the captains is extremely stern. Xavier Rush is leading, exhorting, demanding of his team, and plays from the front, too. Reuben Thorne leads well, but his leadership of a quieter, less abrasive manner. I look for the X-factor in his general play. Instead, the X-factor in the game comes from X-avier Rush.

For the record, everyone is praising Andre Watson's refereeing. He does a superb job. There is not one penalty until the 22nd minute. I feel justified in praising him in the *Herald* the other day.

MAY 25

The papers are full of the Super 12 final. The praise for the game is fulsome. Australia and South Africa, whose teams also contested the Super 12, hardly rate a mention. The final was very much a New Zealand affair, and an All Black trial.

And why not? When the smoke has cleared, Sunday is a day to reflect that New Zealanders dominated the Super 12 all the way.

But will it last into the World Cup? Now we wait for Mitchell, Crowley and Shaw, the three wise men, to name their first squad tomorrow.

TVNZ thinks it is of such shattering importance that it brings to its award-winning showpiece current affairs show *Sunday* a panel of experts to pick their team. Andy Haden, Phil Gifford, Chris Laidlaw and Laurie Mains sit with Mike Hosking and offer their views. Hey Mike, what happened to world affairs tonight? The bombings in Palestine? The troubles of re-establishing a secure Iraqi nation? Our free trade difficulties with the Americans? The Australian governor-general resigning today?

Those stories are nowhere to be seen. They are supplanted for *real* news. There is a Rugby World Cup a comin'. Laurie Mains says that he doesn't rate Anton Oliver as a hooker in the team. Or as captain. Funny that.

For the record (and my editors will not permit me to change this listing after the team is announced tomorrow), my 26-man squad to play England, Wales and France next month is:

Backs: Leon MacDonald, Doug Howlett, Caleb Ralph, Joe Rokocoko, Tana Umaga, Rico Gear, Mils Muliaina, Daniel Carter, Aaron Mauger, Carlos Spencer, Steve Devine, David Gibson. (MacDonald broke his cheekbone in Auckland on Saturday night. If he's not fit, I would choose Christian Cullen at fullback.)

Forwards: Scott Robertson, Richie McCaw, Marty Holah, Reuben Thorne, Troy Flavell, Chris Jack, Ali Williams, Simon Maling, Greg Somerville, Dave Hewett, Kees Meeuws, Carl Hoeft, Anton Oliver, Mark Hammett.

There you are ... from the team of 15 players I offered in Chapter One of this diary, three have not made this squad of 26 – Jonah Lomu, Andrew Mehrtens and Danny Lee. And I still go for Anton Oliver as captain. But from the beatings of the drums, I doubt I'll be correct there.

No-one has mentioned Justin Collins, Keith Lowen or Rico Gear much. And Keven Mealamu must also go close to securing a hooking berth. That's if Mitchell sees it the Mains way.

I can't miss this announcement. I'll rise off the couch tomorrow and, walking bravely, will head for the NZRU's new headquarters. Surely they'll have soft seats there.

MAY 26

When I arrive at the Rugby Union headquarters today, I have with me my precious list written out the night before. I have it so that when chairman Jock Hobbs reads out the names on the live telecast, I will not be like the other reporters and try to scribble down quickly names like Rokocoko and Muliaina, only to get behind as Hobbs moves on.

I will merely, grandly, place a lofty tick against the *same name* he is calling out. This will show me to be in perfect sync with the All Blacks selectors. Right?

So what happens?

This is where an honesty call comes in. I do not do too well in my picks when compared to some of the hotshots around me. I miss on two backs and three forwards.

I felt sure Mitchell would go for forwards Mark Hammett, Simon Mailing and Troy Flavell. None made it. And, among the backs, there is no faith placed in the improving talents of Rico Gear or the darting David Gibson, the sparky Blues halfback.

Oliver survives ... for now.

Yet it's a good-looking and soundly-based All Black squad. I like it, and most of the throng of reporters there seem to, as well. It's a mix of the flash of youth and the toughness of seasoned players. Even the captaincy choice of Reuben Thorne does not raise a murmur. In a theatrical gesture, Thorne does not appear to take his place on the top table until all the names have been called out. Only when Hobbs says ... "and the captain is ..." does Reuben walk in proudly.

After the announcement, the questions come thick and fast. Mitchell fields them comfortably. The co-selectors Kieran Crowley and Mark Shaw are also at the top table. Neither says anything. In Shaw's case, that isn't a surprise. I went around the world with him maybe 10 times when he was an All Black and I was a commentator. Yet he hasn't spoken to me for the past five or six years. (Don't tell me I've upset him too.) He is the Mount Rushmore of New Zealand rugby.

The press conference carries on for nearly an hour. It is carried live on Sky. I am billed on screen as "Keith Quinn, Rugby Guru". We kind of get the feeling that the reporters are running out of questions when Murray Mexted is moved to ask Reuben Thorne if he will be "wearing that beard of yours when it comes to the test matches". This from Mex, who had a Zapata moustache that was at least as silly, or as decent, for all his time as an All Black. John McBeth lightens up things towards the end by asking: "Will any of the team members be allowed to wear white boots when they play?" Good point, John.

My best question to Mitchell is: "How did the team named today change from the ones you chose after each earlier round of the Super 12?" His reply was that after each round of games, the lists were put through a shredder. How curious.

Of course, there are inevitable questions about the absence of Andrew Mehrtens and Christian Cullen. I notice John Matheson, of *NZ Rugby World*, keeps bringing his question line back to the non-selection of Cullen.

This seems strange, as Mitchell had earlier explained that Cullen is, in the selectors' view, now only the fourth-ranked fullback, behind Leon MacDonald, Doug Howlett and Mils Muliaina. Only later does someone snigger and say Matheson's questions were only because he is writing the Christian Cullen biography. We all have our agendas.

At least Matheson does not quote from his own magazine and ask if the All Blacks are going to play with "paradox".

Afterwards, Mitchell lines up for several one-on-one interviews. These are often interesting to see who gets what, as some players and coaches have long memories. For example, it is mentioned that Tana Umaga might not talk to TV3. This is apparently because of that station's manner of reporting him several years before.

And we wonder, seeing that Paul Holmes is at the announcement, whether Mitchell will agree to talk for the *Holmes* show. I recall a vigorous on-camera disagreement between the two after Mitchell had dropped Taine Randell from the All Blacks before the 2001 tour to Britain. (Holmes had asked: "Did you phone Randell and tell him why he was out?" Mitchell had replied, testily: "No I didn't, but he's got my phone number.") This time it's no problem. The two greet each other warmly and disappear into a camera-rigged room.

I have camera time with Mitchell, Thorne and Umaga – coach, captain and vice-captain. In their own ways, each is excellent. Mitch, as I boldly call him (well, I have known him since he worked in Hamilton radio many years ago), launches into his curious Mitch-speak, a kind of rugby talk with Mitchell trendy updates added. He speaks of the team working on "defence compliance" and a dropped player will have to work on his "skill shifts". And this one: "When I get the team from Super 12 play, I have to de-clutter their team cultures." I tell you, listening to him is sometimes a deep concentration effort.

Reuben Thorne grips my hand with all the fierceness and intent of the Todd Blackadder/Alex Wyllie/Don Hayes style. A real eyeball-to-eyeball, man-to-man Canterbury grip (though not as good as ex-All Black coach Ivan "The Grip" Vodanovich – Ivan's was the best). In my brief time with Thorne, I try to lure him away from talking rugby-bloody-rugby and he kind of gets the idea. With a somewhat wistful look, he talks about his desire "to go back to the land after all this is over". He also speaks of his joy in going up to some country property he had just bought at Rangiora "to have fun there in the open air, walking our dogs, away from all the hype. And to also tinker around in my 1971 Ford Fairlane car."

"Gee," I say, "do you drive that around Christchurch?" "Not much these days," says Reuben. "We have to drive these flash ones we get as part of Ford's sponsorship with the Rugby Union."

Actually I am much impressed with Thorne. He is quiet and unassuming and, as coach Mitchell had said moments before, "he doesn't create an atmosphere of anxiety" around him. But can he play with the X-factor, Mitch?

Tana Umaga comes in next and proceeds to philosophise in a superb manner about his life, how it had started in little Wainuiomata (over the hill from Hutt Valley), and how family and his roots always call him back there. He talks of what rugby has meant to him but how important he regards education, which he never showed much interest in as a youth. He says firmly he will tell his kids they "can't play outside till their homework is done". He speaks like a man with many more years on his clock than he has. Could it be he is feeling a mite dreamy today? Tana turns 30 tomorrow.

Getting to know the All Black captain a little better.

Three Wellington players with the World Cup on their minds, Rodney So'oialo (left), Tana Umaga and Ma'a Nonu, celebrate getting over the first selection hurdle of the year.

MAY 27

Happy birthday Tana.

MAY 28

The first flush of the All Black selections this year has gone down very well. This really is surprising, given all the crossfire beforehand. Sure, there has been the odd anxious southerner, wailing on talkback, decrying the low number of Otago players in the team (only two), and a few others are bemoaning the fact that there's only one from Waikato. Generally, though, Mitchell's team has won approval from the public and media.

Sir Robert Jones makes a good point with Graeme Hill on Radio Sport this afternoon. As there have been a few gripes about Christian Cullen not being called into the team, Jones points out: "You should look at the videos of Cullen playing in 1996–97–98 etc, when he was amazing. He is not that player now. You can't pick players on what they used to be."

It's all black for Cullen

The end of a great test career?

For *Gillette Sportsfix* today, I total up those players who have been picked to pull on the All Black jersey since John Mitchell became coach in October 2001. With the recall of Carl Hoeft and the five new caps, the total has now reached 60. Mitchell may say there have been extenuating circumstances for some of these – his 2001 team was heavily influenced by the quick exit of former coach Wayne Smith. Mitchell may also point out that he deliberately rested and recuperated a bunch of players before the 2002 tour to Europe.

Nevertheless, 60 players in 20 months, all swaggering about with the air of being famous All Blacks, is way too many by my reckoning. (Actually the total is 61 if you count replacement halfback Jason Spice, who was flown to the Argentina test in 2001, but did not play.)

Tana Umaga is tonight awarded the Wellington Sports Personality of the Year Award at a flash do in the Duxton Hotel. I go along and present a Wellington Hall of Fame Award to my mate, tennis star Onny Parun.

Straight after, I have to leave for home. Sore backside.

MAY 29

My God, I'll have to go back and delete all critical reference to my old mate Phil Gifford. Radio Sport producer Malcolm Jordan rings to say the station wants me to do a couple of weekly afternoon spots with Phil on his drive-time show from now on. That's okay, but things could get sharpish between us, because Phil and I sure know how to rile each other.

MAY 30

Anne got back from Australia earlier in the week and now, only days later, is off to Korea for 10 days, to catch up with our daughter, Shelley, who lives there. You'd think I was a millionaire, but, in fact, it's all those air points stacked up from three years of travelling on the world sevens circuit. This is the last of them, I think.

So I've got 10 days of peace and quiet ahead at home, and 10 days of frozen home-made dinners in the fridge. I really am pathetic in the kitchen.

MAY 31

A shock tonight. Tony Potter of *The Sunday Star-Times* comes on the phone. "Keith, have you heard the news?" he says in his usual stentorian tone. "Did you know Jonah's gone into hospital for kidney dialysis? It's not looking good." Tony and I talk about Jonah for a few minutes, the thrust of the conversation being about my views on the great man. And this sad and dramatic downturn in his health problems. Tony is writing his bit for the next day's edition.

When we finish, I feel quite stunned, and very sad. To think that when I saw him at the tennis in Auckland in January he had looked so good. From those sunny days through to the harrowing loss of form for the Hurricanes in the Super 12, when the crowds were laughing at him. Now this. It is very sad.

I've known Lomu a long time. I've always respected his talent. A fan, you could say. Earlier this year, I was approached to consider writing his biography. I would like to have done it, of course. It would have been a privilege. But not under the terms offered. The book planners told me that Phil Kingsley Jones, Jonah's manager, wanted to do all the interviews and then have me interpret the tapes into readable text. I have never written another person's memoirs – or an authorised biography, as this one was to be – but the essence of such a book would be to get inside the subject's head with your own thoughts and questions, to write from a trusted insider's standpoint. Not from someone else's question line.

Anyway, I couldn't have done it. This is World Cup year, remember.

JUNE

JUNE 1

The *Sunday News* has a story suggesting Jonah has signed a $3 million advance for a book on his life. Gulp! Did I miss out on a fortune by not showing more interest in writing about the Big Man?

As might be expected, there's a swag of Jonah headlines today – front-page stories in both national papers, as well as lead stories on radio news throughout the day. The essence of what I told Tony Potter was there in *The Sunday Star-Times,* including one of my favourite Jonah stories, about the time he was with the All Blacks in Nantes, France, a soccer-mad city. When Jonah jogged out from the team hotel to get a haircut, about a dozen kids with autograph books followed him and watched through the window as he had his hair trimmed. Then Jonah jogged back to the hotel. About half the French kids ran after him, waving their autograph books, and the rest nipped inside the barber's shop to scoop his hair off the floor.

EXCLUSIVE

RUGBY legend Jonah Lomu needs a kidney transplant to save his life.

SICK JONAH NEEDS TRANSPLANT

Sick Jonah determined to be an All Black again

News that shocked a nation.

93

Incidents like that illustrate that Jonah has been the most sensational rugby player from any country, ever. Argue with me about Jonah as a pure rugby player and I'll concede there were times when he was less than perfect, but from his test debut in 1994 until well into the new century, he did things that no other player has done.

Jonah says no to $10m offer

By JOHN MANUKIA

Yikes! $3 million to write his book and this offer a few weeks ago if he'd play gridiron for the Denver Broncos. Maybe I should have stuck with the big guy.

Of course, his image was helped by TV exposure, but ask any New Zealander who has travelled and they'll tell you that in some faraway place, where the language is different and another sport is be the national game, you can always connect with a local person. You say you're from New Zealand and they'll inevitably say: "New Zealand – All Blacks – Jonah Lomu!"

Tonight the TVNZ show *Sunday* invites me to go on screen with front man Cameron Bennett and John Hart to discuss the impact of Jonah's life and rugby influence. It's a nice 10-minute tribute and is John's first public appearance since a couple of stories appeared in the past 12 months about his marriage break-up and the sad death of his new partner. John looks good. I haven't spoken to him for some time and it is great to chat, before and after the show.

It's funny the way we think. No sooner has John appeared on TV than my office is on to me to check him out for possible inclusion in our TV commentary team for the World Cup. He seems quite keen. Let's hope it works out.

When I get home I have a look at the recording of *Sunday*. One of my quotes seems a bit grandiloquent, but I'll stand by what I said: "I have a feeling that as we of my era thought of Hillary, Hadlee, Meads, Walker,

Snell and Halberg as our heroes, the kids from 2003 might grow up and say Jonah Lomu was theirs."

JUNE 2

It's a dull Queen's Birthday Monday, punctuated by more sad stories about Jonah's plight. I also receive a call from our Auckland office. "We saw you on TV last night Keith. You looked great. Have you been working out at the gym?" I quietly put down the phone and mutter about "bloody Aucklanders".

For the record, lady, I have *not* been "working out". It's just that I have been sick and have lost seven kilograms. My humour over this illness has rapidly faded.

JUNE 3

Tonight's TV news tells us that the England rugby team departed Heathrow for their tour to New Zealand and Australia. On the same day, the Welsh team missed their flight, caught in the horrendous traffic gridlocks that are part of British life. The Welsh team were apparently involved in discussions about player tour payments and their bus had to pull into a service station for a time just north of Cardiff while telephone calls were made and agreements reached. How sad. My regular taxi driver in Lower Hutt, Mort Thomson, snorts, as he does at times like this: "Blimmin' money. When it came into rugby all the fun went out." Though I sometimes try to, you can't argue much against Mort's logic.

Some might feel that instead of the Welsh union paying their players to perform on tour, in view of the team's recent form it should be the other way round.

JUNE 4

The England team arrive with 37 players for three games, plus nearly 20 hangers-on, including 13 coaches, tonnes of travelling kit, gear, and all manner of electronic equipment. And, of course, dozens of reporters, commentators, photographers ("snappers", they're called) and TV staff. It's like an army arriving to do battle.

JUNE 5

The Welsh team arrive a day late and hunker down in Auckland. They'll fly to Australia for their first game in Sydney in 10 days' time.

Tonight Jonah Lomu's on the *Holmes* programme. As Jonah has said nothing publicly since the confirmation of his kidney dialysis needs, this is a scoop for Paul Holmes and his staff.

Jonah looks great. Calm, composed and confidently speaking about his future. Sure, he needs a kidney transplant, he tells us all, "some time in the future". But, he adds, he basically wants nothing more in life than to regain full fitness and play rugby again. And that means playing for the All Blacks. To see him there, looking so positive about a condition that would be life-threatening to many people, is very sad, but inspirational. He is *so* positive it's almost unnerving.

Holmes tries a tone of questioning that, I suspect, is aimed to get a tear rolling down the cheek of the big man. Though at one point a tear does look like sneaking out, it doesn't happen. So Jonah wins the day in that regard.

The programme ends with me, and no doubt hundreds of thousands of other concerned Kiwis, thinking: "Enough Jonah – you've done your bit for the All Blacks over the last 10 years. Now, instead of worrying about getting well at the age of 28 to play for the All Blacks again, why not take it easy and live to be 68, 78 or 88?"

JUNE 6

I fly to Auckland today. This is my first trip for a while, owing to my health concerns. My old mate, Blair Wingfield, picks me up from the airport and looks after me for virtually the whole weekend. Blair has been a buddy since we played cricket for Wellington College Old Boys in the mid-1960s. He has overcome his own serious health problems (leukaemia in 1980) and works selflessly for the Auckland-based support group for the same sufferers. He has been a very loyal friend.

Tonight Blair takes me to a Community Award for Sporting Achievers (CASA) dinner, where I am the MC. A nice night and $45,000 is raised from ticket sales and memorabilia auctions.

JUNE 7

Is this one of the strangest days I've had in my broadcasting career? Maybe. Put it this way, as an attempt to sight the world famous All Blacks in this year of years, you might call it a bit of an eccentric experience.

The plan entails me leaving my room at Sky City Hotel in Auckland and flying to Mt Maunganui to do a piece on *Gillette SportsFix* about the first week of the All Blacks in camp. Once in my room at Baywatch Motel, a phone call to Matt McIlraith, media officer for the All Blacks, tells me that the All Blacks' public appearances have finished for today. I have, quite simply, missed them. I'd told the producers in Auckland this was going to happen but they insisted I do a piece in Mt Maunganui anyway.

In the morning the team apparently had great fun staging canoeing races across the bay. My secret source (Matt McIlraith, actually) tells me that John Mitchell really struggled in his craft, much to the mirth of his team. No doubt though, they weren't laughing too loud. Never laugh too loud at the boss, right?

So there I am, in the motel in Mt Maunganui for the afternoon (but checked in for the night), waiting for my 5pm appearance on TV. Not having seen the team all week, I have little to contribute. However, being resourceful types, Eric Young, the front man, and I work out in advance a couple of questions and responses between us that might not alert folks at home that Quinn has been nowhere near the team all week. I am to rely on TV, radio and newspaper reports for my information. It's the lazy man's way of sounding authoritative. I don't like doing it. But there you go ...

So, come 5pm and there I am, all dressed up ("like a pox-doctor's clerk", the late and much-lamented Glyn Tucker used to say before he went on TV). I'm positioned in front of Mt Maunganui as the sun goes down, ready to do my bit with Eric. It makes for a scenic shot.

I tell how hard and eagerly the All Blacks have worked all week, how they have pleased the public, how they have signed autographs by the thousand, have had dinner with the sponsors ... I have on my most serious and earnest face. It goes okay, but it lasts only two minutes. I kid you not. Afterwards, I walk back to the motel, pick up some Chinese takeaways and settle back to watch the rest of the show by 5.15pm. Such is the giddy world of TV.

And yes, you guessed it, when the programme finishes my cell phone rings. I *looked* great on the programme. Thank you, Auckland staff. Even though my backside still aches, I'm starting to believe I really do resemble Robert Redford.

Later, when *One News* has finished and the sweet and sour plate lies empty on the table, I set my alarm for a couple of hours' snooze. I wake mid-evening to watch Australia thump Ireland 45–16 in Perth, followed by South Africa beating Scotland 29–25 in Durban. The march towards the World Cup has begun in earnest for me.

A funny place to begin? You bet. In the Baywatch Motel in Mount Maunganui, with not a soul with me in Room 14. Will it end with me shouting my lungs out in a packed stadium with an audience of millions in Sydney in 126 days' time – and New Zealanders celebrating World Cup success?

JUNE 8

7am Sunday, and thanks to my friendly Tauranga taxi driver ("John-Boy", another authority on rugby), I comfortably make the early flight back to Auckland.

Tonight, while enjoying a glass of the cleansing stuff in the Albion Hotel, my mate Paul "Doy" Hafford, the manager, confirms that he has received my entry in the hotel's competition for guessing the run-on All Black team to play England next Saturday. Before he took up hotel management, Doy was known as "the last butcher in Queen St". He says I'm the only person picking Doug Howlett to be fullback. The potential winnings are $700.

JUNE 9

Today it's my privilege to be the MC for the farewell breakfast for the New Zealand Special Olympics team heading to Dublin for their trip of a lifetime. In the afternoon I fly to New Plymouth to watch England begin their World Cup campaign, with their second XV in action against New Zealand Maori.

The flight from Auckland is so smooth I sleep all the way. When I stand, three or four sweets fall out of my lap. The stewardess had obviously, and delicately, placed them there. Almost coinciding with the plane's landing, a southerly change comes across Taranaki. Rain and wind whistle in from the south and howl around New Plymouth.

I go to the Plymouth Hotel to meet John McBeth and Peter Marriott, who have driven from Wellington for the game. They tell of bad weather all the way up the island. Our plan had been to watch the game under lights, then drive back to Wellington, a journey of four-and-a-half hours. But John and Peter had noted the forecast of further storms and booked a motel for us half-way home.

The rugby is spoiled by the weather. England win 23–9, scoring just two tries. But the margin between the teams is much wider than the score suggests. The Maori team are far from the best they have fielded. Still, the touring team's performance is a signal to New Zealand fans of the depth of English rugby and some of the problems the All Blacks might strike on their journey ahead. I particularly like Andy Gomersall (when he comes on to replace Kyran Bracken at halfback), the front-rowers Trevor Woodman and Phil Vickery, and big wing Dan Luger.

We three intrepid travellers eschew press conferences and aftermatch functions. They're usually incredibly boring, the only fun being watching people like John Mitchell and Clive Woodward bat away serious questions with rugby-speak non-answers. Instead we head into the tempest. McBeth drives, I navigate and from the back seat Peter takes it upon himself to be the one who repeatedly inquires about the prospects of finding something to eat.

Dozens of my touring media colleagues will attest that the art of navigation is not my strong suit. Consequently we soon find ourselves taking Taranaki's Surf Highway home in the storm, rather than the much better-lit State Highway 3. The drive is horrendous, with rain bucketing down and swooshing against the windscreen. It's so bad we are extremely grateful to pull off the road at Patea to take refuge at the Windmill Motel, where the nice people have put the heaters on to warm up Room 2 (of three units), which we crowd into.

Over late-night cups of tea, and some very average fish and chips (bought from the only shop open between New Plymouth and Hawera), we reflect on the game we've just seen. We agree that the top England combination is going to be extremely tough for the All Blacks come Saturday. We wonder whether Mitchell's team has the wherewithal to keep at bay the Six Nations champions.

JUNE 10

This morning Peter Marriott and I are given the dubious privilege of watching John McBeth broadcast his morning summary of last night's game. If only the *Morning Report* listeners could see McBeth lying in bed in his baby-blue pyjamas.

Later, we complete our drive home. The storm has weakened considerably, though we learn that we drove through a once-in-a-decade outburst last night.

I have to be home as early as possible, because Anne is flying back from Korea after her holiday. I make it just in time to vacuum the house, empty the dishwasher and clear the kitchen rubbish.

JUNE 11

Tonight the England and New Zealand test teams are announced. England go for a clean sweep, with no players included from the team

Howlett gets full backing

But can the Blues bullet defuse deadly Wilkinson's bombs?

Howlett at fullback. Fair enough, I say.

that won in New Plymouth. The inclusion of Jason Leonard at prop ahead of the vigorous Woodman or Vickery hints that Woodward has merely rubber-stamped the England team that completed the Six Nations Grand Slam in Dublin at the end of March.

New Zealand's team, sure enough, has Doug Howlett at fullback, ahead of the still recovering (from concussion) Leon MacDonald and Mils Muliaina, who goes into the reserves. Despite many calls from the public and the media, Christian Cullen is still not wanted. I had hoped Howlett would take the fullback slot, because he was clearly the most explosive fullback in New Zealand's Super 12 teams.

A number of other questions are raised, like Justin Marshall being preferred at halfback to partner Carlos Spencer, the Wellington pair of Tana Umaga and Ma'a Nonu together in the midfield, and Rodney So'oialo being picked at No 8 when he will be much shorter than his counterpart, the towering Lawrence Dallaglio.

How will the team stack up against England? Meeting with a bunch of my English touring media mates, it sticks in my craw to have to admit I feel England will win.

I phone the Albion Hotel in Auckland. Doy tells me five of his customers have picked 12 of the starting 15. I'm one of those winners. So we get $130 each.

Tonight McBeth and I go to the New Zealand versus England netball match at Wellington's Queen's Wharf Events Centre. We see various members of the England and New Zealand rugby teams there, seated well apart.

The hard seats in the stadium are killing me. I'm very relieved to take part in a netball-throwing contest with John out in centre court at half-time. John wins a washing machine for a nice woman with a lucky number in the crowd. I don't care – I'm just pleased to stand for a while.

New Zealand win the netball comfortably. A portent for the All Blacks? I'm dubious.

JUNE 12

A quiet Thursday. Both teams have gone into hiding. That's the usual way these days. If you're a reporter chasing the team and your editor is demanding a story from you, there's interview time available for you only if you have organised it way ahead. This entails endless phoning, sometimes days before, to each team's media liaison officer's cell phone. Usually on days like this requests are declined and you are directed instead to a mass question-and-answer session at the end of the afternoon. No wonder stories in many newspapers and electronic outlets carry the same quotes and storylines.

This afternoon the final filming schedule comes through for the advance TVNZ World Cup film trip through Australia. It looks like a fantastic few weeks. The list of possible stories has been trimmed from 59 pages to 14. The organisers are whittling things to only the best 35 story opportunities. I must be physically ready for all this. My backside is giving me more grief. I feel it's getting worse. You forget how much you rely on your behind as a soft cushion on which to achieve your happy daily rituals. The community nurses who make daily visits tell me that once you get these abscesses they are often hard to shrug off. I'll agree. Let me add here: the nurses are bloody marvellous.

There's a strange interview on TV3 tonight. The programme is called *Home Truths.* Newsreader John Campbell talks to a significant, newsworthy personality for half an hour each week. Tonight the interview subject is Laurie Mains. I stay up and watch but the programme is a disappointment. No home truths are exposed. I'm left wondering about the problems that have put Mains in the headlines lately.

Nothing is asked about the Highlanders, or Anton Oliver, or John Hornbrook, or Mains' future with the southern franchise. No hard-edged questioning. Maybe the normally courageous Campbell is not permitted to ask about these and other recent subjects at issue in the life of Laurie. (Remember, it was Campbell's grilling of former Prime Minister Jenny Shipley that, some say, brought down the last National leader.) It is only nicey-pie stuff from TV3's showpiece hard man. Did TV3 edit out all the good questions? Or did Mr or Mrs Mains lay down the rules of combat beforehand?

I get confused with one reply Laurie gives. He offers a slightly ambiguous response to a question concerning coaches who influenced him in his early years in Dunedin. Laurie looks whimsical and says: "Ah yes, Eric Watson, God bless his soul ..." It sounds as if Laurie thinks Eric, the ex-Otago and All Black coach, has died. But as of June 12, 2003, Eric Watson is still hail and hearty, retired, and living quietly in Dunedin.

Enough of Laurie for the moment. Apparently he has responded positively to our offer to come on to several TVNZ discussion panels for the World Cup in Sydney. I look forward to that.

JUNE 13

On *Breakfast,* when asked by Eric Young which team is going to win the test tomorrow, I pull myself up to my full height and say: "Not New Zealand." How's that for courage? Throughout the day on various radio stations I pick England to win.

The *Breakfast* programme also plays some black-and-white videotape of the 1973 All Blacks versus England game from Eden Park. It was the last time England won a test in New Zealand and was a young Keith Quinn's first test rugby commentary. Listening to it today, the voice sounds like that of a choirboy!

Pre-test drinks tonight at the Backbencher pub are with my old Busaco Road flatmates. We are a bunch of friends who flatted together more than 30 years ago. We meet two or three times a year. Tonight there is a 100 per cent turnout of the boys. We talk rugby endlessly, but when it comes to moving on for the traditional steak, eggs, peas, chips and tomatoes dinner at the famous Wellington restaurant, the Green Parrot, I excuse myself and head home. I am not well again, folks. You don't want details, I know, but I can hardly stand because of the pain.

At home on the couch, with much TLC from Mrs Quinn and everybody's friend, Mrs Panadol, I am only slightly cheered when I watch Sky TV's replay of its first *Steinlager Speeches* dinner from Wellington. The programme's special guest speaker, Peter Wheeler, the ex-England captain, admits from the podium to having read "one of your commentator Keith Quinn's books" while flying to New Zealand. I try to muster a cheer for myself, saying with a measure of glee: "Peter, I am *not* one of Sky's commentators. I actually work for its rival." But I'm deflated when Wheeler then adds: "How sad to be reading one of Keith Quinn's books!"

JUNE **14**

Test match day. I wake in such pain that my first "journey" is to the doctor. I'm advised to go straight to hospital. "But I can't go today," I plead. "This is a rugby test day and any rugby test day is the most important day of one's life. A rugby test day overrides all pain." Nevertheless, I inquire whether I can go to the hospital *tomorrow.* My motto for today is: forget the pain Keith, stack up on Panadol and thrill to seeing the All Blacks begin their journey to the World Cup.

I defied death to get to this game!

Tonight I am once again at Wellington's Westpac Stadium with my rubber cushion in my supermarket plastic bag, hoping the security people will allow it to pass. They do.

I sit at the back of the press room. My rear end is killing me, but I don't move. The ever-thoughtful and sympathetic John McBeth brings me coffee and a match programme. Would that I had him as my test match manservant all the time.

It's good to see my mates in the press benches again. Not just the Kiwi blokes – Wynne Gray, Duncan Johnstone, Marc Hinton, Phil Gifford, Jim Kayes et al – but the Brits as well, people like the commentators Ian Robertson, Stuart Barnes and Miles Harrison and writers David Norrie, Peter Jackson, Chris Hewitt, Stephen Jones, David Hands and Paul Ackford. Also Ian Borthwick, from *L'Equipe* in Paris. I've known some of these blokes since the golden age of touring Britain in the 1970s. I really enjoy their company. (Thankfully only Lynn McConnell, formerly of Wellington's *The Evening Post,* notices I am not moving far and am perched on a soft cushion. Lynn, a man of discretion, inquires quietly about my discomfort and doesn't mention my predicament to a soul.)

The test is a classic, with the team with the better tactical match plan winning. Simple as that. My version is that England, under the powerful presence of their captain, Martin Johnson, out-think the New Zealanders with a cunning plan. It is to lumber their ageing forwards around the field, killing the ball in rucks and mauls whenever possible. This is done for two reasons – to deny the younger, speedier All Blacks more effective running chances and to slow down the game so the England forwards will be able to go the distance. Johnson, meanwhile, also makes his presence felt by invading Australian referee Stuart Dickinson's personal space and getting into his ear as often as possible. Therefore Dickinson is not inclined to do anything too drastic about England tactics that are, in effect, spoiling the game.

Sure, lots of penalties are dished out. At one point of the first spell there are 12 in succession to New Zealand, but no yellow cards are issued for repetitive offences. Maybe there should be. It is only in the second half (after the touch judges in their half-time break no doubt alerted Dickinson to the wily ways of the English) that both Neil Back and Lawrence Dallaglio are sent to the sin bin at the same time. Even then, when it is 15 players against 13, the All Blacks, who have been dropping passes all over the slippery park, cannot use their advantage to score another try, or points of any kind. Lack of leadership prevents plans being

An aberration or an omen of things to come?

put in place to capitalise on the chances on offer.

The match finishes 15–13 to England and the 38,000 crowd troop away disconsolately. I walk with them, in a hurry to meet my ever-faithful Mort Thomson, who always parks his taxi for me outside the gates of the Ngati Poneke marae. I listen to the wise and worldly comments of disappointed New Zealanders. Some are amusing, like the bloke who tells me: "I think we need Jonah and his dialysis machine for the next test!" And the woman who calls out: "Well, they might have won, but two players in the England team will still be sad. They're the two without coaches!" There is the inevitable snarl from one bloke, who, yanking his young son by the arm, says: "Of course *you'll* be happy, Keith – I saw you on TV the other morning when you picked England to win."

JUNE 15

The aftermath in the Sunday papers is predictable. Big headlines front and back asking why the English won. Most doubts are centred on the All Blacks' inability to win after having possession, territory and refereeing advantages. "Why could our team not score a try when we had 15 on the park and they had only 13?" is one oft-asked question on radio talkback. Not to mention leadership – where Martin Johnson was a powerhouse figure, Reuben Thorne was Mr Meek by comparison.

Carlos Spencer's goal-kicking lapses are a big concern, especially when stacked against Jonny Wilkinson's efficiency in scoring all of England's points.

To be fair, New Zealand did score the only try, through an excellent chase by Doug Howlett after a kick by Spencer. Howlett was New Zealand's best player, followed closely by Richie McCaw and Spencer. There was disappointment in Caleb Ralph's showing. He wore Jonah's jersey but looked way too slight to concern England's magnificent defenders.

As to the manner in which England played the game, most of the criticism was directed at the referee. I did see some balance when Dallaglio appeared in a sound bite on the TV news saying he had expected to be sent off when he dived in and hung on to save a certain try. ("What I did just had to be done. I've got no complaints about being sent off.")

To me, the quote vindicated Dickinson's persistent whistling. Dallaglio confirmed that the English knew from the start what they needed to do to stop the flying New Zealanders. What a shame Murray Mexted led the way on TV in whipping up nationwide acrimony towards the ref. Mex's harsh words could have been directed more against the English cheating. Mexted commented on the number of penalties as a horror total – it's true, there were 33 in the match – but overlooked how many were the result of Dickinson's attempt to police the laws correctly. Murray wants games to end with a low penalty count, and there is merit in that, but a referee who doesn't blow for infringements against the game's law would equally be criticised for allowing too much illegal play.

So, it's a loss the team and the public have to swallow. Now we are left wondering if New Zealand's planners for this year's World Cup have the nous to work out how to beat such tactics.

And here's a nagging feeling I have. The All Blacks need a more dynamic captain if they are to win the tight games this year. I'm starting to lean towards Richie McCaw taking over. Why not? He is surely destined to be an All Black captain at some point. Why not now? Wilson Whineray and Graham Mourie, two of our greatest leaders, were promoted to captaincy early in their careers. Why not the man who is easily the most dynamic young forward of the current crop?

Unfortunately, I don't think there is momentum for a change in captaincy. Thorne sits atop the throne, followed by Tana Umaga and Anton Oliver (both of whom had a disappointing test). So far only Phil Murray, a Wellington journalist, writing in a local giveaway paper, *Contact*, has pushed for McCaw, plus there was a small mention a couple of months back in the British-based *International Rugby World*. I'm joining those people today.

JUNE 16

"Good morning everyone. This is 'Post-mortem Monday!'" begins Martin Devlin on his Radio Sport breakfast show. And so it is, all day ... questions, discussions, debates – you name it. Thanks goodness I can turn it off and concentrate on getting my health right. I'm back in Hutt Hospital today for more minor surgery on my unmentionable backside problem. A second abscess has appeared. Further surgery is required and the recovery will mean I have to spend another night in the GSG (General Surgery) Ward.

The doctors and nursing staff are great. They are so supportive and considerate, especially Burton King, who assures me that after this week's work, and more surgery next week, I should make the July 13 departure date to Australia for the film trip. And there's Dr Andrew Cameron, the lifelong family friend from our street, who visits to explain things about my problem in layman's terms. And the dozens of nurses and staff who make me feel at home.

Two of the nurses are rugby fanatics. During my overnight stay I call for an extra blanket at 3am. Cherry appears to make me more comfortable. Before she heads back to her station, she asks me if John Mitchell is doing okay as coach? In the dead of night, with my bum throbbing, I have to smile at her enthusiasm. Shona, another nurse, says she asked Mr Mitchell in "a very loud voice" during the test why he hadn't included Christian Cullen in the All Black team? She had lots of "other advice" for him, too, she says. "If these international teams have so many hangers-on, I want to be the first groin-o-cologist the All Blacks choose!"

JUNE 17

Today I creep home and head straight to bed. In a loud voice I tell Anne I *will* be okay to travel to Hamilton for the Wales versus New Zealand test on Saturday night. Anne says, equally adamantly: "You will *not* be going to the test."

I grumble (quietly). She wins.

Mitchell announces the team and it's "all change", with most of those in the All Black squad who did not appear against England getting a run. Marty Holah will play on the side of the scrum in place of McCaw. Is that because the game is in Hamilton?

I have another theory: if Holah proves as dynamic as he was in Europe at the end of 2002, there might be a case for McCaw and Holah to go left-right as flankers for upcoming big games. Why not? Our team must still be searching for a point of difference for the World Cup games. And if that happens, why not have McCaw as the All Black test captain? Reuben is just not "cuttin' the mustard" for me.

Mitchell uses another new term today. "This team," he says, referring to the large number of changes in the line-up, "is a 'block-building' one."

There you go folks, not "building-blocks", but "block-building".

JUNE 18

A shock today. Fullback Leon MacDonald, who missed the England test but was chosen for the game against Wales, withdraws from the team. He has apparently suffered post-concussion headaches, which arose after practice this morning. This is yet another example of trouble for MacDonald. Will he ever risk playing again? Who among the medical staff will give him a clearance now?

JUNE 19

What generous thoughts for me at home today from a number of my mates. Not only have I received phone calls at home over the past couple of days from the likes of John McBeth, Stu Dennison, Steve Jamieson, Grant Nisbett, Gavin Service, Colin McRae, Blair Wingfield, Cyril Delaney, Kevin Black, Mort Thomson, John Davies and Garry Ward, plus visits from sister-in-law Pat Quinn, Joseph Romanos, Alan Honey and sundry other neighbours and family, plus a long letter from Peter Sellers in Dunedin, but today a very nice bouquet of flowers arrives for me. It's from Nicky and Jock Hobbs. Their message is simple – "Slow down and get well". Anne nods in agreement. Today, I have to say, I'm taking heed. Thank you all.

JUNE 20

I'm in bed most of the day. But there is a significant anniversary. Wasn't it on June 20, 1987, that New Zealand won the first World Cup, beating France 29–9 on Eden Park? It was, you know. I look for a reminder on the TV news. Alas, no mention.

That's the All Black flag flying above the Red Dragon of Wales outside the Quinn house in Lower Hutt.

Another test day. This time, in the refurbished stadium in Hamilton, it's New Zealand versus Wales. I'm picking Wales to go a lot better than most Kiwis expect.

I have a really bizarre day today. I get up at 6am to watch the All Whites soccer team play Colombia in the Confederations Cup in France. New Zealand lose 3–1. Maybe getting up early makes me feel drowsy, but I need a snooze later in the morning. Anne takes me to Petone Recreation Ground to watch the Petone Police team play. They lead my old club, Wellington, 35–0 at half-time. Feeling slightly off colour, I head home.

Anne goes to work (she works as a civilian at the Lower Hutt Police Station). Our son Bennett comes in to tell me the final score was 49–3, then leaves. I am therefore alone when the test kicks off at 7pm.

I lie on the couch in our front room, and, with the heater on, fall into a deep sleep. I see the first 10 minutes, but when I awake it is 55–3 to the All Blacks, with just eight minutes left .

I'm shocked. Me, sleeping through a rugby test? It's hard to believe. I'm starting to understand that these antibiotics and the Panadol I'm taking, plus my debilitated and incapacitated state these past few days, plus standing in the wind at a rugby match for an hour or so, are reminders that my wife and all the doctors and nurses might just be correct. I am still way less than 100 per cent. But sleeping through a rugby test? I can't believe it!

With numerous repeats on Sky Sport 2 and the Rugby Channel, I record the game and by later in the evening am as well-versed on the action as anyone. New Zealand were impressive, but rugby fans will be left wondering about the quality of the victory when weighed against the inferiority of the Welsh team. I am surprised how meekly Wales folded.

Reuben Thorne led the team more decisively. He was in the play much more than last week. At one point the referee, Alan Lewis of Ireland, even waved Reuben back, saying: "I don't need you chirping in my ear all night." That's a big change from last week, when Martin Johnson was the verbal champion by a mile. My theory about McCaw becoming captain has probably taken a knock in this game, but I'll stick with it anyway.

The ease with which the All Blacks wiped away the Welsh could be judged by the glum faces of the New Zealand reserves. When a try was scored (there were eight in all) the on-field players danced and hugged, and the crowd roared and waved flags. But when the cameras caught the All Black reserves, like Oliver, Mauger and McCaw, they looked far from pleased. A sign, perhaps, that being on the bench is an insufferable experience for them. A sign, too, that competition for the starting XV is really hot.

JUNE 22

I'm up and into it today. Time to peruse the Sunday papers. Phil Gifford is back writing about Canterbury players, seeing debutante Daniel Carter played well and scored 20 points. Fair enough, I guess. There's also time to reflect on England's 25–14 thumping of Australia in Melbourne. That was a much more impressive performance than the one they gave in Wellington and clearly places the Poms top of the pile, at least for the moment.

One thing I admire about Clive Woodward's team is that they came Down Under with nary a whinge about touring at the end of a long domestic season and with no qualms about playing the other two leading teams in the world, when a rest at home might have been preferable. They came, they saw – the Maori, the All Blacks and the Wallabies – and, quite frankly, they stuffed them all. It was a stupendous performance by the English. Though some New Zealanders might quibble, I think from listening to some talkback today, more rugby-heads are starting to believe England are the team to beat in the World Cup.

I'd even go so far as to say that the England team in New Zealand and Australia in 2003 might rate alongside the great South African touring sides of 1937 and 1956, or the British Lions of 1971, or the Australians of 1998. What a pity the English couldn't have stayed and played more games. I'd have enjoyed watching their 30-metre forward rushes, the efficiency of their forward play, the brilliance of Jonny Wilkinson and the emerging capacity of their back play. And the way they execute tactics that, while not always pretty, win games.

JUNE 23

Tonight on *Holmes* did we see a further sign of the new attitude of New Zealanders towards All Black rugby? More interested in fashion than footy? Several of this season's flash, skin-tight, stretchy-stretchy adidas All Black jerseys ripped against England and Wales. What does the *Holmes* show do? It goes nationwide with the story, as if it is some kind of rugby crisis. And wait, there's more – the story is also on the TV1 and TV3 network news.

What's the world coming to? Can we not instead have a discussion about what the All Blacks need to do to counter an English team that have gone home, cock-a-hoop after an unbeaten tour? England have assumed the No 1 world position and favouritism to win the William Webb Ellis Cup. There's a crisis here for New Zealand rugby, but we get a discussion about jerseys getting torn! I reckon it's part of the Auckland attitude that is being foisted on the rest of us sensible New Zealanders. They say: "It's how you look that's most important." The rest of us say: "Yes, but how are we going to win the World Cup?"

I turn to *Deaker on Sport* on Sky TV and there, thank goodness, is a good breakdown of the problems New Zealand rugby is facing. The panel is Deaks, Brad Johnstone and Ofisa Tonu'u. Johnstone says he'd like to see more "strength on the side of the scrum". That's just after he has praised Richie McCaw and Marty Holah to the skies, so he's obviously referring to Reuben Thorne. The doubts about Thorne continue.

My friend Doc Williams, the first touring TVNZ All Black commentator, emails me from Blenheim. He says: "Thorne is one of the great All Black selection mysteries of recent times. Someone up there must like him."

JUNE 24

The French team fly to Christchurch ahead of their test with New Zealand this weekend. The All Blacks team is named tonight. Last week's front row is replaced. That's interesting, as Kees Meeuws scored a try and had two others disallowed against Wales. He is playing out of his tree. One radio caller, whom you'll never please, contends: "If he's scoring tries, he's obviously not doing the work a prop should do in the tight." Yeah, right mate.

The other change is McCaw back for Holah. Would the selectors dare to substitute the captain during a game to allow the experiment of Holah and McCaw working together? Fat chance, I say.

There is the same backs line-up as against Wales. That means that Ma'a Nonu has been overlooked. Summarising the team on *One News,* reporter Stephen Stuart suggests Nonu could be a "one-cap wonder". I hope not.

JUNE 25

I make it into town tonight to MC a big dinner. I have not done much speaking of late and my radio work has been put on hold while I try to recover from my illness. But when it's Olympic Day and my good friends John Davies and Clive Moon have asked me so nicely, I cannot refuse. Especially as John has become so ill. He has cancer and, with wonderful support from his wife Patsy, has been battling in private for more than six months. His profile as president of the New Zealand Olympic Committee has been lowered considerably while he's had a number of operations and trips to Australia for medical checks.

John probably should not have travelled from Auckland to Wellington today. When he enters the room for the dinner many of his friends are shocked at his frail and emaciated condition. The Olympic Academy awards him the Leonard A Cuff Medal, for a lifetime of espousing the

My good friend John Davies making his inspiring speech as he accepts the Leonard A Cuff medal.

principles of Olympism. Leonard Cuff was the New Zealand sports official who was an inaugural member, alongside the famous Pierre de Coubertin, when the International Olympic Committee was formed in 1894.

John Davies has lived his life by believing that just attending the Olympics, as John did as a 1500m runner in 1964, is a privilege. Winning a medal, though, is secondary in John's belief. He has always held dearly to the wider conviction that the opportunity to attend an Olympic Games is a badge of honour one has for the rest of one's life.

When John stands to receive his medal, there is hardly a dry eye in the room. When Clive Moon, who is blind, embraces him, I look at Patsy, who is proudly in tears. They are such a devoted couple.

I expect John to sit down immediately after the presentation. He is in no condition to speak. But without hesitation he comes to the podium and, without notes, proceeds to calmly launch into one of the most courageous addresses I've heard. He comments about his health, stating simply to the audience, with each word said on its own: "I have been better." He then continues to warmly thank those who have helped him in his life as a follower of Olympism, and also his many friends from the Hellenic Community who are in the room, and his colleagues from the New Zealand Olympic Committee who are there. He finishes by gently reminding us all of what he stands for, not as a bronze-medal-winning runner, but as one who firmly believes in Olympism first as a way of life, as distinct from just being part of a medal count. He sits down to a thunderous ovation and many tears.

How dreadfully sad that Tay Wilson, New Zealand's International Olympic Committee member, should speak from the same podium only minutes later and churlishly attempt to diminish everything John has said. Wilson, an advocate of the "let's win more medals" school of Olympic thinking, completely misses the point of the function. In view of John's precarious and life-threatening condition, this is not the time nor place to air such a vigorous, contradictory view.

Anne and I drive home afterwards, uplifted by John's courage and seething at Wilson's thoughtlessness. "My God," I think, "my health problems are minuscule compared to John's. I *must* get well again, to do my very best at the World Cup, and maybe TVNZ will then see fit to send me to Athens for the Olympic Games next year."

JUNE 26

At 7am today I enter Hutt Hospital for more surgery on my backside. I meet again the lovely nurses of the GSG Ward – so bright, so knowledgeable about rugby and so professional in their work. Thanks again, ladies.

JUNE 27

Home after my third 24-hour surgery this year. Straight to bed. With a throbbing backside, I don't even care that I cannot be in Christchurch for the test tomorrow night.

JUNE 28

I sleep most of the day. But there is method in this. I rise tonight to watch two intriguing tests. The All Blacks beat France 31–23 and South Africa beat Argentina 26–25 in Port Elizabeth.

I'm glad it is such a close battle for the All Blacks. Even though there are moments when it is possible New Zealand might lose, it's better that it was a tough contest to wrap up the first stage of John Mitchell's "long journey" to the World Cup.

If the All Blacks had won by 30 or 40 points (as many New Zealanders picked), that might have left our rugby in a state of smugness. Now, at least we know there will be many more tough games, apart from England, if we are to win the big one in November.

I'm delighted for wing Joe Rokocoko. He scores three tries and now has five for the All Blacks in three matches this season. His second try is scored after the fastest run by an All Black in recent years. He scythes downfield in a 40-metre burst after taking an in-pass from Carlos Spencer. In terms of speed, the try rates ahead of anything Doug Howlett has done recently. That's not surprising, given that young Joe was faster than Doug in the 40m time trials this season. Joe's run makes me wonder why there was all the fuss earlier this year about Rupeni Caucaunibuca being in the All Blacks.

There are other things about the game I note.

Will the New Zealand public finally realise that just because they aren't familiar with a foreign name, that doesn't automatically make that player second-rate? The French prove in Christchurch that, though their names might not be familiar to us, they are of top-drawer quality. The French team reflect the depth in French club play, more depth, I suspect, than we have in our NPC teams.

I like the zip that is added when Keven Mealamu, Byron Kelleher, Brad Thorn and Kees Meeuws come off the substitutes bench. The squad is building impressive depth. It's a shame there isn't time tonight for Marty Holah to do the same. He has only a few minutes on the field. Meanwhile, of those on the bench who don't get called on, Caleb Ralph continues to look perplexed, as though he knows he is not going to get much more test time. Aaron Mauger also continues to look a sad chap, sitting out the whole of a test for the second consecutive week.

Jerry Collins has a rousing game at No 8, consistently breaking the line. But others, like Tana Umaga, Ali Williams and Doug Howlett (for once), seem off the pace. Chris Jack is excellent, though the French give the All Blacks many headaches at scrum and lineout time.

I admire this French team. Sure, they did bring a team of so called no-names, but their best-known man, halfback and captain Fabien Galthie, rallies them superbly from being 3–19 down after 20 minutes to scoring two tries and closing the gap to within five points in the last minute of the game. The All Blacks can score only four penalties in the second half. The best compliment to the French performance is that it opens the lines on talkback radio straight after. Calls for Christian Cullen to come back, and Andrew Mehrtens, too, come thick and fast. The other main discussion points concern the abilities of John Mitchell and Reuben Thorne.

The All Black captain has another match where he is not seen in a line-breaking role. He "distinguishes" himself only when he is sin binned by Andre Watson for punching late in the game. Still, Thorne is admired by someone important, and, with the first part of the journey over, there's no chance of Mitchell replacing him now.

JUNE 29

The headline writers work overtime.

The general view in the papers today is that the win over France merits a pass mark and not much more. It was not impressive enough to inspire thoughts of victory at the World Cup. Both Sunday papers indulge in "clever" headline writing. The *Sunday News* has a front-page story under a headline "French Fried", which ignores the fact that the French had a chance to win until the final moments. *The Sunday Star-Times* is slightly closer to the mark with its "... almost French Fried" front-pager. It follows inside with a story headlined, "French Resistance after Fijian's First Half Coup". I suppose that's okay, if only as a play on words to introduce Joe Rokocoko's family background.

The *Sunday News* takes the prize with a "French Dressing" back page heading on a story that included this sentence, written by Neil Reid: "The All Blacks beat France 31–23 last night – but the win lacked any French Polish!"

In view of the change to the prostitution laws in New Zealand last week, it's a wonder French Kissing and French Letters aren't mentioned by either paper.

Apparently not, according to Marc Hinton.

Incidentally, it will be interesting to see how *The Sunday Star-Times* goes in future. Today was the last day at the paper for two of its accomplished writers, Marc Hinton and Duncan Johnstone. Both have taken the redundancies offered by the paper with its change of ownership from INL to Fairfax. Who will take their places?

Both are in top form today. Johnstone details how he feels the All Blacks have slowly slipped as a world rugby power during his 12 years covering them. Hinton's last assignment was to study Reuben Thorne, and Thorne alone, throughout the French test, to gauge his contribution. Hinton concludes that Thorne's punch was by far his biggest contribution in 80 minutes. "Instead of our captain being Mr Invincible, he was Mr Invisible," writes Hinton.

JUNE 30

Today marks the end of the first half of this momentous year for New Zealand rugby. From now, the World Cup will race towards us. Far from being satisfied, rugby fans are still asking questions about the All Blacks. There are a number of main issues:

- Is John Mitchell driving correctly?
- Will Reuben Thorne be the equivalent of a soaring eagle for the All Blacks this year, or an albatross around their necks?
- What is the truth about Andrew Mehrtens and Christian Cullen and the others? There are all sorts of rumours. Are they gone for good as All Blacks?
- Are the All Blacks on a journey to somewhere, or to nowhere?

From today it's 100 days to the World Cup kick-off.

JULY

"A very sad day for New Zealand rugby."

JULY 1

Might this be a quieter week for we rugby-heads? It's been a strenuous three Saturdays for everyone. Perhaps we need a break from all the yabber about everything concerning the All Blacks and the World Cup.

For Wellingtonians, at least there's a rep match to watch today. Ahead of a Ranfurly Shield challenge in Christchurch next week, Hawke's Bay come to town. They are despatched to Upper Hutt to play the Wellington Lions at Maidstone Park and barely a thousand turn up to watch. The weather is awful and I stay home.

On his way home afterwards, John McBeth stops by for a cup of tea. He has plenty of good gossip from the high-flyers he was talking to around the touchlines. Local attention was on Christian Cullen, the Wellington fullback. But with only Mark Shaw watching from the New Zealand selection panel, it's not a vote of confidence in Cullen being in line for an All Black recall. "He played okay," says John, "but the word is he's not going to make it." John reports the whisper that Cullen has signed to play for Munster in Ireland.

This rings a bell with me. I've had two emails in the past two days from Irish reporters looking for Christian's phone number. It points to Cullen's departure. But getting his phone number? You might as well try to get George W Bush's!

JULY 2

Rumour has it that Ben Blair is to be the replacement fullback in this week's All Black squad of 26 for phase two of the journey to the World Cup. So this afternoon it's another session on the couch for me, watching Canterbury's first Ranfurly Shield defence of the year, against North Otago.

Blair scores a million points in an 85–22 romp, but did he play any better than Cullen yesterday? North Otago score four excellent tries, but are not as strong as Hawke's Bay. Anyway, the All Black selectors will have decided this one weeks ago.

JULY 3

Today it's official. Wellington – and the rest of New Zealand – wakes to hear that Cullen has signed for Munster. It is a sad time, as Cullen has been one of the great players, but it's been obvious for some time that he has not been in John Mitchell's plans.

The phone lines run hot. On Radio Sport Brendan Telfer milks the story for all it's worth. "This is a very sad day for New Zealand rugby," he intones, and callers rush to agree. Brendan is so unreserved I almost expect to hear him say that there has been an "outpouring of grief" over the departure of Christian. (Media types use that expression for occasions of deep national sorrow.)

It goes on all day. Tonight on all the TV news it's the same. But there's no sign of Cullen. He is not speaking, behaving instead with his usual evasiveness. By signing he has ended his All Black days.

JULY 5

The Cullen debate rages. Most people are up in arms. Today there is snow down to 200 metres around Wellington. It's the worst weather seen in the city for years. But good old club rugby goes on, of course. Cullen makes further progress up the popularity pole when he turns out for his club, Northern United, at Porirua Park, where 3000 maniacs huddle to cheer him on. It's the biggest club crowd of the season. He plays soundly and Norths win to go to the top of the Jubilee Cup table. The man is a hero. But he is still saying nothing.

I sneak a peek at the Internet and see that in Australia David Campese is rubbishing Mitchell roundly. Campo says: "The coach is the star these days," and then adds: "Mitchell doesn't want to promote a superstar he hasn't brought through himself." It's an interesting theory, out of the Campese left-field thinking.

In *The New Zealand Herald*, Wynne Gray has had a chat with Mitchell, who discusses the shortcomings he believes are keeping Cullen out of his thinking. This is unusual for an All Black coach, but a scoop for Gray.

Fans back culled Cullen

Fullback focuses on match not Mitch despite coach's criticism

Christian's still the people's champion ... but not John Mitchell's.

JULY 6

You guessed it – Cullen is big news in the Sunday papers today. Chris Laidlaw writes a sympathetic piece in *The Sunday Star-Times*. He concludes that Cullen has not been at his best lately, but that his place as one of our rugby greats is secure. Nicely written under a headline "Farewell Cully the Legend".

In the same paper, the main story about Cullen also has a nice headline. Co-written by Dylan Cleaver and Jonathan Milne (they are the replacements for Johnstone and Hinton) the story banner mentions Cullen playing in the rain. It says, "Fans back culled Cullen; Fullback focuses on match not Mitch".

No sooner have I folded away those papers than the second All Black squad of the year is released. Cullen's name is missing. Ben Blair is back in the squad. That much was expected.

But there is a shock to take away the breath. Anton Oliver, the eight-year veteran, former captain, and hard-working hooker, has been dropped in favour of Mark Hammett of Canterbury. No newspaper picks up on the obvious headline involving the players' nicknames – "The Hammer replaces The Hatchet". More questions are asked, though surprisingly not nearly as many as for Cullen.

I contribute a column for *Rugby News* today and give it my best shot on both men.

On Christian Cullen:

"Sure, we can pull out the videos of Christian Cullen ducking and weaving and counter-attacking to score all of those wonderful tries for the All Blacks from 1996 to 2001. They were superb. And how we rightly cheered him.

"But when trying to be hard-nosed in making a call on Cullen's form this year, I have seen a different player. When I interviewed him for TV this year, I noted a relaxed, more mature young man, who openly talked about having 'before and after' ability on the field. It was a virtual admission that last year's knee injury prevented him from being the player he once was. Being honest, Cullen knows the recovery process has left him a few notches short of the player we see on the videotapes.

"Playing for the Hurricanes this season, he did not show the counter-attacking confidence of yore and has become less surprising to opposing teams. The knee injuries prevented the outrageous confidence in his sidesteps and speed at which we once gasped. His main repertoire this year seemed to be the run-forward-and-chip-kick type of thing

CHRIS LAIDLAW

Farewell Cully the Legend

THERE IS a measure of sadness when a great athlete's career at the top begins to turn downward. Some players, no matter what the sport, invoke intense emotions when their time to move over finally comes. Some don't want to go and have to be dropped. Others go with dignity

A sympathetic piece by Chris Laidlaw.

"The loss of confidence showed in the TV close-ups, with him looking about blankly, not communicating with those around. Christian is a quiet bloke, but at the top these days they want players who point, whisper and gesticulate to keep team-mates aware of what is going on.

"I wish Cullen all the best in Munster. He must leave our country with the knowledge that his place as an All Black great is fixed firmly in our memories. But no-one can stop the march of Father Time. Not Jonah, nor Taine, nor Anton, nor Razor, nor Sharkey, nor Cully. Even Mehrts, maybe.

"At Munster, Christian will have to ignore the names of the 1978 players (from the team that beat the All Blacks) on the plaque on the wall of the new grandstand at Thomond Park, Limerick. Munster will welcome him warmly and I know he will give of himself there. The rugby there is strong and they will want him to play well. My hope is that they haven't contracted one of our greats on the basis of those old videotapes."

On Anton Oliver:

"In the two-page blurb from the NZRU that went out mid-morning there was one very sad sentence. It read: 'He [Mark Hammett] comes into the squad at the expense of Anton Oliver.'

"That was it. There were no other mention of Anton Oliver. As an old mate of mine used to say, there were 'No thank yous, no kiss my bum, no nothing at all' for Oliver.

"Can I remind the NZRU that the man they churlishly dismissed in one sentence has played for the All Blacks over a span of eight seasons? He has appeared in 41 tests and 48 games in all, he was their test captain 10 times, and in all that time never shirked an opportunity to give anything less than his guts for the famous black jersey.

"Yes, true, maybe he did throw in crooked to a few lineouts (and I mean just a few across his whole career), but never has one act of one player's role in the All Blacks been so scrutinised as Anton's at the lineout. There has been little balance in reporting the tremendous effort he gives to rucks, mauls, scrummaging, tough tackling, forward rushes, power running, leadership and general hard-nosed play.

"Maybe the NZRU will say that it did not make any further mention of Anton because he is still in Mitchell's 'wider group' and is available for recall should there be injuries to Mark Hammett or Keven Mealamu in the run-up to the World Cup.

"But following the weekend comments by Mitchell, you and I know this is the beginning of the end for Anton the All Black. I want to salute him as a very fine wearer of the black jersey, one who always played with the vigor of his father Frank, also an All Black captain.

"And remember this, too. Anton once had the decency to drive hundreds of miles from Dunedin to a North Canterbury farm to be with Todd Blackadder on the day the end came for Blackadder as the All Black captain, when Anton had been chosen to replace him. Not many men have the quality to do that."

JULY 7

Suddenly John Mitchell seems to be appearing in the media a lot. Yesterday he was on Murray Deaker's Newstalk ZB *Scoreboard* programme. Today he's on the TV news. When you add in the comments he gave in *The New Zealand Herald* a few days ago, the weeks of silence from the coach seem distant. Is this a message from the Rugby Union that the public wants to know more about what's going on with the All Blacks?

I had a wee smile when I read this quote from Mitchell: "Actually, I don't read papers or listen to talkback." I find that one hard to believe.

What's gone on over the past weeks – the lineout problems against France, the captaincy qualities of Reuben Thorne, the dropping of Cullen and Oliver – has thrust Mitchell and his thinking into the spotlight. The rugby public is nervous. Mitchell is the target. His unique way of speaking, using his distinctive style of language, is picked at and mocked every day. Today on TV he seems to be looking down at the interviewer, which induces some churlish radio callers to comment: "Why doesn't he look up at us and look us all in the eye?"

People are voracious in their desire to know more about Mitchell's thinking. "What's goin' on?" is heard more often on radio talkback. "I'm getting pretty disillusioned with this All Black team," is another regular comment. Maybe even John Hart had it easier in 1999.

Which reminds me ... Hart has agreed to join the TVNZ commentary team at the World Cup – good news. I haven't worked with John in a commentary since the 1995 World Cup final. He is a detailed and canny observer, so will add a lot of authority when the time comes. Laurie Mains has said he is unavailable for us in Sydney. I am sure there's no connection between the two decisions.

JULY 8

Apparently Andrew Mehrtens failed to make Canterbury's team practice a few days ago and has been dropped to the reserves for the Shield game against Hawke's Bay. The rule in the team is that if you don't turn up to training, you don't play. It's being called a "misunderstanding" and a "communication breakdown", but coach Aussie McLean has dropped Mehrtens. A young lad named Cameron McIntyre gets his place.

Rumours about lack of concentration by Mehrtens have been raging all year and he hasn't played any significant rugby. He still has much support from his adoring public, with some calling for him to be drafted straight into the All Blacks at the expense of Carlos Spencer. This latest omission won't help his cause. Mind you, Mitchell said last weekend that "Mehrts is still very much in the frame for the World Cup".

So am I, by the way. This week I can declare I am fully recovered from recent health problems and I make it back to work just in time to fly to Australia on Sunday as part of the advance filming trip for back-up stories around the World Cup TV coverage.

Taine Randell is in *The Dominion Post* today. In a Jim Kayes story, Taine adds fuel to the debate, saying "John Mitchell's criticism of Christian Cullen has hurt the team at a time when public support is crucial". He feels the point-by-point criticism of Cullen's play (as outlined in *The New Zealand Herald*) was wrong. "People want to support the All Blacks, but the public towelling of a real favourite like Cully doesn't go down well," says Randell.

This is sensational stuff. An All Black captain of only months ago, criticising the coach who picked him. It's a bit like tit-for-tat, as Mitchell was quoted in the *NZ Rugby Monthly* earlier this year as being critical of Randell's captaincy on the tour to Britain and France.

Today I pick up the July issue of *NZ Rugby Monthly* and, in a regular column in which he usually discusses refereeing problems, Paddy O'Brien has given Sky TV's Murray Mexted a burst for his habit of climbing into refereeing decisions. Paddy makes some valid points, but when all's said and done, is he just nervous about whether *he* will get to go to the World Cup?

JULY 9

TVNZ's *One News* runs an interesting piece tonight. It is not in the sports section and is basically about a call for the public to support the All Blacks much more. Interview grabs, all begging encouragement for the team, are taken from Stu Wilson, John Hart and John McBeth. Their words are interspersed with shots of All Blacks in test struggles this year. It's like a rallying call – "pleeeease support the All Blacks", is how it looks to me.

It doesn't always work like that with the hard-edged New Zealand rugby public. In the mood of this month, and with the Tri Nations tests looming, the public is demanding excellence from our top players. Almost everyone's form is being questioned.

There is a bizarre twist to this season's Otago rugby saga today. Our old touring mate, journalist, author and columnist, Ron Palenski, who has had a superb book on 100 years of All Black test rugby published this week, has swept to power as chairman of the Otago Rugby Union. This is a surprise to us outsiders, though obviously Ron has a swag of support. We in the world of the sports media wonder if Ron will continue his newspaper column-writing. If he does, how valid will his opinions be on anything to do with Otago? Not since Trevor McKewen, who was formerly sports editor of the *Sunday News*, then *The Sunday Star-Times*, before moving into high-ranking rugby league and rugby union administration, has a working reporter jumped to the "other side".

"Ron's switch is a bit like poacher turned gamekeeper," says Phil Gifford on radio tonight.

JULY 11

Those glorious women of the Lower Hutt Community Nursing staff have been visiting my house almost every day for the past three months. Today they make their last visit. Praise be! I've been given clearance from them to travel to Australia to film. Ladies, you were all superb. I thank you from the bottom of my heart, or is it from the heart of my bottom?

JULY 12

The three-week epic begins today. In some ways I'm glad to be out of New Zealand for a while. The public expectancy ahead of the World Cup has become almost unbearable. Every word, every flicker of comment by John Mitchell, or any of those around the All Blacks, becomes headline news.

The All Blacks also left today, for South Africa and the start of the Tri Nations.

I fly to Auckland, in preparation for an early flight to Melbourne tomorrow.

This afternoon I visit John Davies, who I haven't seen for some weeks. He's rather frail and is relaxing on the couch when I arrive. The paleness and weakness we'd noted during his courageous visit to Wellington a couple of weeks ago is significantly worse. But John is such a kind man. He steers the conversation to my problems, not his.

After an hour-and-a-half, Patsy drives me to my next destination and, as we go, she talks with great love and affection for her "Davies" (as many of us have always called him). She says: "If he is to die, Keith, I hope he doesn't suffer long." There's the sound of resignation in her voice. Though Patsy is very much a fighter, there is nothing more we can do but hope with all our hearts for our dear sick friend.

My next stop is the Grace Joel Hospital, in St Heliers Bay Road. I tiptoe quietly into the room of Sir Terry McLean, who is bed-ridden these days. Tomorrow he will celebrate his 90th birthday. There's to be a small celebration at his rest home, and family and friends are gathering. I'm really sorry I won't be able to attend.

TP asks about my trip to Australia and I tell him that one of my first interviews in Melbourne will hopefully be with John Clarke, alias Fred Dagg. TP's powers of recall are 100 per cent. He instantly remembers Clarke's great quote when asked by a New Zealand reporter why he'd left New Zealand. Clarke had replied: "Because it's there." Recalling the quote, good old Terry crinkled his face in delight at its cleverness and relevance.

Tonight I enjoy the company at a kind of pre-party party for Terry. It is mainly Terry's family. Son Jock and daughter-in-law Kate offer drinks and high humour, which I really enjoy. Another of the McLeans who is there is Bob, whose father was Hugh McLean, the All Black of the 1930s. Among the stories told is the one about Terry and Hugh's mother travelling from New Plymouth to Auckland in 1930, to see Hugh make his test debut at Eden Park against Great Britain. As the big Southlander Bill Hazlett always refused to wear jersey No 13, the newcomer McLean (from Wellington) therefore had to. This made the numbers published in the programme incorrect.

So when young Hugh McLean made an early run of some length, the crowd cheered the play of "Hazlett". This incensed Mrs McLean, who stood up from her seat in the stand and shouted in a loud voice to anyone who cared to listen: "That's not Bill Hazlett, that's my son Hugh!" The crowd around her erupted in delight. The story is still good 73 years later.

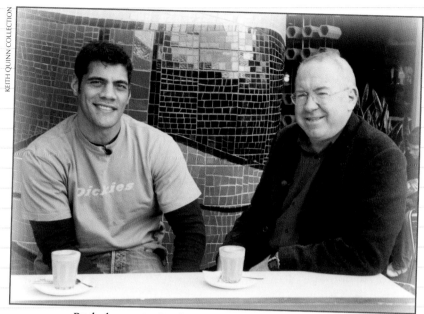

Rugby league star Stephen Kearney made a good tour guide during our stop in Melbourne.

JULY 13

Help! If the rest of the trip is like today, I wonder if I'll be able to battle through. My taxi, driven by the loyal and ever-efficient professional Shirley Waru, is waiting when I come downstairs from my room at Auckland's Heritage Hotel. It's 4.45am. I've been up half the night watching South Africa beat the Wallabies in the Tri Nations opener, so am only half-there all the way to Melbourne on the Qantas flight.

It's cool in Melbourne as our filming begins. At each stop we are to be guests of the state's Tourism Commission. Our guide in Melbourne is Diana Morgan. We're straight into work.

The afternoon is spent in the company of Steve Kearney, the big Kiwi league star who plays for the Melbourne Storm. Steve acts as our guide in a story about the city's trams. The idea works nicely, so one of our proposed 35 stories is in the can, as we Hollywood hotshots say. Everything takes time, though, especially getting Sunday travellers to move from their seats as the tram on which we're filming rolls along. Everyone is very helpful, but by the time producer Steve Jamieson, cameraman Graeme Patrick and I get back to the hotel, we're pretty much knackered.

The cheerful Diana then points out that we are expected at a new restaurant in the Docklands area, so off we troop for seafood at Livebait.

When I finally climb into bed, I realise I've been on the go for nearly 20 hours, and have hardly thought about the All Blacks.

JULY 14

Today is even longer. We film four stories and then fly to Canberra in the evening. We do one story about the planned changes to the Melbourne Cricket Ground and another inside about the four museums and sports exhibitions on permanent display there.

Then it's out to the Yarra Valley for shots and an introduction for a piece on "Melbourne's Favourite Retreat", as they call this beautiful piece of countryside. With 35 wineyards, there is much to attract people.

The highlight today, though, is meeting John Clarke. He strolls out of his office and we immediately feel at home in his infectious company. He has lived in Melbourne since 1978, but is still profoundly Kiwi by nature. John's knowledge of sport is astounding. He recalls playing primary school rugby with men who went on to become All Blacks, he remembers several

He might be John Clarke to millions of Aussies, but he's still Fred Dagg to many New Zealanders.

wild drinking sessions with Grahame Thorne (well, we *all* have those kind of stories) and he tells us how an incident involving one All Black changed his attitude to life.

"In the late 1950s I wrote a fan letter to Terry Lineen, who was then the All Black centre," says John. "He was a hero of mine. He replied very nicely, sending me a signed autograph sheet of that year's All Black team. The thrill of receiving the letter, and the kindness of it, remained with me. A few years later, when I was doing the Fred Dagg thing on New Zealand TV, I used to get a lot of mail, and much of it was from kids. Because of the thrill I got from the Lineen letter, I made a point of replying to every one."

I tell John of Terry McLean's memory of him and we tee up an appropriate beginning to our interview. I solemnly ask John why he left New Zealand, to which he replies in the voice that is still, thankfully, delightfully Kiwi: "Well Keith, because it's there." Terry will chuckle when he sees it.

Then we rush across the city to pick up a massive pile of luggage and camera gear and head to the airport. It's necessary to fly to Canberra tonight, as the fog in that part of the world can be bad, and a closed airport will disrupt our schedule.

JULY 15

Today our ACT guide, Neil Guthrie, takes us on what proves to be a fascinating trip. We are the all-day guests of the Australian Institute of Sport, and are given access to film the entire massive complex. When I say massive, I mean halls of residence for 260 athletes across 35 sports, an Olympic-size swimming pool, a 400m running track, a six-court basketball stadium, tennis courts, a multi-faceted gymnasium, a biochematics laboratory, a talent-identification programme, a biomechanics complex, a video performance analysis room and many other places we don't have the time to enter. Even the lunchroom is monitored. It has to be, because some athletes in training are eating up to eight times a day. For us it is an exhausting tramp from one place to the next, but eye-widening. Now I have some idea why the place produces so many champions.

The day ends with a brief visit to Bruce Stadium, where I talk to Danny Harley, the chief executive of Canberra Stadium. He is generous to his visitors, but tells of the glee in the city when New Zealand's bid to sub-host the World Cup fell over. Canberra, the home of Australia's most consistent rugby team, the Brumbies, wasn't going to get any games under the original plan. Now it will have four. New Zealand's pain is Canberra's gain.

The rush around town means I'm able to spend only 20 minutes with my older brother, George. He has been head of Asian Language Studies at the Australian National University for nearly 20 years, and hasn't lived in New Zealand since 1965. He has never seen his baby brother work. Even so, there is instantly a bit of brotherly assistance when we stop at Lake Burley Griffith so that I can record a piece to camera. I make a slight mistake in the way I word the introduction about his adopted hometown, so, like any helpful big brother, George steps forward and corrects me. Nice work Big Gee, as we in the family call him.

We hump our gear to the airport and catch the 7pm flight to Sydney.

JULY 16

Sydney-based New Zealander Spiro Zavos tells it like it is, as always.

Where are the All Blacks? There's hardly a peep in the papers here about them. But today in *The Sydney Morning Herald* former New Zealander Spiro Zavos' regular column is headlined "Coach Jones may be a good talker but his transitional team is incoherent". Substitute the word "Mitchell" for (Eddie) "Jones" and wasn't that the All Blacks when I left home?

Today we start with a short feature shot covering the workings of the Sydney fish markets. Did you know, for instance, that 54,000 tonnes are Dutch-auctioned there every weekday morning?

Then comes a highlight for me, an afternoon drive to the country town of Bowral. Our story here is about the Sir Donald Bradman Museum. It is well worth the three-hour drive. It is a thrill to stand and look across the picturesque oval to where Australia's greatest sports icon made his senior cricket debut, at the age of 12, in 1920. He played with a sawn-off bat, scoring 37 not out. Our interview subject is Ian Craig, the 1950s Australian test cricket captain. He lives in Bowral and is chairman of the Bradman Foundation board of directors.

One highlight of a fairytale trip to Australia – I get to meet "The Don" at Bowral.

JULY 17

The highlight of today's filming around Sydney is a visit to the headquarters of PMP, a massive printing and paper company in Chatswood, of which New Zealand's only World Cup-winning captain is the chief executive. Bounding in his usual vibrant manner into the room in which we have set up our cameras, David Kirk greets us typically warmly.

Now established in Sydney's business world, he asks about the state of rugby in New Zealand. He has excellent memories of the time in 1987 when he gave a thumbs-up to the crowd after scoring, to signal that he felt the All Blacks had sewn up the World Cup final against France.

133

David Kirk has settled comfortably into commercial life in Sydney, but his passion for New Zealand rugby seems as strong as ever.

He admits to being slightly amused every four years getting media calls, mostly from home, asking him to reflect on that great day at Eden Park. He says he would dearly like another All Black captain to win a World Cup.

One good story he recounts concerned his boots coming out of retirement. It happened after the 1987 season, when he retired and took up a Rhodes Scholarship in England. David presented his Cup final boots to the New Zealand Rugby Museum in Palmerston North and they were displayed proudly. Six years later, when David had returned to New Zealand, he was invited by the Barbarians Club of Auckland to play in a celebratory match in Rangitikei. He agreed, but having been retired for years, had no boots.

He phoned his mother in Palmerston North and asked if he had left any old pairs around the family home. She said he hadn't, but had an idea. Mrs Kirk popped around to the Rugby Museum and explained the problem. The curators allowed her to uplift the donated boots from their display cabinet and they were returned to David for the weekend. He played for the Barbarians and scored several tries. The boots were then returned to the museum, where they went back on display.

JULY 18

It's on to Brisbane for several days' filming. Among our activities today is a meeting another former All Black, Grant Batty, at the newly-revamped SunCorp Stadium. Security there on a non-match day is ridiculously stern. I sign three small documents and two people follow us wherever we go.

Batts is coach and general manager of the Gold Coast Breakers rugby club, the home of Wendell Sailor. We lament the passing of Lin Colling, news of whose death came through last weekend. Colling was the first of the 1972–73 All Blacks to pass away. Batty mentions that some members of that All Black team are formulating a plan to find the much-missed Keith Murdoch and try to bring him back to New Zealand from the Australian outback, where he has lived in self-imposed exile since being sent home during the tour of Britain all those years ago.

Batts and I remark on the poor quality of the playing surface of the new stadium. As we speak, a group of workmen start what looks like a complete "sand-slitting" of the turf. Let's hope the ground is at its best for the nine World Cup games in three months' time.

It's terrific to catch up again with that dynamic winger of the 1970s, Grant Batty, who these days is doing good things for rugby in Queensland.

JULY 19

We journey three hours into the bush today, to Woodenbong. To get there we cross back into New South Wales. The purpose is to film an outback rodeo.

Back at our Brisbane hotel, I snooze for a couple of hours before the All Blacks play their first Tri Nations match. At least in Australia test rugby in South Africa comes through at a reasonable hour.

At 11pm the All Blacks run out to meet the Springboks in Pretoria. There is simultaneous coverage on two stations. You can choose Aussie commentary on Channel 7 or the South African angle on Fox TV.

After a faltering start, New Zealand are soon steaming towards one of their most significant recent wins. The final score is 52–16. As Reuben Thorne comes off the field, he tells a reporter: "It's always tough to come here to Loftus and win, so we are *very* pleased today." It is Thorne's best media quip this year. And he has his best game, too. Have we all been wrong about him?

What I like most is the emphatic way the team thing works. The forwards, encouraged at the start by a storming midfield run by Chris Jack, work over their Springbok opposites clinically and ruthlessly. Given front-foot ball, the New Zealand backs flourish. The seven tries are extremely well taken. Rokocoko goes from strength to strength. He scores two more tries, as does Howlett, in a return to form for him.

Several other factors help the win. One is the return of the solid Aaron Mauger at second five-eighth. Another is the fact that the game is played in bright afternoon sunshine. The All Blacks relish it. On the other hand, poor South Africa ... the only thing they win is the singing of the national anthems.

JULY 20

A day off. Well, partly. Up at the gloriously late hour of 7am, it's out to the airport, the three of us humping 12 boxes, bags and suitcases, for a flight to Proserpine. Once there we check into the Coral Sea Resort at Airlie Beach for two nights.

There's just time to watch TV coverage of the Australian cricket team beating Bangladesh in a test match at Darwin. It is a right old thumping, but one hard-case radio man on the ABC is heard to say: "On the basis of what we saw the All Blacks do last night in Pretoria, is it possible the Wallabies could get a rugby test next week against Bangladesh?" Don't you love that wry Aussie humour? There does seem a sense of doom in much of the rugby humour here at the moment.

JULY 21

A lovely day weather-wise, but a terrible one in every other aspect. Our hardy film crew is on the dock at 8am, set to embark on a cruise around Great Barrier Reef. Life is looking pretty good as the blue sea streams out behind our cruising launch. Then the cell phone rings and it is John McBeth calling from Wellington to say John Davies has died.

I am shattered. I saw John just a few days ago. Though he looked fragile, he said to me: "You have a great time in Australia, Quinn." So typical of him to always think of the other person. At the time all I could do was give him the simple native South African parting of: "Stay well old friend."

Now he is gone. A gentleman and a gentle person. John was one of the best men I have known and one of my soundest and closest friends. I hope he gets the kind of send-off he merits as a great New Zealander, who believed fervently that through sport the world could be a much better place.

Steve and Graeme are also upset at the news, but, being so far away, what can we do? Our every step of every minute for the next fortnight is mapped out and there are commitments we cannot avoid. If we had been in Sydney when this news had come through, I would have gone home for John's funeral, but on Friday I will be at Uluru, in the heart of outback Australia. "At least it is a spiritual place," I tell dear Patsy tonight when I speak to her on the phone. She is generous enough to say: "Keith, I know you'll be there with us in spirit on the funeral day."

At home in Wellington, Anne says she will definitely be going to Auckland on Friday. I have to admit that today, in faraway Great Barrier Reef, I do not do my best work. I have other, sadder things on my mind.

JULY 22

The filming schedule is still a bit of a blur today, though it is full of Australia's exotic experiences. We fly into Cairns and begin a story about the Royal Flying Doctor Service. We'll shoot the second half of it in Alice Springs later this week.

Then we zoom through steamy Cairns to the home of David Hudson, Australia's biggest-selling didgeridoo player. From the time we see his cheery wave to us from the porch of his house, he makes us feel very welcome. His stories of the traditional Aboriginal musical instrument are captivating. The fact that he is a composer and painter, and that with his brilliant talent is able to accompany himself on guitar while playing the didgeridoo, adds to the fascination of being in his company. Via several of the 27 CD albums he has released so far, we pound out his rhythms in our rental car as we drive away.

Dave makes a wonderful gesture – he makes me a didgeridoo to take home. I am taken aback. On it he paints a silver fern logo and a wallaby. Plus, his hand imprint in paint, as a gesture of friendship. He is bringing it to the hotel tomorrow.

JULY 23

It's Wednesday today and we are about 3000km from the All Blacks, who are in full training in Sydney for Saturday's Bledisloe Cup match. What are they saying and thinking? What quips has John Mitchell made that I should have written down? In *The Cairns Post* today is one small item about the team. There's much more about the rugby league test this Friday night in Sydney and the second cricket test against Bangladesh, which starts here in Cairns on Friday.

Our filming today is about the Kuku Yalanji tribe's life in the rainforests of far north Queensland. Our guide, Roy Gibson, announces he is feeling "crook" when we meet him, but says he will be okay once he goes into the forest. The forest has that effect on him, he says. Like David Hudson yesterday, Roy proves a fascinating subject. Why didn't I know more about the Aborigine tribes and their customs before this trip? They are fascinating and wonderful people.

Roy tells us that every day when he comes to work as a guide he goes by himself into the woods and talks in his native tongue, either out loud or "from inside", to his elders and forefathers. He can hear from the trees and streams how they advise him to live his life. He says they had told him that morning that everything would go well in our interviewing of him. And so it did.

No disrespect, but I'd have preferred to stay in the rainforest, with its tranquillity and peace, and learn more from our new friend, than to move on to film at the Crocodile Farm in the afternoon. Still, the crocs, 2500 of them, at Hartley's Crocodile Adventure complex, are on our schedule. Given the human fascination with this 60-million-year-old creature, and the sight of them leaping out of the water and snapping at pieces of dangling chicken, I'm sure it will make for an interesting item.

JULY 24

We're up early and on a 6.30am flight to Ayers Rock. That means a 4am wake-up call and baggage in the foyer by 5am. Just when I imagine that a flight across Australia will be like one from say, Auckland to Wellington, I'm wrong again. I'm reminded every day that Australia is such a massive place. It is a three-and-a-quarter-hour flight from Cairns to Ayers Rock. On the way the stewardess reminds me that you can fit all of Europe into Australia, with room to spare.

Coming in to land we can see Uluru in all its magnificence. This famous giant red monolith stands in the middle of the desert in the centre of Australia. It's a beautiful place to be, so peaceful and serene. As we prepare to film, we are reminded to be respectful of the Anangu, the traditional owners of the land, and the rock surrounds.

The weather is a contrast: freezing cold in the morning for our filming shortly after we arrive, burning hot in the afternoon, dropping towards freezing again as the sun sets. It is great to be here today. Another highlight in the life of a lucky man.

Would it be possible to film in front of a more dramatic setting than the famous Ayers Rock, in the middle of Australia?

JULY 25

If I cannot be at John Davies' funeral today in Auckland, then Uluru is a worthy substitute location. We leave the hotel in dark, freezing conditions and watch the morning sun peek over the edge of the rock. What a sight, with its shafts of light and blossoming colours, bringing back warmth to everything by the minute. What thoughts it also empowers a man to have about life and its importance. Make the most of life, is the powerful message to me from this deeply inspirational place.

Later, I phone Anne. She tells me of the very appropriate and moving service for John, which nearly 1000 people attended at St Mary's in Parnell.

Tonight I have another very persuasive experience, spooky even. At Uluru you can partake in a wonderful evening called the "Sounds of Silence Dinner". For this, about 60 tourists from many countries climb to a high point in the desert away from the hotel, and the red soil is flattened down hard to make a perfect viewing place. There, sipping drinks, we chat and watch as the sun goes down. The midday brilliance of Uluru changes from bright red to a glowering grey before disappearing into the darkness. To see it change and disappear is quite something.

When it has gone and the temperature is heading towards freezing, we are ushered to an open-air silver-service table settings area, where a full four-course dinner of the most elegant cuisine is served. Yes, it is cold, but braziers of glowing embers warm each table as dinner is served. It is a fascinating setting, with the red dust underfoot.

Among the dishes offered are some from the desert, like kangaroo and crocodile steaks and casseroles. It is all superb and is washed down with the best Aussie wines. And yet, just when we are lulled into thinking it can't get any better, a local identity named Laksar Burra, born in New Zealand but resident in the area for many years, steps out of the shadows. The candles at each table are extinguished and we are invited to quieten down and listen to the desert's "sounds of silence".

With 60 people totally silent, in pitch blackness, with no cell phones rattling, no passing cars, or kids chattering, no TV sounds, no doors slamming, the only sound able to be picked up is the light rustle of the gentle desert breezes kissing the grasses on the edge of the dining area.

Then, in a powerful and measured style, Laksar Burra launches into an identification of every major star and constellation that can be seen above us. To aid his performance, he points out each one with powerful spotlights and laser beams. It is a brilliant show. There has never been

One of the most moving moments of my life – meeting the inspirational Laksar Burra at Uluru. On this most poignant of days for me, Laksar was John Davies.

better viewing of the night sky, or a better staging place. The blackness is as total as the silence.

Maybe my mind is powerfully sensitive on this day and distracted by what I know has been happening in faraway Auckland, but in that moment this mystery man, Laksar, assumes for me something of another form. While I am interviewing him for our show, I am struck by what I see as his powerful and eerie resemblance to John Davies. I cannot explain it. Tears keep clouding my eyes while the interview is in progress. For a start I make out it is the brightness of the last of the afternoon sun that is the problem. Laksar asks me if I am okay. I tell him it is just that he resembles a friend of mine, who has been buried in Auckland only hours before. Call me silly if you like, but to me, on this night, the tall, slim, bespectacled, stylish and quietly-confident Laksar *is* John Davies. It is Davies talking about the stars and looking towards the heavens.

Laksar seems intrigued by my story, but I think it is only me being emotional. My next thought is to "get a grip". I recall wondering whether I will try the sizzling kangaroo meat that smells so good. Laksar disappears from the dinner area. I do not notice that. Later, though, he returns, coming out of the pitch darkness. As we are all enjoying coffee and still gazing skywards and marvelling at the show he had put on, he says he had slipped back to his home, a number of miles away. He has returned with a piece of his beautifully hand-worked glassware, a piece that depicts a local Anangu Aboriginal story. "Take this," he says to me, "for the connection you have made here. This place, Uluru, does that for many people in many ways. I see it all the time. I'm glad you felt it here tonight."

I am speechless. The piece of intricate, heavy-worked glassware will always have pride of place in my home. I will see it as Laksar's work and a memory of beautiful John Davies.

JULY 26

I'm halfway through one of the most amazing travelling experiences I've been on. Meanwhile, in Sydney, the All Blacks will today meet a Wallaby team smarting from their recent loss to South Africa. I know that, because through the Internet I read the Sydney papers. In the cities they're worried, but not many out in the bush care a jot about rugby union or any upcoming World Cup.

We fly today from Yulara (the resort village that services tourism around Uluru) to Alice Springs. Fancy watching an All Black-Wallaby test from there. Steve, Graeme and I retire to our hotel rooms to watch the game and later gather with glazed eyes to discuss the amazing result.

The All Blacks sweep aside the Aussies 50–21, a remarkable score. Never have Australia lost by so much to the All Blacks. Being so far removed, I cannot imagine how the New Zealand public is going to view this result. What about the previous disquiet and unease? From Alice Springs I half-wonder how I can tune into Radio Sport to hear the previous whiners about John Mitchell, Reuben Thorne and co now warmly applauding their wonderful talents. Mind you, a flick back through the pages of this diary will reveal I've had uncertainties about them, too. We all have, haven't we?

I once again find myself vigorously applauding wing Joe Rokocoko's brilliance. His three tries are superbly taken. I especially like his sprint from halfway. No Australian can catch him. The sprint comes after Tana Umaga's best pass to one of his wings in years. And from that incident Tana himself seems to burst back into favour. Doug Howlett, too, with a couple of tries, adds further to New Zealand's sting out wide.

Even though it is a wonderful victory, there are one or two areas of concern. The lineout timing and jumping are not good again. Keven Mealamu does not always make contact with his designated targets when throwing. Australia win six or seven balls off New Zealand throws. The Aussie Channel 7 commentary team, led by my old mates Gordon Bray and Chris (Buddha) Handy, are amazed that New Zealand can win by so much with only 40 per cent of the set-play possession.

It also crosses my mind that if the World Cup, now only sevens weeks away, goes as expected, New Zealand will meet Australia again. Can a World Cup semi-final result in a score like this one? Surely not. Other outside influences, like injuries to star players, wet weather, ground conditions and home support, might combine to make it a lot closer. For the sake of the tournament's solidity and credibility you'd hope to have close, exciting matches all the way.

However, favouritism for the Bledisloe Cup, not to mention World Cup, has swung back to New Zealand. The All Blacks have to win or draw in Auckland in a fortnight's time to clinch the Bledisloe Cup for the first time since 1998.

Australia, meantime, is in a right state of worry. I am now saying to anyone who will listen over here: "If you have any spare change, back Argentina to beat Australia on day one of the World Cup." The Wobblies seem right for the plucking.

JULY 27

There's no time to celebrate the win. In worse-than-freezing conditions, we're tossed out to another filming job today, at 5am, in Alice Springs. It's with a locally-based former Hawke's Bay man named Jason Livingstone. He has us sailing across the desert in our first giant hot-air ballooning experience. Jason and our TV crew have a few cheery words with the Australians present about the rugby score last night. Not all of the locals appreciate which game we are talking about. Apparently, Port Adelaide beat Brisbane Lions yesterday in a thrilling AFL game.

JULY 28

Last night we flew two hours from Alice Springs to far-flung Coober Pedy, a town of 3000 that is famous for three things – the world's best Opal "noodling" opportunities, the eccentric lifestyle of half of the local population (they live in cave houses to keep out the searing summer heat) and Peter Rowe, who knows everybody and everything in the town. All three impress us.

Now we are really out the back of beyond. When people here talk about "down the road", they can mean 400 kilometres away. Often a neighbour is 200 kilometres away.

The hard case and hard-working Peter Rowe takes us on his mail run to some outlying homesteads and farms. Some are massive. For example, Anna Creek Station is bigger than Belgium, Wales or Israel. If you rode a horse its length it would take a week. The station runs 16,000 head of beef.

We film the remarkable dingo fence, which keeps the wild dogs from the north from harassing the docile sheep in the south. The fence runs for 5291km and stretches from Queensland to South Australia. It is longer than the Great Wall of China.

We stop in William Creek for lunch at the tearooms there. It is said to be the smallest town in Australia. The population was 12 until wee Patrick, only six weeks old, raised it to 13. (He was working on his mother's hip, helping sell excellent home-made pies and sandwiches to weary travellers.)

JULY 29

Tonight Peter Rowe bundles 12 of us (the TV crew plus some tourists) into his mini-bus and takes us 40 kilometres out to Manguri, where he requests each of us to get out and wait in the dark by the side of the railway tracks. We are killing time for the arrival of The Ghan, the daily luxury train that runs from Alice Springs to Adelaide. There is no railway station. Standing there in the middle of nowhere, it is *cold*. Undeterred, Peter lights a lovely warm fire by the side of the track. "The driver will see this and stop for you," he says, "and you'd better drink this," he adds, handing out glasses bubbling with Australia's best, along with platters of local cheese. It is so dark you can't see a foot in front of you without a light ("It's blacker than a black dog's guts at midnight out here," is how Peter, our lovely Aussie mate, puts it).

Eventually, the train chugs in, slowing in the dark as we 12 strangers huddle around the fire. It's wild west stuff. We clamber on, heaving up our voluminous baggage, filming for a train story as we do so. We are given a royal welcome by the train officials, Trevor White and Debbie Munn, and settle down to ride in luxury and to sleep overnight on our way to Adelaide. Where is that World Cup again? Which teams are playing for it? Who cares? Who are Collingwood playing next?

JULY 30

News about the World Cup is *really* sporadic now. We've passed through Adelaide for a day and have headed to the Chardonnay Lodge in the Coonawarra region of the south-east of South Australia. Our host at the lodge, James Yates, is formerly from Whangarei. He and his wife Anne have built a superb establishment, with fine food and excellent hospitality. Coonawarra is the place they call Australia's "other" red centre (the main one being the red dust of the Northern Territory). The "other" one here is a tribute to the beautiful red wines produced by dozens of vineyards around this Limestone Coast region.

James and Anne, and others in the past two days, have been wondering about the news from New Zealand about the All Blacks squabbling with the Rugby Union over money. Peter Bissell, formerly of Hokitika, and now one of Australia's finest winemakers, and resident here at the Balnaves Estate, is well-briefed on the game back home. But when he asks me about the squabble I can't offer much on the subject. It has not been talked about here. Surely it will be sorted out soon, we feel.

JULY 31

Well, it is sorted out after all. Like the Doug Howlett "going overseas" story earlier in the year, this one took time to work through. Now we know the All Blacks will get a bigger bonus if they win the World Cup. Up to $80,000, it's reported. And they get some of that money even if they don't win. It's all rather academic to me.

First, the team has to actually win the thing, don't they? And though South Africa and Australia have been turned back with impressive ease, there is still a long way to go on the "journey".

AUGUST

*"In rugby you have to
win your grinds."*

AUGUST 1

Day 21 of our trip. I'm in Melbourne, and feel like it's time to fly home. But our schedule says we must fly in the opposite direction. So, here we go again ... baggage in the foyer at 6.30am, pay the bill, then fly to Perth on the 8.10am flight. We arrive in the west at 10.10am (the time difference is against us). We film two local stories, followed by a drive for four hours in a mini-bus. We finally rest our heads in Margaret River at 11pm. It's been a 15-hour working day – and I know that back home they'll be calling this trip a "holiday".

One of the stories today is about Trent Croad. We think he's the only Kiwi playing in the Aussie Rules football competition, the AFL. He's a nice young bloke, and very proud he is of his All Black connection, via his granddad, the 1946–49 wing Eric Boggs.

AUGUST 2

The Perth weather lets us down on our last day of filming. Wild winds sweep the southwest coast and we can't do a planned story on surfboard riding. However, there is compensation in visiting Voyager Estate, where some of the finest young red wines in Australia are produced. They are part of the emerging region of Margaret River.

Our driver on the last afternoon, Jeff Cottrell, tries to get us to Perth on time, but we reach the Sebel Hotel only in time to catch the last minutes and highlights of the South Africa versus Australia Tri Nations game in Brisbane. According to the commentary, this is "Australia back to its best" but I can hardly agree. From what I see, and have confirmed in replays, this is a case of "two bad teams having an off day", mixed in with a couple of nasty incidents. And this from two teams who had conceded 50 points to the All Blacks in their last outings. Australia win tonight, 29–9.

147

AUGUST 3

A sleepy Sunday in Perth. From the last of the 16 hotels we have stayed at over 23 days, the baggage, cameras, sound gear, cables, lights, videotapes, tripods and all the other stuff that makes up a travelling TV crew (nearly 200 kilograms in all) is lugged into the mini-bus and the three of us head home. It has been a splendid experience, finding out about the great expanse of the real Australia. The loading and unloading of the gear from the hotels has been a pain, but hey, life is great when we can say we have done all that we have done. We reached our goal of 35 stories, five more than was originally asked of us.

Leaving Perth. Not long now till kick-off.

For Steve there is a massive job ahead over the next month. He must trawl through the 10 hours of video we have shot to make the travel features that will play between games during the TVNZ World Cup coverage. We think they will look good.

Home to Wellington at midnight, with only a slight delay getting my didgeridoo through customs. "Just wait, I'll have to ream it for termites," says the officer on duty, with a determined look in his eye. "Ouch," I whisper to myself, giving me my first thoughts in weeks about my earlier health issues.

Anne is waiting in the airport, which for such a late hour is a marvellous and much-appreciated effort. She takes one look at the weary traveller and announces quietly that she has a few days off from work and we are to head away for couple of days R and R.

AUGUST 5

The world has changed. I tune in to the radio and read a couple of old newspapers. What has happened to the doom, gloom and misery of the country I left three weeks ago? I have been home for only 48 hours and already can sense a new feeling of optimism among Kiwis about the World Cup. People seem to be whistling as they go about their daily lives. Gone are the reservations about everything to do with the All Blacks' on-field performances.

The doubts and fears from those early test performances have disappeared – well, maybe not completely, there are still mutterings about lineout throwing – but in my listening and reading I detect no great depression now. The dark clouds have lifted, helped no doubt by the recent big wins over our old foes.

A scan of last weekend's *Sunday Star-Times* shows me that dear old Phil Gifford is back writing about Canterbury players. All *must* be well in the world!

The Springboks arrive in Dunedin from Brisbane for their match with the All Blacks. There are claims and counter-claims about dirty play from the test against Australia at the weekend. Corne Krige appears on the *Holmes* show and on *Deaker on Sport* to put his side of the argument. He says that though Bakkies Botha and Robbie Kempson have received suspensions following their actions, the South Africans are not a dirty team. Eddie Jones, the Wallaby coach, disagrees. He and George Gregan have said some very aggressive things about the Springboks' on-field attitude.

I go along with Krige. Every Springbok team I've watched has been tough, mean and hard, and might have pushed the boundaries on several occasions, but, per se, they are not dirty rugby players. Tough yes, dirty no.

Be quiet Eddie and George. You should be concentrating on getting your own house right.

The self-belief in New Zealand rugby has allowed John Mitchell to announce five changes in his All Black team for this Saturday in Dunedin. He says on the TV news tonight that he is not working a rotation policy, rather it is "faith in the squad", a nice way of putting it. It is an expression I have not heard before.

In will come Brad Thorn for his first starting test, and there is a re-shuffle of the forwards. There is a complete change in the front row, with Greg Somerville, Keven Mealamu and Dave Hewett stepping aside for Kees Meeuws, Mark Hammett and Carl Hoeft. At openside flanker Richie

From drama to chaos

The man ... cent ... at ... World Cup bonus dispute ... sports and being busy ...

Boys who cried 'more'

Agents maligned in bonus ruckus

There's a moral side to working for players says the agent to some of New Zealand's top sportspeople

The player bonus row ... I'm glad I was away while this storm raged.

McCaw will rest and his back-up, Marty Holah, gets the reward of a starting place. Holah's name was mentioned to me a lot in conversations in Australia. They like him over there. I recall how well he played at Twickenham last year against England. A towering game.

We are right back into the action. John McBeth rings to say he and I are off to Dunedin this weekend to see the test. But, he adds, there are no hotel rooms available on the Saturday night. So I ring my brother Max, a long-time Dunedin resident. He says: "Sure, you can stay with us." He adds: "Tonight we had to move tables in the Jizo Japanese restaurant, as we diners were told by the staff that 'the All Blacks are coming to eat'. Sure enough, in came all of the backs in the team."

All Blacks eating Japanese food? Such a gastronomic option would never have happened in the old days. I recall an All Blacks tour of France in 1990 when two of the younger players were assigned to find a nice dining place for the squad. In turn, the full team would assemble in their "number one" dinner jackets for the much-anticipated culinary experience. The two young players then announced that for the outing they had chosen the McDonald's outlet across the street from the hotel.

Since returning from Australia, I've spoken to a few people about the money squabbles last week between the All Blacks and the NZRU board. The story was obviously huge all over the country. Some say it was the biggest rugby story of the year. I don't doubt that. The fact that the discussions, debates and late-night arguments all happened and were resolved last week is a blessing for me. Being in Australia meant I have been kept away from that acrid odour. I cannot stand arguing about money.

At least the two parties have settled. For the record, the 30-man All Black squad will each receive up to $NZ80,000 as bonuses from their World Cup games. That is up from the $40,000 the Rugby Union originally offered each player but down on the Players Association demand of $120,000 each.

It underscores several things. In this age of professional sport the public is being made to understand more each year how mean and nasty dealings between players and their employers can become. There is no loyalty any more to the previously blessed colour of the All Black jersey. To even talk of such loyalty is to indicate your advancing years. Such blind attachment to the colours is outmoded.

I have a very recent CD by the black American Toni Braxton. In one of her sultry songs she sings: "In life you never get what is fair, you get what you negotiate." Is that the All Black theme song these days?

If it is, then it is very sad, but a sign of the times, I'm afraid.

AUGUST 7

I'm back on Radio Sport this morning, and guess what? Martin Devlin welcomes me back by saying: "And how was your junket through Australia, Keith?" I knew it, I bloody knew it. We should have contracted the bugger to come with us, even if just to be in charge of the baggage handling. Then we'd have seen how much of a junket he thought it was.

AUGUST 9

Test day. I fly to Dunedin and check in at Hotel Quinn. It was a lovely day but freezing cold tonight. Everyone is asking: "Why could the game not have been played during the day?" It's a fair question, and is asked more by Dunedin people when they have a lovely day for a test and their game is scheduled for a night kick-off. What they might say if it was hosing down with rain is another matter. The discussion confirms my view that there is still a delightful air of innocence among Dunedin's sporting populace. It is one of the city's nicest points. The issue of money is not raised much today, but there is much discussion about the weather.

The All Blacks win, 19–11, in front of 36,000 people. A score as close as that sits comfortably with me. There is an assurance about the future of test rugby while games are a true contest like this one. But afterwards many people are disappointed that the All Blacks haven't run up another 50-plus total. It doesn't work that way. Never has.

There are only two tries in the game and both are remarkable. First, Aaron Mauger chips through a low bouncing kick behind the South African defence. From my view in the press box the ball looks like it might run into the dead ball zone. In a flash though, Joe Rokocoko is on it, sprinting through to claim the ball and score. The crowd gasps at Joe's speed.

But even that try's brilliance pales when compared to big Richard Bands'
run to glory for the Springboks. The roly-poly prop bursts away from his
mates and, from 45 metres out, begins a charge. He pushes off Kees
Meeuws, then Carlos Spencer, and gradually increases, not speed, but
momentum. When he comes thundering past where I sit one can almost
sense him saying: "I'm going to have a crack for the line." It's astonishing
when he makes it, crashing over in Mauger's grasp. The crowd cheers
the prop's effort. It is one of the best long-distance tries I have seen.
McBeth and I can't think of one better. (John nominates Wilson
Whineray's effort for the All Blacks against the Barbarians in Cardiff in
1964, while I have vague video-memories of Welshman Graham Price
thundering away for a match-winner in Paris in the mid-1970s.)

AUGUST 10

The Sunday papers offer muted praise for the All Blacks' win. At the
same time, there is grudging admiration for the way the Springboks had
played so stoutly, in the face of their recent defeats. It's good to see them
coming back, I say, though many others offer the "We should have kicked
them some while they are down" theory.

John McBeth relates a conversation he had over the weekend with a
prominent NPC coach, who has been in recent contact with John Mitchell.
"Mitchell reckons," says John, "that the key to the World Cup for All
Blacks lies in viewing last November's test against England at Twickenham.
That was when an inexperienced New Zealand team scored four tries
against the same English defence that operated in New Zealand this year.
The methods of scoring that day were not attempted at all in Wellington
when England came to play. The successful moves remain locked away
in the All Blacks' arsenal of attacks. They are practising them this year,
but so far haven't used them."

AUGUST 11

We're on the road again, filming. This time it's McBeth and I, with
cameraman Steve Croy, and we are spending a couple of days cruising

around the Otago and Southland provinces. Our aim is to capture ordinary Kiwi people on video talking about their interest in watching the TV1 coverage of the World Cup. It's different from the type of coverage we attempted in Australia last month. Today it's more like getting "grabs" from people, rather than making full stories. We travel all day from Dunedin, through Rae's Junction, Gore, Waikaia and Winton to Invercargill.

AUGUST 12

More filming, starting in Bluff and wending our way to Dunedin. McBeth and Quinn fly home, 29 stories and faces achieved in two days.

I leave my cell phone in Steve Croy's van and ring him to check if he has it. Steve tells me he was assigned to film the farewell dinner for Taine Randell tonight in the Dunedin Town Hall. According to Steve, Taine made a gracious thank you speech, mentioning that he was leaving Dunedin tomorrow, probably forever, but when it came to leaving the stage, perhaps distracted by emotion, he tripped on the steps and tumbled awkwardly to the floor below. "He was okay, but it was a sad way for him to leave," says Steve.

AUGUST 13

The All Black team is announced for the game this weekend against Australia in Auckland. John Mitchell shows his hand by returning to the top XV that beat the Wallabies so well in Sydney. So, at last we're seeing a pattern. These now seem his top men. The worry is, I suppose, that they must play through the last of the build-up tests injury-free.

Oh no! Our old friend Suzy is back in the headlines. You wouldn't believe it, but memories of the 1995 World Cup final in Johannesburg come flooding back today. The theory is that a hotel worker called Suzy deliberately poisoned the All Blacks before the final. Now, in 2003, some bloke in the hotel industry in South Africa has announced in a South African newspaper that he knows for sure that the reason the All Blacks lost the final that year was because the players had eaten a prawn meal on the Friday night before the game and had got sick from that. The hotel man said the players kept this dinner news from coach Laurie Mains because Mains would have been wild to know they had eaten such a dinner the night before the test.

This version of events has been quickly rubbished today. Laurie himself reminds us that the illness struck on the Thursday night before the final and by Friday night the sick players were very sick indeed. The prawns theory is just another to add to the list. According to historical records (an increasing stack of newspaper clippings) the All Blacks were poisoned after taking on bad water, bad tea, bad coffee, bad hamburgers, bad milk, bad chilli sauce, bad fish and now bad prawns.

AUGUST 14

I'm in Auckland today for a Trans-Tasman Business Luncheon. Held at the Carlton Hotel, it is a very flash do and Peter FitzSimons is his usual bubbling self as the other speaker. "Don't go too long Keith," he says to me, "and be boring, won't you. They've come to hear me, not you!" If that sounds bigheaded from him, it's not. Peter is a great guy and *together* we seem to satisfy the crowd. We agree, however, that the 650 attendees are not our usual rugby audiences. As a speaker you can tell when the significance of a rugby story doesn't quite hit the mark. The vivacious organiser Alison Parker tells us we were great. That's all that matters.

AUGUST 15

I edit a small pre-Bledisloe Cup story for *Gillette Sportsfix* all day today. Tonight I am one of the so-called celebrity barmen at the Albion Hotel. You see, we *are* allowed an hour or two of freedom. John McBeth, Stu Dennison, jockey Alan Peard and I pull pints for the throng. I am starting to believe that the big city is really getting into this test match thing. This promotion – the "Hi How Are You Party!" – has been the idea of Paul "Doy" Hafford for the past 10 years. This time it really gets the crowd going, with lots of pre-test buzz. Not like some other years, when a test match has taken place in Auckland and you would hardly have known it the night before.

A slightly disconcerting thing happens today. I take a call from a sports journalist at *The Sunday Star-Times*. He wants me to comment on the rumour that he says is "racing around town". The rumour says: "Keith Quinn and John McBeth are to be replaced for TVNZ's coverage at the World Cup. The company is looking for younger people to do the job." What can one say to a question like that? I ask the journo where the rumour came from, and he, understandably, doesn't tell me. Except to say: "Out of a good source inside TVNZ."

I'm flabbergasted. All this at a time when the station is running promotions that clearly show the portly, dashing Quinn and the slim, dashing McBeth as part of the commentary and presenting team for the Cup. And I have a schedule that shows when I fly to Sydney, where I will live while I am there, and when exactly I will come home. Somehow a rumour has flared. Later in the day, after phone calls from the TVNZ Sports Department to the writer, the man on the phone turns up for a drink at the Albion Hotel. I ask him: "Have I still got a job?" He says sheepishly: "Yes you have mate. We've dropped the story."

Still, it's disconcerting to be dealing with stuff like this with only 56 days until the Cup kicks off.

AUGUST 16

Test day, and an on-and-off day for the weather. I am reminded of the Crowded House song "Four Seasons in One Day". Raining one minute, sunny the next. I look at *The New Zealand Herald's* super sport edition from yesterday and try to work out how they got a photo of Reuben Thorne holding up the Bledisloe Cup in triumph. It's amazing what computers can do. And the *Herald* also publishes a picture of all of the captains from previous Wallaby and New Zealand tests. It is a beauty.

McBeth and I go to Eden Park early and do our TV thing there. I buy a match programme to check the teams and so on, and find that it costs me $10. I also buy one for my old mate Cyril Delaney, who is such an avid collector. Expensive, but it is an excellent publication, full of information, stories and statistics.

We go to the press box and Graham Reddaway, the hard-working media officer, finds me a seat. I am to be next to Phil Gifford, and he and I chat to all of our media mates in the row behind us. But when I sit down I find that a late-arriving media person has nicked one of my precious $10 programmes. The bastard! I hope I am not a mean man, but I did spend my cash to buy two copies.

The All Black and Wallaby teams go through the national anthems. Ali Williams jumps up and down throughout both of them. That's eminently sensible to me – after all, it is a cold night, and the anthems can last up to 10 minutes. Who wouldn't be cold standing around in their underwear doing nothing for that long?

The game kicks off with a high state of excitement from the 45,000 crowd and it stays that way throughout. It's a good game to match the mood. New Zealand win 21–17 after scoring two thrilling tries, both by Doug Howlett, and, though somewhat wayward at times, Carlos Spencer adds the rest of the points via his goal-kicking.

The most important facet of the win is the teeth-rattling defence of the All Blacks. The Wallabies play at a much-improved level than they had at Sydney and Brisbane. They launch many storming attacks, all of which are repelled until George Smith goes over with five minutes to play. Before that, referee Jonathan Kaplan twice has to call on the video referee to judge on two very close try-scoring attempts. Both times the All Blacks defenders have somehow clawed their way under the Wallabies as they lunge at the line.

The best individual of the New Zealanders is hooker Keven Mealamu, who makes many thrusts and in one move makes like a centre as he bursts through to draw the fullback and send Doug Howlett away to score.

The other player who catches my eye is the All Blacks skipper himself. Reuben Thorne excels, with a true leader's game. His confidence is growing in every game. He makes a number of critical tackles, runs aggressively several times into gaps and, in the last 10 minutes, when Australia are within striking distance, calls the lineout throws to himself and grabs the ball each time. These are all critical takes. Thorne's stride about the field now has a more commanding leadership look, too.

At the end of the game, with only a four-point winning margin, the All Blacks fling their arms about in wild celebration. These gestures are, no doubt, for tonight's victory, but also for bringing home the Bledisloe Cup, which has not been in New Zealand since 1998.

I look closely into the faces of the coaching and captaincy staff of the two teams afterwards. Eddie Jones and George Gregan come in first to face the biggest media scrum of the season. Far from being downcast at Australia's loss of the trophy, the two are bright-eyed. Gregan says: "We still have areas of improvement to make, but we are a team which knows where we're going. We showed that tonight." That is true enough, when one considers their improvement from a 50–21 loss three weeks ago to just 21–17 tonight.

And when Jones is asked about whether he is feeling better about playing the All Blacks in a possible World Cup semi-final, his eyes flash. "Yep, can't wait," he says.

John Mitchell, Robbie Deans and Reuben Thorne are next and, while not looking like their grannies had died, their faces show only strong, resolute and stoic features. They are behaving in the true All Black tradition. Remember the "Unsmiling Giants" tag of the 1960s? The big three of this year's All Blacks look anything but like they have just been part of a solid win at the end of a long build-up season.

Mitchell agrees that it was a tough, grinding match and adds: "In rugby you have to win your grinds." I glance at Doug Golightly, of *The Truth* and Radio Sport, who is standing near me. He and I had just been lamenting the fact that there had not been many additions to "Mitch-speak" in recent weeks. But "winning your grinds" is a good new one.

Then Thorne breaks from tradition (which might earn a rebuke from the coaches afterwards). He allows a wide smile, one that hasn't been seen this year. Perhaps it is a further sign of his growing confidence. When asked about who made the calls for him to be the target of those last three lineouts, he replies: "I did, it was an option." This again had Doug and me exchanging sly winks. "It's an option" is right out of the old Alex Wyllie phrase book.

There is no doubt Reuben Thorne has moved solidly upwards into the captaincy role. His confidence has come with the recent wins, of course, but he must be inwardly smiling now, especially when he sees headlines like the one *The Otago Daily Times* offers: "We Love You Now, Reuben Thorne". I should check to see what the same paper was saying earlier in the season, when their Anton Oliver and Taine Randell had been passed over. *Rugby News* has a cover story headline this week titled, "From Captain Invisible to Captain Invincible". That pretty well represents the national swing in opinion about this man.

Robbie Deans sits quietly for most of the press conference, but when some bright spark asks whether he had forgotten what the Bledisloe Cup looked like, Robbie, who had been in a team that won it in 1984, replies with the best quip of the session: "No, I haven't forgotten, and down in the dressing room we've just been reminded that it still holds the same!"

Everyone in the room laughs heartily. Then John Mitchell says: "We'll see you all for the World Cup team announcement on the 25th." With that, and resuming their serious faces, they file out. One reporter over to my left claps heartily. This is not done in a press conference, you understand. A Winston Churchill quote jumps into my head. "This is, perhaps, the end of the beginning."

Out in the street, as McBeth and Quinn try to flag down a cab, a wild-eyed man gives the first indication that a percentage of New Zealand rugby supporters are *still* not satisfied with the All Blacks. "Why didn't Mitchell use more players off the bench? The Aussies did," the man yells at me, while his wife tries to persuade him to keep walking. Our replies are along the lines of: "Hold on, sport, we *won*, didn't we?" But the man keeps shouting as he disappears into the night.

The All Blacks just cannot satisfy some Kiwi fans. The wild-eyed man merely confirms for McBeth and me our earlier beliefs, which we have grown to understand from years of travelling around New Zealand and overseas – our rugby public do not know how to lose with honour, or how to win with grace.

AUGUST 17

Home again today via a mid-morning flight. Today I have a short conversation with Mark Shaw. We are getting on the same plane. It is the first chat we have had for years. I am not sure why Mark and I have never clicked – after all, he was a player and I was a reporter on five or six world tours. Could it have been my regular condemnation of rough play in rugby, which he was sometimes involved in? Or maybe a testy little story I wrote about his short conversational abilities, which amused

Bring on the world

Happiness is beating Australia.

us in the media more than 25 years ago while on tour to Britain? Anyway, well done the two of us today.

The National Provincial Championship began over this weekend. While Wellington sneak a win over Southland, the most pleasing aspect might have been the form of Rodney So'oialo and Ma'a Nonu. Both look fitter and fresher than their colleagues and opponents, testimony perhaps to their continuing involvement in the All Black training squad for each test this season. They must go to the World Cup.

One of the biggest issues facing John Mitchell as he goes into a final week of deliberation over his World Cup squad is what to do with Andrew Mehrtens. The fact that Carlos Spencer missed three kicks out of seven in the test yesterday seems to have again fuelled vigorous discussion over whether Mehrtens should come into the side. The logic of many of the callers to Radio Sport seems to be that Mehrts would have kicked each of the kicks Carlos missed. Nonsense, of course.

It doesn't get better than stuffing Ockers

JUSTIN MARSHALL summed it up before the game. Does it get any better than bringing back the Bledisloe Cup? "Well, if things go really well in November that mi...

Phil Gifford strikes a chord with rugby fans.

I don't think Mehrtens will make the World Cup. Too much has happened with the squad this year that he has missed out on. Even if he is chosen he is never going to start a game at the Cup, because Spencer is doing the *playing* of the Mitchell plan this year. And doing it, I believe, so much better than Mehrtens ever could. This year's All Black backs are a sharp, decisive and fast-moving unit, whereas Mehrtens has not been showing that kind of form. He is a reader of the game, more tactical, and more considered than the sparkling Spencer.

The case of Jonah Lomu is even more clear-cut. The big man was sighted at the Wellington NPC training last week, and though he did play half of a warm-up game against Taranaki, having to fly back to Auckland each day to continue his kidney dialysis is not conducive to playing rugby at the highest level. Jonah did not play in the NPC this weekend because of a slight calf problem. He continues to be in the news and there is worldwide interest in whatever he does, but, sadly, it seems certain that his brave efforts to make the World Cup will come to nought.

AUGUST 18

All Black supporters seem to be enjoying "the journey".

AUGUST 20

While the country is in a state of limbo waiting for the final World Cup team selection next Monday, the Aussie jokes have started to surface. Most of them are tiresome and I don't really approve of them but, what the heck, it has been five years since the Bledisloe Cup was in New Zealand, so let's go for the jugular.

The best joke so far is this: what has four legs, weighs a tonne and echoes? Answer: the Australian Rugby Union trophy cabinet.

Tom Scott captures the national sentiment, yet again.

AUGUST 21

There is a slap in the face for the slumbering news media today. Jonah Lomu has been in the news, of course, with his ongoing kidney dialysis, his attempt to gain All Black selection and his struggle to recover in time to make the Wellington team. For all of those stories he made headline news. But no-one was prepared for the latest Jonah news – he and girlfriend Fiona Taylor got married today. Apparently the very secret nuptials took place, with only 16 guests, at a top reception location on Waiheke Island.

I say good luck to them. I'm glad I'm not on "Jonah watch". Those reporters all missed out today.

And congratulations Fiona, for becoming Mrs Lomu. I hope the news media treats you more courteously than one newspaper last month, which churlishly described you as "Jonah's latest fiancée".

Sad to hear, though, that Jonah chose not to have his parents present for the service. Whatever could the man be thinking?

AUGUST 22

Of course there has to be scandal over the ticket prices for a big sports event such as the World Cup. This year is no different than the 1999 World Cup and the 2000 Olympic Games. Tickets and hotel rooms become scarce when supporters and fans from all countries come surging in for major events. And so prices go up to match the interest.

My view is coloured because I sit on easy street over such matters, having gratefully accepted a free ticket, provided yet again by TVNZ, to fly to the Cup for the fifth time. But a percentage of Kiwis expect to take a trip across the Tasman for the same prices as they'd pay to attend a Bledisloe Cup game. People just don't understand that at big international events (the Olympic Games, the Soccer World Cup) it doesn't work that way. Under pressure, ticket prices always rocket.

The main complaints today seem to be that the IRB is putting a levy on top of each ticket price, which will force up prices for big games at the World Cup. The fans in New Zealand are suspicious of anything the IRB does, and suspicious of any profit that the IRB might dare to make. New Zealanders have no interest in the work the IRB does in bringing the game to a wider audience.

Tonight NZRU chief executive Chris Moller appears on *Holmes* and explains that the NZRU will encourage fans seeking tickets to skirt around official methods, and encourage them to go on to the Internet and obtain tickets by legitimate, but slightly backdoor methods. I wonder what the official travel agents/ticket sellers think of that?

AUGUST 25

All is in readiness today for the announcement of the final 30-man All Black team. The announcement will be made live on Holmes at 7pm.

In all the radio discussions today the most commonly used terms are "bolter" and "back-up".

According to the weekend papers, various "bolters" are now being mentioned to make the All Black team. (The dictionary meaning of the word "bolter" is "an outsider in a horse race".) Players mentioned as bolters are Angus McDonald, the Auckland lock/flanker, Sam Tuitupou, the Auckland midfield back, and Sam Broomhall, Simon Maling and Troy Flavell. Or maybe the last three are "back-up" players?

A distinguished four-man panel in *The Sunday Star-Times,* consisting of John Hart, Ian Kirkpatrick, Frank Bunce and John Schuster, also showed considerable support for Christian Cullen (three votes), Anton Oliver (four) and Maling (three). For the rest, they stuck with the members of John Mitchell's current squad. Curiously, no panellists picked Caleb Ralph.

Suddenly tonight on *One News,* at 6.45pm, a few minutes ahead of the team announcement, there is another twist to the bolter's saga. TVNZ's Stephen Stuart appears in the sports news slot, talking about Canterbury's Corey Flynn as a late bolter prospect. This is bizarre. Flynn has been injured since May. He's had no rugby since then. How did Stuart reach this conclusion?

And, curiouser and curiouser, over on TV3, in its equivalent sports news session at the same time, Flynn is being tipped as a bolter.

Is it possible that naughty reporters, having had the team slipped to them earlier than the 7pm embargo (to allow time for production staff to make graphic captions) decided to make themselves look a wee bit better by pre-empting the selectors' announcement? After all, no-one, but no-one, had even thought of the sidelined Flynn.

Sure enough, minutes later, when the live broadcast starts on both stations and on radio, there is chairman Jock Hobbs, all dressed up in his best bib and tucker, announcing Corey Flynn in the team. You've gotta laugh at these TV types, don't you?

Chairman Jock reads out a team that will satisfy the majority of the public. All Mitch's winter squad of 26 will be at the World Cup, including Caleb Ralph, whom no-one in the Sunday newspaper picked. But, as with any All Black announcement, there are a number of discussion points.

- How come Corey Flynn makes the squad when he hasn't played since breaking his arm in May? He comes in as third hooker, behind Keven Mealamu and Mark Hammett. There is no place for Anton Oliver. I, for one, am sad.
- How many of the sports media picked all of the other four places in the squad? None that I can find. That's because of Flynn, but also because Daniel Braid, the Auckland openside flanker, is also a down-the-outside bolter. The other two to make the squad are Byron Kelleher and Ben

Blair, whom many people had been confident would make it. They have been in the training squads at differing times this year and Kelleher had been on the bench against South Africa.

- If there is a quibble it might be that there is not great height for lineout time. Simon Maling has not been selected. Chris Jack and Ali Williams will almost completely carry the burden of securing lineout possession. And remember, that burden is for up to seven matches. The Thorn(e)s, Brad and Reuben, appear to be the back-up locks, though neither is very tall, nor has either had much time as a lock at the top in recent years.

- It is sad about the veterans Andrew Mehrtens, Anton Oliver, Christian Cullen, Taine Randell, and even Sam Broomhall and Tom Willis. There's no place for any of them. But then who is surprised, given the hard-nosed attitude John Mitchell has used to pursue his dream of taking a fresh, youthful-looking team to the Cup this year?

Anton Oliver might deservedly feel most miffed tonight. He started two tests this year and was only as bad (or good) at lineout throwing as the other hookers, Mealamu and Hammett. It must be said that Mealamu has made strides since being given his opportunity, but the axing of Oliver for a man who has not played since May is a slap in the face. There would seem to be much more to his non-selection than not "running the right lines" or whatever it was that Mitchell said earlier about Oliver's shortcomings. Maybe the internal squabbles at the Highlanders harmed his chances.

AUGUST 26

Nationwide reaction to the team is favourable. There is puzzlement over the selection of Flynn but comments about the absence of Cullen, Mehrtens and Oliver seem muted. Almost as if it was always suspected they were not going to make it.

One issue for some callers to Radio Sport is that some players are not going to get game time during the tournament. That is open to dispute, I believe. People are tending to forget that there are seven games to be played for the two teams that will play in the final. And those games will be played over six weeks, rather than the eight weeks the All Blacks have just had in playing their seven lead-up tests. So, for a start, it is going to be a tighter time schedule.

Mitchell might well say in a few weeks: "Look, we've played Italy, and our next game is against Tonga in six days. I think I should protect a couple of players from their potential hard hits." That will mean changing the team around to suit that particular opposition, which will mean most players will be included for at least a couple of matches. Well, that's my theory, anyway.

AUGUST 27

Today my thanks go to Bevan Sanson of the Auckland Rugby Union. He phones and says "a little bird" told him that my test programme(s) had been pinched from the press box in Auckland last weekend. He says he has a few left and will send some down for Cyril Delaney and me. Thanks mate.

How about this for a similar incident? Tonight I travel to the Police College at Porirua to speak at the launch of an excellent book called *Police and Sport*. It is written by retired policemen Ray Reid and Joe Franklin, and they have their families and many police mates there to help them celebrate. Afterwards they kindly present me with a copy of one of the first books off the press. I feel chuffed, and place it behind my chair at the dinner.

The dinner carries on – top food, excellent wine, great company. But when I decide to head home my book is not where I had put it. It has been "uplifted", you might say.

The World Cup story doing the rounds today concerns the Rugby World Cup organisers announcing that *Waltzing Matilda* will not be allowed to be sung at games Australia play. This has not gone down well across the Tasman. In recent years the song has been a kind of Aussie response to the New Zealand haka. Even Prime Minister John Howard has weighed in, issuing a statement of scorn about the decision. "Matilda" will not be stifled, the Aussies cry.

Let's put this bluntly. There is now far too much stuffing about before international sports fixtures. Sometimes at rugby tests involving the All Blacks, the teams, on a rainy, bleak and freezing winter's night, have to run on and stand through 10 to 15 minutes of meet-the-president (as in Dublin), sing the two interminable national anthems (New Zealand's is now twice as long as it used to be, while Ireland has three anthems for games played in Dublin), then perform the haka, then listen to the dirge of *Waltzing Matilda* (at tests in Australia), then check with both the referee and sideline for TV floor managing timekeepers, before at last being allowed to start playing. I say, why not, run on to the field and get on with it.

As for the haka ... I'm a Kiwi and love it to bits, but why can it not be done as the All Blacks did at the end of their famous test win in Pretoria in 1996, or the New Zealand sevens team at whatever successful tournament they are in? At those events that haka is launched into only in celebration at the *end* of the game. It is then a challenge to the beaten opposition to come back and try to take on our team on next time.

AUGUST 28

McBeth and I are up to Auckland and back today for a "photo-shoot". There we are, all TVNZ's planned commentators and presenters for the Rugby World Cup, gathered in a downtown studio. All dressed in black, we face the cameras. Click-click-click. God, we look a dashing lot! Well, Bernadine Oliver-Kerby does.

In the photos, and therefore signed up as part of the TV team, are John McBeth and me (we are TVNZ staff members, of course), experts John Hart, Grant Fox, Gary Whetton, Richard Loe and referee Colin Hawke. Bernadine will be doing news reporting for us (as she did so well at the World Cup in 1999), and we welcome Jason Fa'afoi, who will host a daily late-afternoon version of the coverage, which will be directed at a younger audience, or for those who weren't able to sit up all the previous night to watch games.

It's good to see and hear the crossfire of the ex-World Cup reps in our group. They are men with strong views, and within minutes of arriving their various discussions are fascinating. It's great to see again Hart and Fox, whom I enjoyed working with so much at previous World Cups. They agree that they would have both chosen Christian Cullen. Interesting, say McBeth and I on the way home on the plane.

The only one missing from the photo-session is Jeff Wilson. He is keen to come as part of our broadcast team but cannot make the trip today from his home near Christchurch. "Don't worry," says Zara Potts, of the TVNZ publicity department, "we can always 'screen' him in later as well."

AUGUST 29

Today I meet my joined-at-the hip mate John McBeth again and we're off to Nelson for a few days' filming. We build in attending a sporting dinner tonight, organised by the Haven Sports Trust, which does excellent work supporting young people's sport in the Nelson area. Former Olympic boxer Jeff Rackley is the main organiser. He puts in a tonne of work and gets a packed house every year at the Rutherford Hotel. McBeth is the MC for the dinner and takes the chance to put in a plug for our World Cup TV coverage. He says: "You'll notice TVNZ are going to wheel out Keith Quinn and myself in our Zimmer frames to bring you the games." That gets a hearty laugh from the crowd, but when the Wellington NPC team's win over Auckland is announced from tonight's game on Eden Park, a *huge* roar goes up. It just goes to show you that the South Island can appreciate a Wellington sports team.

AUGUST 31

A day of filming more of the vignettes from ordinary Kiwis around the country. In glorious Nelson weather I work with the local husband-and-wife crew of old friends Bev and Murray Creed. They certainly know their way around the town, and within a couple of hours we have completed filming in enough beautiful locations with enough bright Nelsonians to set off for the Buller and West Coast regions.

As for the All Blacks this weekend? The month has ended with a number of them reportedly on holiday with wives and kids in Fiji, or at home resting. This is a weekend off for most of them, although Ben Blair and Caleb Ralph are in great form helping Canterbury turn back a tough challenge from Taranaki to retain the Ranfurly Shield (and the unwanted Mehrtens plays a cracker, too).

The weekend papers seem strangely quiet. Not much to write about, although France did beat England overnight in Marseilles, and Wales, shock-horror, have ended the week with two test wins in four days, over Romania and Scotland. There is a picture of Corey Flynn playing for the Canterbury Maori with a huge cast over his forearm. It is his first game for 17 weeks.

Many people have asked me in the past few days: "How come Flynn made the World Cup team?" I can only give the dumb and dumber shrug of the shoulders.

The Police book turns up today. It hadn't been pinched. One of the organisers had put it in a safe place while the celebrations raged. Thank you, sirs.

SEPTEMBER

"He is not doing any interviews."

SEPTEMBER 1

Today I wake in Westport and during the day Murray, Bev and I film our Buller and West Coast people, after which I fly home via Christchurch. It's a pleasant day and a nice way to celebrate my birthday. Yes, I've made it to another year, and I'm sure the best is yet to come.

One of our stops in Westport is to interview Rodney Dawe, the 1995 NZRU president. He was the man who introduced the All Black players to President Nelson Mandela before that year's World Cup final. Rodney confirmed that he knew of the joke that had been going around about his famous meeting with Mandela. The joke alleges that when the greeting between the two took place on that fine day at Ellis Park, the great South African said: "Hello, I'm Nelson Mandela and I lived on Robben Island for 27 years." To which the New Zealander replied: "That's nothing, I'm Rodney Dawe and I've lived in Westport all my life."

SEPTEMBER 2

This afternoon I'm off for one of my first experiences with the All Black World Cup team. McBeth and I fly to Whangarei, where the players are beginning the first of their pre-Cup camps.

As TVNZ is the rights holder for All Black coverage up to and including the World Cup, we supposedly will have the advantage for the moment over other TV outfits. It has been arranged with the All Black management that tonight we will do interviews with most of, if not all, the New Zealand players. Along with executive producer Stu Dennison, director Alan Barnes, and two camera crews, who travel from Auckland, and all our lighting equipment and gear, we converge on the Quality Inn in Whangarei. We hope to set up in two rooms and it is planned that John and I will split up the individual interviews (about half each) and, with set questions for each player, build a series of potted profiles. The arrangement also includes interviews with John Mitchell and Robbie Deans.

Alas, we didn't bank on the players not seeming very interested in fulfilling their part of the bargain. Well, that's my take on the situation. On arrival at the hotel, ever-earnest media man Matt McIlraith presents us with a list of players' names, and we note there are only four players each for John and me to interview. "Only four each?" we ask. McIlraith replies: "Yes, well, the others are either out on visits, too tired after training, wetting the head of someone's baby, or are visiting friends. And as for interviewing Mitch, well, I haven't asked yet, but he won't be interested, I can tell you. He isn't doing one-on-one interviews for anyone. Now that he has won the two trophies he isn't doing any more interviews."

We look at Matt, we look at our gear, which has been transported all the way to Whangarei, and we look at each other. We have come a long way for very little.

Matt is a nice bloke and I suspect he's hamstrung by the workings of the team around Mitchell. On Mitchell's part, no doubt he is trying to protect himself and his team from the media. Tonight though, I can't help thinking: "Mitch, old son, wait till you get to the World Cup. It'll be worse there."

But what can we do? Here we are, waiting to do the interviews, but hardly any of them turn up. I'm sure this situation would not be foreign to reporters like Grant Nisbett, Tony Johnson, Bob Howitt, Don Cameron, Sir Terry McLean, Graeme Moody, Wynne Gray and many others from the travelling media over the years. They will probably tell you that the All Blacks are the All Blacks. Since time immemorial, the very famous All Blacks of New Zealand have never had to keep appointments, or be on time, or have the same social graces as the rest of us. They are the All Blacks. Therefore they are above all the decencies that we mere mortals live by.

I get wild about this. We are all mad, actually, but not surprised. We have collectively come thousands of kilometres to be here, but cannot say a peep in protest. We must remember that we are in the company of All Blacks, and that we have to be sycophantic to the players' needs at all times. That's the way it works – we cannot afford to "lose" them before the Cup, because the public will want to hear from them as the next weeks unfold, and so will our bosses at TVNZ.

Oh well, as we regular touring reporters have said down the years: "The All Blacks, their managers, coaches and the players, all come and go. Only the reporters stay constant."

Nevertheless, we're grateful for the eight players who arrive. They all perform well on camera. Our thanks go to Reuben Thorne, Caleb Ralph, Dave Hewett, Marty Holah, Aaron Mauger, Greg Somerville, Dan Carter and Ma'a Nonu. The other 22 players, Matt McIlraith assures us, will be there for us in New Plymouth on September 17. We will be there, never mind the cost.

Tonight I do a little reading. A book called *A Whole New Ball Game* has just hit the shops. It is writer Paul Thomas's view on what has happened to rugby in New Zealand in the professional era. In one chapter there are comments from former All Black manager Andrew Martin that in the current All Black era there is too much drinking of alcohol.

This is curious statement from Colonel Martin, because his only observance of excessive drinking by the team would have been while he was the team manager, from 2000–2002. He would surely have had the authority to stop excessive drinking, wouldn't he?

SEPTEMBER 3

The Australian World Cup team is announced today and of course various bolters are discussed in the media. However, the main talking point is the loss of Toutai Kefu because of a cracked shoulder blade. I've always liked Kefu's rugby – tough and uncompromising. He tells the media in Brisbane that missing the Cup will be a huge disappointment but that he is grateful that he has a great family and a new baby on the way. Nice sentiments.

SEPTEMBER 4

As if South Africa needed further problems, a bitter race row breaks out today. We heard a few days ago that big Geo Cronje, along with team-mate Quentin Davids, had been kicked out of the Springbok World Cup training camp because the pair had had some sort of race row. Cronje, it is alleged, declined to room and share bathroom facilities with Davids.

Initially I didn't make too much of this (inasmuch as the World Cup is concerned), as neither player was a strong candidate for selection. However, today the story takes a much more sinister twist. The Springbok team's

SA probes racism in Bok camp

South African rugby's governing body has ordered an independent racism investigation after the national team's communications spokesman has announced he does not want to be part of a "squad in which prejudice is tolerated"...

A festering sore in South African rugby.

media man, Mark Keohane, a former touring reporter, resigns over the incident. This with less than four weeks to the World Cup.

To an outsider this may not be seen especially significant. But Keohane departs making strong charges about more episodes of racism inside the team.

Keohane, from my observance, has a keen eye for correctness and decency. I have personally noted several examples of white not getting along with black in recent South African teams. One time, Anne and I were in Dubai having an evening meal in the same hotel where the 16 teams of an IRB sevens tournament were staying. We noted the South African squad of 12 players come in and sit down at the table designated for them. The half-dozen black and coloured players sat at one end of the long table, the white players sat at the other, with space between the two groups. It was very sad and very noticeable to others.

That same year I was approached by two South African coloured rugby writers who wanted me to help secure funds for a documentary series on the history of racism in South African rugby. "It still exists, believe me," they insisted.

Today, with a heavy sound in his voice, Andy Capastagno tells Radio Sport listeners that "we still have to face the facts here in South Africa that, basically, there are still many of us here who don't like each other".

SEPTEMBER 5

Chris Jack is 25 today. Happy birthday, big fella. Please relax today if you can and contemplate what lies ahead. Your country is going to need you over the next few weeks. Maybe like no other player in the All Blacks' recent history. The decision by coach Mitchell to select only three specialist locks has put incredible pressure on Jack's big frame. Without his presence at the World Cup, who will consistently win good lineout ball for our speedy backs?

The alarm clock rings at 5am and it's out of bed to catch the live telecast from Twickenham of England against France. By the time I've rubbed the sleep from my eyes the game is effectively over – England are running in so many tries. The commentators omit to mention that the French

It's not just the New Zealand media that trumpets about its rugby team before the World Cup. Here's a selection of what the English papers had to say about their team after the win over France.

team is nearly a "B" selection. England win 45–14. They look, as everyone says, bloody awesome!

The space-ship impersonation uniforms of both teams catch my eye. Skin-tight, muscle-shirts are de rigueur for both teams. The jerseys are a bit like the adidas ones the All Black backs have been wearing this year. But the English and French are going even further in modern design in their Nike jerseys. They also have the forwards wearing them. So the big roly-polys of the front row have all their sticky-out bits there for all to see. And there are no collars – nothing to grab on to in a flailing tackle.

The South African weekly TV show *Boots 'n All* does a clever edit tonight of the highlights of last week's first test between the same two teams. Hands grappling for, but missing, players in the tackle can be clearly seen. Writing in *National Business Review,* columnist Paul Verdon suggests that the All Blacks should not have shown off the adidas jersey in the early tests this year, "so it could not be replicated by competitors in time for the World Cup".

Also today is a column in *The Sunday Star-Times* in which Chris Mirams laments lack of media access to the All Blacks this winter. Sounds like Chris is having the same sort of filibustering relationship with the team that many others are having. Still, the public doesn't give a cuss about the media's problems. Media people are, after all, the enemy to many, aren't they? Does John Mitchell believe that too?

SEPTEMBER 8

Several World Cup teams are announced today. By virtue of their win over France, England are now firm favourites. And Clive Woodward has a wealth of talent available in some places. He leaves out the 2.03-metre (6ft 9in) lock Simon Shaw. This monster of a man had been most impressive only 48 hours earlier at Twickenham, not to mention my memory of him on a rainy night against New Zealand Maori in New Plymouth in June. All I can say is, if Shaw were a New Zealander there would not be so much pressure on Chris Jack in the locking position. In fact, Shaw might be chosen in the All Blacks ahead of our best lock.

The three England locks chosen are captain Martin Johnson, Ben Kay and Danny Grewcock. All are powerhouse players. I reckon all would comfortably make our team. The loose forward cover for their position will come from the experienced Martin Corry of Leicester.

Elsewhere in the England squad there is no place for Austin Healy or Graham Rowntree. That, again, is more a commentary on the depth of talent than their poor form. The absence of Healy will rob the Cup of a colourful character, while the non-attendance of Rowntree will at least mean the contest to find the best/worst cauliflower ears (depending on your view) will be much more open.

Scotland also announce their team, and there's no place for the ex-pat Brendan "Chainsaw" Laney, formerly of Otago. This is a rather strange decision by coach Ian McGeechan, given that Laney was lured by the same man to Scotland in 2001 with the World Cup uppermost in the Scottish union's mind.

That means the only "Kilted Kiwis" in the Scottish squad will be the utility back Glenn Metcalfe and flanker Martin Leslie. The Scots lost 29–10 last weekend to Ireland and have been doing some way-out things in preparation for their time in Australia. They underwent some sub-artic cryotherapy in Poland. You'd "cry-o" too, if you had to stay in a sealed chamber with temperatures as low as minus 126 degrees Celsius for up to three minutes. Somebody swears it aids the recovery and repair of muscle strain.

Today, after a weekend off, the All Blacks reassemble in Auckland before a trip to Gisborne for another week of training. But the country is being lashed by rain and Poverty Bay's forecast is terrible for the week. Manager Tony Thorpe must have been bitterly disappointed when he had to cancel the five-day excursion to his home town. Sad also, because the All Blacks have never played in that town.

SEPTEMBER 9

The news from South Africa worsens. Somehow Mark Keohane's 12,000-word summary of his views on racism inside the Springbok camp has been leaked. It's such a damning document that TVNZ's *One News* gets correspondent David van der Sandt live on screen from Johannesburg tonight. He tells New Zealand there is a good chance Springbok coach Rudolph Straeuli will be relieved of his position in the next 48 hours.

SEPTEMBER 10

It's 30 days till the whistle blasts and Argentina and Australia do battle on opening night. I still say Argentina could cause an upset on day one. And yet, I'm also nominating Australia as one of the teams capable of upsetting the favourites. In the past couple of days my view has firmed that England will win the World Cup.

SEPTEMBER 11

Another shock – an unknown ex-Kiwi from Auckland, Rima Wakarua, has come out of nowhere to claim a five-eighths berth in the Italian World Cup squad. Coach John Kirwan obviously thinks the defence of his Argentinian-born regular, Ramiro Pez, is not up to scratch. It was exposed badly last weekend in their last warm-up game (a 31–22 win over Georgia in Turin), so the unheard-of Wakarua will make his debut against the All Blacks. I make a note to email Frank Bunce, who coaches in Italy, and see if Frank can provide any background on this newcomer.

Wakarua's presence raises the number of Maori players who will turn out for other countries in the World Cup. This no doubt will please those in New Zealand who pushed for a while for a Maori team to play in the World Cup. The late Alby Pryor would be delighted at these numbers. I can name 10 Maori players who will be playing for other countries at the World Cup: Wakarua, Scott Palmer and Matthew Phillips (Italy), Morgan Turunui and Jeremy Paul (Australia), Sonny Parker (Wales), Tony Marsh (France), and George Konia, Adam Parker and Reuben Parkinson (Japan).

SEPTEMBER 13

The South African Rugby Union has postponed any inquiry into racism in its team until next year. What a joke! Rugby in that country lurches from one disaster to another. How can the team expect to play well when so much of the world's attention will be on their every move? Very sad. At least Rudolph Straeuli didn't get sacked.

SEPTEMBER 14

I get an email today from a despondent Frankie Deges in Buenos Aires. He has distressing news for the Pumas' hopes. In a practice game in Tucuman, the Pumas' captain, the stylish and solid Lisandro Arbizu, twisted knee ligaments and is out of the Cup. What a disaster for the man who has captained his country to several World Cups and sevens World Cups. He is Argentina's most capped player by a long shot. No doubt Agustin Pichot will replace him.

I note a superb Tui beer advertising billboard up in Ghuznee St, Wellington (it's also in the October edition of *Skywatch* magazine). It says: "I never doubted Mitch – Yeah right."

I love this advertisement, which was found on various billboards and in **Skywatch**.

SEPTEMBER 15

It's slightly like poacher turned gamekeeper for a selection of the rugby media today. Grant Nisbett (Sky TV), Chris Mirams (The Sunday Star-Times), Graeme Moody and Kevin Sinnott (Newstalk ZB), and Keith Quinn and John McBeth (TVNZ), arrive at NZRU headquarters in Wellington at 9am sharp. We're ushered into a room and tea, coffee and muffins are offered. The doors are then shut.

With us is the union deputy-chief executive, Steve Tew, one of the media staff, Joe Locke, and two consultants with accountancy backgrounds. We are there as an unofficial think tank, to discuss ideas about the direction of the game in New Zealand. We are told there will be grim days ahead for the game unless methods can be found to make the NZRU, and the National Provincial Championship in particular, run more professionally and cost-effectively.

So there we are, we who often criticise the Rugby Union for the way it organises its game, being invited to offer our views on how we think the future should go.

I go to the meeting with a rather haughty attitude of, "I'm busy with the World Cup, so I don't need to think about this". But I find myself enjoying the ideas and issues raised, such as which players should be professional. Tew seems generous in the reception of our ideas, which range from the old chestnut, "We must have All Blacks playing club rugby every season" to "They should play only tests, tours and Super 12".

The meeting ends cordially, which, in the case of Mirams and Tew, is worthy of note, considering the two have had public words of difference in the past few days about the access of the All Blacks to the media. I'm starting to believe that anyone in the media who hasn't had a difference of opinion with the assertive Mr Tew has no opinions of merit anyway. That man loves to present his side in strong rebuttal.

(It crosses my mind that two of the country's keenest observers of the current rugby set-up in New Zealand, Joseph Romanos and Paul Thomas, were not at the meeting. Both are resident in Wellington and both, in the past year or so, have published books that deal precisely with the subject we discussed today.)

The All Blacks fly to New Plymouth today for another pre-World Cup training week. They're hoping for better weather than last week. The chief executive of the Taranaki RFU, Paul Easton, is quoted on the website allblacks.com as saying: "Schools are closing for the day tomorrow – and businesses will be shutting down early too."

SEPTEMBER 17

Today we at TVNZ are back on our mission to gain pre-Cup interviews with each member of the World Cup squad. So far we've done eight out of 32.

At 4pm, on yet another of this season's endless succession of flights, McBeth and Quinn are off again. It's a blustery, rainy evening as we land in New Plymouth. We set off to meet the rest of the TV crew, who have arrived from Auckland. This time it's Adelle Wintle and Graeme Patrick, who have driven down, swaying about in a van laden with camera gear. Alan Barnes, the producer, who will oversee then edit the interviews, flies in from Auckland. We check in at the Grand Central Hotel.

We taxi to the Auto Lodge Hotel, where the All Blacks are staying. The staff there have generously given us two rooms to set up our interviews stations. Beds and furniture have to be moved around. But nothing is a problem for the hotel people.

Matt McIlraith arrives with a crumpled piece of paper. He announces: "Tonight we should be able to offer you another 12 players for interviews." Our disappointment and frustration rise again. Will we be able to secure all 30 players before the World Cup starts? Only one media day remains for us.

It seems that, unbeknown to us, seven players have been released to play NPC games this weekend. Among the seven are some we managed to grab in Whangarei. Others are not, so we will have to get them later. Many of the remaining players, for reasons not made clear to us by the unrelentingly enthusiastic Mr McIlraith, are again not available tonight. Neither is Mr Mitchell. No reason is offered for Mitchell, beyond the standard response that "he is not doing interviews". Some of us reflect wistfully on the good old days of John Hart, when everyone in the media was able to talk to the All Black coach.

Thanks tonight go to Joe Rokocoko, Doug Howlett, Chris Jack, Jerry Collins, Mils Muliaina, Leon MacDonald, Keven Mealamu, Tana Umaga,

Mark Hammett, Corey Flynn, Steve Devine and Ali Williams. To make the epic and expensive filming voyage to New Plymouth more cost-effective, we snap up the offer to talk to referees Paul Honiss and Kelvin Deaker. The Honiss piece will be useful on opening night, because he is to be in control of Australia versus Argentina. But, with respect, interviews with those two fine gentlemen are not what we are here for. So again the evening ends with a lot of public money having been spent and the All Blacks proving yet again they do not have to fulfill their obligations.

For the purposes of the World Cup coverage, we at TVNZ are supposed to be working *with* the team, to show them in the best light during their quest to be world champions. They, however, seem not to care about our requirements.

We will try again, with more expense, in a fortnight's time, probably in Methven, to achieve the last 10 interviews.

John Mitchell's mood has been interesting to observe in recent days. He is becoming an increasingly distant figure. Apart from being not available again tonight, he seems aloof and distant to everyone, even those around him in the team. Even at his place of employment, the NZRU, not many are saying kind words about Mitchell or his moods. Stories are being murmured that he believes he is above reproach and beyond accepting advice. Some, it is said, are afraid of him.

Tonight, after accepting a table in the restaurant at the Auto Lodge Hotel, we see Mitchell come in. He walks through the place with his eyes fixed on a point high on the furthest wall. I feel disappointed for him. In New Zealand, when you are a recognisable figure you create immense goodwill with a "Hello" to all people, wherever you go. It's not a burden and those of the public who receive even the slightest nod of recognition go away and convey to others that so-and-so is a good bloke.

I think back to the bright-eyed Mitchell who shook the media by the hand when he was announced as the All Black coach in Wellington late in 2001, or the tremendous interview McBeth and I got from him one Saturday afternoon on TV1 when members of the public called in live and offered their best wishes to him. Then Mitchell talked of his hopes and dreams. And even earlier this year, when he gave excellent interviews on the day his first team of the season was announced.

While I appreciate that being All Black coach can be a lonely job, I say wake up John, you're missing the best days of your life.

(To be fair, at the end of his short stay in the restaurant tonight, Mitchell does squeeze John McBeth on the shoulder on his way out. Mind you, not a word is directed downwards to McBeth, and Mitchell's gaze stays fixed on some mythical spot high on the room's far wall.)

I have a nice chat with Jerry Collins tonight. We get to talk about how far he's come in his young life. From being a knockabout four-year-old in a Samoan family that arrived in New Zealand, he is now about to strut his powerful presence in front of a multi-million-member audience at the World Cup.

Jerry gives the impression that he can hardly believe it. "I remember when we came here from Samoa and settled in Porirua, our family had to eat on the floor. Not only that, we had no dinner set to eat with. My sister and I shared one plate between us. That's all we had. And Mum cooked us rice, spaghetti and corned beef. We loved it so much we used to ask for it for breakfast, lunch and dinner. The nutritionists around the All Blacks will probably be horrified to know, but that's still my favourite dish."

Thanks Jerry, for bringing some sanity and perspective into tonight's proceedings.

SEPTEMBER 18

Up early and on to an aircraft. Today is a commentary and outfitting day for the TVNZ presenters. We fly to Auckland and meet John Hart, Grant Fox and newcomer Jeff Wilson. Our World Cup TV producer, Stu Dennison, outlines his hopes for the broadcasts ahead and I'm asked my opinions of how a rugby commentary should go. I say to all three blokes: "Let's keep our disciplines, let's each stay in our own areas of the broadcast and let's not talk over each other. It's a simple formula." I feel like I'm giving a team talk before a test match.

Then we take up headsets and microphones and, watching a video of the All Blacks versus South Africa game at Dunedin last month, we commentate intensely in a practice session that goes for about 30 minutes. To me, the results sound just fine. Hart and Fox come in with their expertise at the end of each play and we wait for each other to finish speaking. There's a bit of finger waving and "stop" signs being waved about, but overall we are delighted. It's the way I believe TV commentary should be done. I do not prefer the Murray Mexted style of the "comments man" butting in whenever he wants to. To me Mex comes in over the top of Grant Nisbett's flow of description far too often. I do not hear any other commentator in the world do that. Nisbo (and other callers Tony Johnson, Steve Davie and Ken Laban) must love it when they work with the more laid-back Sky expert commentators such as John Drake, Matthew Cooper, Chris Laidlaw and Ian Smith.

Jeff Wilson then has a turn at the mike. Because of his summer cricket commitments for Otago, he can be with us at the Cup for only about six commentaries. But I think he will be great. He slips into commentary mode as if to the manner born. Jeff has done some radio work with Paul Allison in Dunedin and I reckon he has a real future at the microphone.

SEPTEMBER 19

Was I mean in my assessment of John Mitchell the other night in New Plymouth? I might have been, I suppose. It's just that we in the media get frustrated when nothing happens to honour previous arrangements. I still hope Mitchell takes the All Blacks to victory at the World Cup, but I wish he'd take time to smell the flowers on the journey. Plus give more access to the media, of course.

SEPTEMBER 20

I feel elated today. But, being a modest Kiwi, I'll try to keep my feet on the ground. The NZRU's official All Black website, allblacks.com, has released the results of a poll it has been running all week to find New Zealand's favourite TV rugby commentator. Last week it asked the same question about the favourite rugby writer and Wynne Gray, of *The New Zealand Herald*, polled highest.

The poll result today suggests K Quinn is the favourite TV commentator of the 1226 people who responded. I admit to being surprised, and feel quietly chuffed. I have no idea where the voters came from. Presumably they are New Zealanders.

An NZRU official pointed out the poll to me two days ago. He shook my hand, saying, "Well done", because I was polling heavily. The final totals were Quinn 760 votes, Murray Mexted (Sky TV) 254, Grant Nisbett (Sky TV) 64, Hamish McKay (TV3) 56, Tony Johnson (Sky TV) 53, Gordon Bray (Australia) 33, and David Fordham (Australia) 6.

The result is surprising, given that my only 15-a-side commentaries this year have been two efforts (sitting on a rubber ring) for the local radio station, *The Breeze*. On TV I have done the sevens circuit for three years but my last 15-a-side rugby was the All Blacks tour to Britain and Argentina in 2001. I think the "familiarity breeds contempt" expression may have applied to some of the regular Sky blokes, while "absence makes the heart grow fonder" may have helped me.

However, Kiwis are a funny lot. When news of the poll has reached several radio stations today, suggestions were made that all my relatives and friends must have been working hard, on my behalf, to vote for me. Oh well ...

Actually, while pleasing, the poll result adds pressure on me to do a good job next month.

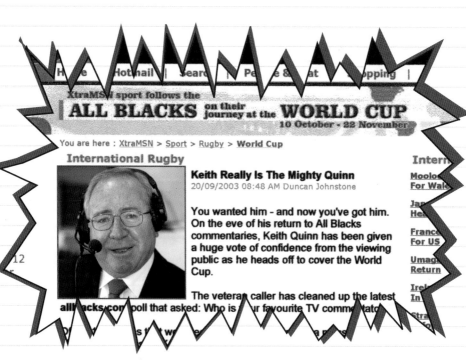

12

So absence really does make the heart grow fonder.

SEPTEMBER 21

A great day today for the whole world! Well, my view anyway. Wellington, by virtue of a 48–18 win over Taranaki this weekend, now lead the NPC. Whether they will stay there is open to question, as four of the players in their team this weekend (Ma'a Nonu, Rodney So'oialo, Lome Fa'atau and Kas Lealamanua) are heading to the World Cup, for New Zealand or Samoa.

Seven All Black players were released by Mitchell to play for their NPC teams, but not all took the field. Some NPC coaches preferred "regular" men to hold their places.

The new Sky TV nightly news show *Sport 365* claims tonight that Ali Williams has had a stress fracture in his foot checked by medical staff. To me that throws a scare into the All Black plans. Williams is a vital element to the New Zealand team. We need him, along with Chris Jack, to get us at least 40 per cent of lineout ball in key tournament games.

By the end of the night, no other media outlet has gone with the Williams injury story. Mind you, Norm Maxwell was at the camp in New Plymouth this week. Was he there as scrum practice cannon fodder, as Mitchell more or less announced, or was there another reason he was called in?

SEPTEMBER 22

Nineteen days to go. There is very little World Cup news today. "It's like the calm before the storm," says Brendan Telfer as he begins his Radio Sport slot.

One item that does catch my eye comes from the Wellington Rugby Union, which asks Manu Samoa if Wellington can retain their two Samoan internationals, Lome Fa'atau and Kas Lealamanua, for Wellington's Ranfurly Shield challenge against Canterbury on Saturday. Samoan coach John Boe cheerfully clears the two to play for Wellington, but wonders out loud when the NZRU might do something similarly favourable in return for Samoan rugby. It is a very fair point, more so, when you consider that none of Wellington's four All Blacks (Tana Umaga, Ma'a Nonu, Rodney So'oialo and Jerry Collins) are cleared to play.

SEPTEMBER 23

The main news today concerns Jonah Lomu. He hasn't been included in any Wellington team plans for the rest of the season. Is that it for Jonah?

The All Blacks begin another training camp, this time in Nelson.

Tonight Colin Meads appears on a pre-recorded "Heroes" cooking show on TV2, with current All Blacks Chris Jack and Richie McCaw. Meads gives another of his great quotes: "In the modern world of all of this nutrition and stuff, I say if you eat it and you like it, it *must* be good for you."

I go to the doctor tonight for a final World Cup check-up. Everything seems fine for me, which is great. Thanks again, Dr Reid. In the waiting room at the surgery a woman I've never seen before approaches me. She announces that she wants to shake my hand, because I was the one who changed her life. Her name is Suzanne Davis and she lives in our neighbourhood.

I do recall that nearly 10 years ago I received a phone call one night from a man who asked me, out of the blue, if I knew the occupations of each of the Welsh players in the 1950 British Isles rugby team in New Zealand. I sometimes get requests like this.

I looked up an old book, and gave the man information about the Welsh students, doctors, lawyers, a policeman and a railway worker in that Lions team. I hung up and thought no more of the call.

Later that year – 1994 it was – came another call, this time from a Suzanne (Suzy) Davis, who began by saying: "Keith, you don't know me. We've never met, but I want to thank you very much for helping me find my birth father."

Apparently Suzy had always known she had been adopted. She had been born "up north" in Hastings, in February 1951. Many years later, as an adult, and a mother herself, she had wanted to find her birth parents. She eventually found her birth mother, who was quite elderly and living in Dunedin. But finding the identity of her birth father was more difficult. Her mother did not want to talk about him.

Eventually, from snippets of conversation offered by her mother, Suzy surmised that her father had been a strong Welshman, a sporting type and a railway worker. Suzy also reached the conclusion that her conception might have been the result of a "one-night stand". She therefore counted back nine months from her date of birth and, checking the records of Dunedin's *Otago Daily Times*, where her birth mother had always lived, concluded one of the members of the Lions rugby team might be the "one" she was looking for. She asked a writer with whom she had made contact, Des Williams, to ring me, thinking I might know of the Welsh players' occupations.

Hence the phone call to me from the mystery man. From the information I gave them it was worked out by Suzy and Des that Don Hayward, a burly Welsh front row forward, as the only railway worker in that Lions team, must have been the father. The facts were placed before Suzy's mother, who confirmed them.

The story didn't end there. The irony was that Hayward, on returning to Britain in 1950, decided that New Zealand was the place he wanted to live permanently. So he emigrated to Wellington, where he played in the Wellington rugby team for several seasons. He married and settled in Lower Hutt, becoming a butcher. Meanwhile, Suzy Davis had also moved to Hutt Valley. Unknown to each other, the two lived close by for years.

Tonight, Suzy confirms the happy ending to the story. She met Don Hayward and announced she was his daughter. By then Don was a publican in Otaki. He was delighted with the news. He and his late wife had together produced only a son, Gareth. Tonight, at the surgery, Suzy tells me that dear Don had become like a second grandfather to her own family. Sadly, he died in 1999.

"And what about Gareth?" I ask. "Do you keep in touch with him?"

"Of course," replies Suzy. "Remember, he's family now; he's my half-brother."

So tonight in the surgery is my first meeting with Suzanne Davis. See what happens when you answer the phone nicely? See what happens when you keep clippings and papers and books for 50 years or more?

(Des Williams, the New Zealander from Rotorua who had phoned me to make initial contact, became so engrossed in the 1950 Lions team that he wrote a book about them. It is an excellent work, and as far as I know is the only book written about that hugely popular touring team.)

SEPTEMBER 24

Having a look at the teams as the World Cup gets closer, a survey of the England squad tells me that 16 of their players are aged 29 or older. There are 13 over 30 and three aged 29 (with Martin Corry turning 30 during the Cup). By comparison, New Zealand's squad of 30 players has 25 *under* the age of 29.

Well done to *Sport 365* on Sky TV. Their story about the Ali Williams injury four days ago has finally been followed by other news media. The new Sky sports show is battling for recognition, but by breaking stories ahead of other news organisations it will soon have viewers watching with interest.

The Williams scare must be serious – the NZRU makes a press release today. If Williams is unable to go to the Cup, who replaces him? Many of the leading candidates are out of the frame – Simon Maling of Otago is still hurt, as are Waikato's Keith Robinson and Canterbury's Norm Maxwell. Maxwell is still playing, but is said to have an ankle injury. We note with interest the appearance of Troy Flavell at the All Blacks camp in Nelson. The big North Harbour man has drifted out of favour recently with doubts about his fitness and his tendency to play outside rugby's laws. Mitchell is a stickler for discipline on the field. Still, Flavell looks to have the front running.

SEPTEMBER 25

Alan Jones, the former Wallaby coach and a radio star in Sydney, is on the news today, saying the All Blacks won't win the World Cup because they are "haunted by failure". He adds: "They've got very good players but they've been bruised by failure, and whether they've been able to purge themselves of that, I really don't know."

Earlier this month, Nick Farr-Jones, the former Wallaby captain, suggested that the All Blacks might crumble under pressure at the Cup.

Quinn and McBeth head to the beautiful far north today. We are filming Kiwi "World Cup faces in the crowd" again, capturing short, pithy and supportive comments about the World Cup. We have almost completed a full sweep of the country. These little pieces, each only 30 seconds

I couldn't go past this eclectic collection of mailboxes just outside Kaitaia without stopping for a photo.

long, have been a delight to collect and collate.

Today we are reminded yet again of this country's continued love of the game and everything involved with it. Today we meet a family who are holidaying in Whangarei and whose young son is Todd, named after a famous rugby son of Canterbury. Then there is Branko Clinac, selling delicious Kerikeri oranges by the roadside. Branko tells us of his lifetime devotion to watching rugby, even down to collecting videotapes in his retirement years. We end the day at the Kaitaia RSA, having been advised to go there for dinner. Tonight we listen to any number of local characters tell of their hopes and dreams for John Mitchell's team, "the boys", as they are lovingly referred to by most.

McBeth and I later remark that we hope the NZRU fishheads travel on similar trips to what we have done this past month, meeting grassroots rugby people, who are keeping alive a loyal love of the game, far away from the corporate plonkers who populate much of the city rugby scene.

SEPTEMBER 26

Still filming in the north, we are guided expertly out to 90 Mile Beach by local authority Toto Thompson. He takes us high above Shipwreck Bay to film a superb view along the beach. Then ex-All Black Percy Erceg is visited on his 10-acre block. As we go, Toto can lovingly tell us where every person in the district who has attained All Black status was born, raised, lived or went to school. Toto's club, Awanui, has produced Peter Jones and Mike Burgoyne (Mike still works in the town); Victor Yates is back from Auckland again; Wayne Neville now works as a builder in Auckland; Pat Walsh was born "in that house there" as we drive through tiny Ahipara.

We thank Toto for his wisdom and then journey south, via tiny Kohukohu. There, we spy a friendly chap named Bunny Slade in the local bowling club garden and, unannounced, we ask him to lean over the fence and tell us about the tiny town's interest in the World Cup. He does it in one take. He then goes back to work and we drive away.

Then we cross on the Rawene Ferry – the great commentator, Winston McCarthy, spent some of his retirement years here, and loved the place. I can see why. Then through Opononi, Kaikohe and Kawakawa and back to Whangarei. Our scan of New Zealand is over.

Waiting to fly home, we stop for a coffee. Clambering into a taxi, the driver looks at *me* and asks: "Aren't you John McBeth?" In the back seat I can hear the real McBeth chortling. A local rugby man stops by and tells us that the whisper around town after the All Blacks had had their week in Whangarei was that John Mitchell is not enjoying his job at all these past few months. "It's all the pressure, apparently."

We reply: "Hold on mate, that's only a rumour."

But it makes us wonder once more about Mitch, given our recent dealings with him. Poor bugger, we're now saying. Who'd want the job of coaching the All Blacks at the World Cup, given the expectations we've heard from New Zealanders around the country these past few weeks?

Just when we were thinking more anxious thoughts about the All Black coach, John McBeth's cellphone rings and it is a cheerful Robbie Deans, telling us that we can interview him and Mitchell next week in Methven at the next All Blacks camp. No problems at all.

You could knock us over with a feather. McBeth had decided to circumvent the Rugby Union's media-blocking systems and simply rang Deans and left a message. The quick affirmation that the interviews are okay to do makes us wonder if Mitchell was ever told of our needs.

SEPTEMBER 29

I feel refreshed today after a weekend spent with our beautiful granddaughter Maggie at our holiday place at Riversdale Beach by Masterton.

I could not bear to write an entry for Saturday the 27th, as that was the day Wellington challenged for the Ranfurly Shield in Christchurch and came away with only a 38 38 draw As they say, close but no cigar. The draw means Canterbury retain the Shield. It turned out to be a great game but I thought Wellington played poorly.

How could a team score six tries to three, as Wellington did, plus score more NPC points, three points to two, *and* retain their lead on the NPC championship table, and yet not win the Ranfurly Shield? Amazing.

Bad news for a staunch Wellington supporter, whichever paper you read.

Watching in Riversdale, I immediately went for a walk along the beach afterwards. When will Wellington ever win the Shield again?

Today, a week out from our departure for Sydney, we hear of a slight hitch in this week's Mitchell/Deans interview scenario. Apparently, NZRU media staff have told our people the interviews are to be secret. No-one but us at TVNZ is to know the meeting. Especially none of the other media sniffing around for crumbs off the Mitchell/Deans table.

And the interviews are to be aired only *after* the All Blacks have left for Melbourne. The arrangements suit us fine. We can play bits on the opening day of the World Cup on October 10, and then more the next day, before New Zealand play Italy. But were Mitchell and Deans actually asked to be available to us at Whangarei or New Plymouth? We'll never know for sure. If the interviews are good, who'll care?

The Dominion Post reports that Norm Maxwell is on official standby for the injured Ali Williams. The NZRU denies it.

SEPTEMBER 30

To Christchurch today to meet producer Alan Barnes and cameraman John Robertson. We are off to see the man who began the year a lot more open and approachable than the coach who has been showing signs of withering under pressure these past few weeks.

We drive towards the Southern Alps and see more snow on the roadside. By the time we arrive at the Terrace Downs Golf Resort, the grounds are covered in a heavy layer of snow. Can this be true? The bad weather plaguing this team's training camps has been incredible.

But we're not here to worry about that. We want to finally complete our very expensive filming requirements, spread now over nearly a month.

We set up in a chalet, with snow all around. And we wait. This time Matt McIlraith arrives with his lists. The news is promising. Matt says that all the players who missed interviews while we were in Whangarei and New Plymouth *will* be appearing tonight. And so, too, will the All Black coaches.

Snow in Methven – hardly ideal preparation for rock-hard grounds in Australia next month.

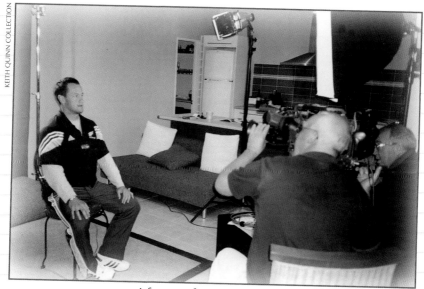

A few gems from Carlos Spencer.

Soon after, out of the darkness and mushing through the snow, come the remaining players. Their interviews go fine. The best response comes from Ben Blair ("Critter" seems to be his All Black nickname). I ask him: "What was your favourite food at your house in your young days?" He replies firmly: "Whitebait, fried in fat by Dad, put on white bread with lots of butter, and, though some West Coasters like to add mint sauce, up in Ngakawau in Buller, I always preferred a dash of lemon juice."

Once again, you nutritionists can go stick your heads in a bucket!

Then a car from another Terrace Downs chalet pulls up. Out of the darkness step John Mitchell and Robbie Deans. We of the crew do a silent clenching of the fists and a mute shout of triumph.

The two are as welcoming and friendly as I have ever seen them. True, Mitchell, with his beanie pulled low, looks pale and gaunt, but once under the camera lights his face is open and warm. The interview goes sweetly. He answers any questions I pose from my prepared list with a straightforwardness that belies my previous concerns. He is on camera for about 20 minutes. Deans is the same – open, honest and thoughtful.

When the interviews end we can't be happier. The thousands of kilometres covered to collate them all is behind us, so naturally we feel it's all been worthwhile. I thank Mitchell, who says: "It's never a problem to talk to you Keith." I swallow and feel mean at the dark thoughts I had had in New Plymouth a fortnight ago. It's such a friendly scene – I pose

Pre-interview discussions with John Mitchell.
Robbie Deans (background) catches up on what's in the papers.

for a photograph with them, taken by Alan Barnes.

The coaches head into the black night and we are left to pack up. Matt McIlraith repeats the interview rules: "Nothing from them must be shown before the All Blacks leave for Australia. And no mention must be given of the media advantage you have been given here tonight. Especially not to other reporters."

All smiles as the interviews take place at last.

OCTOBER

"A hallmark of this All Black selection panel is lateral thinking."

OCTOBER 1

It's only six days till I fly to Sydney, 10 till the World Cup, and 11 till the All Blacks' first game.

I wake at 5.30am in a narrow bed at Mount Hutt Lodge, in the wilds of North Canterbury. We arrived so late last night that the people running the lodge were in bed. We had to feel about in the cold and find our rooms by checking which ones had our names cellotaped to the glass-fronted doors. The rooms were unlocked, so we let ourselves in. It could happen only in rural New Zealand.

By 6.30am we've slung our gear into the van and drive off. We leave before the owners have woken, so we never see them.

Returning to Wellington, I take the mid-morning conference call from our office in Auckland. I report that the interviews with the All Black team and management have finally been accomplished. I feel like Paul Revere bringing the vital news. A triumphant report.

And thank you Frank Bunce for emailing back from Italy today. It turns out Rima Wakarua is no stranger to Frank. In fact, Rima has come under the Bunce influence at the Leonessa club in northern Italy. Rima is a former Takapuna Grammar player and helped his Italian club win promotion to the top division for this season. "This bloke can do everything," Frank says. "He's been the best first-five in Italy for years. Only the politics of Italian rugby have kept him out."

OCTOBER 2

The Carillon Club holds a pre-World Cup luncheon at the Beehive today. This club raises funds for youth sport in the Wellington region. I've been the president since its inception eight years ago. We've raised and given away nearly $500,000 in grants. We are proud to announce that we supported Jerry Collins's start in the game. Now he's off to the World Cup. Previously our club's pride and joy had been the weightlifter

Olivia Baker, whom we identified early and assisted during her rise to Olympic Games status in 2000.

Today John McBeth and I are on stage, outlining our TV coverage to the audience of 250. Minister of Sport, Leisure and Recreation Trevor Mallard and Earle Kirton are the guest speakers. The "do" is a big success.

The people love what Earle has to say. Earle reckons the winning of the World Cup will depend a lot on the refereeing. "Get into those buggers early," he says to me. "Our three refs have already flown over. I bet they're being brainwashed for a fortnight by the IRB refereeing people. And the IRB people, being from the Northern Hemisphere, will encourage a style of reffing like we see from the Pom refs and the others up there – all slow stuff and allowing the killing of the ball."

Earle is convincing. He tells the crowd: "England, with their big pack, will have to slow the ball down to win. Their defence is such that if we play them and all our line-breakers come at them through the backs, they won't know who to go for. So we have to 'encourage' the refereeing to allow that to happen."

Afer the speeches I ask for a show of hands on who will win the World Cup. South Africa wins one vote, France about 10, Australia 15, England about 100 and New Zealand nearly 120. Earle says emphatically: "The referees will win the World Cup." It's sobering that 40 per cent of a good, average Kiwi crowd think England will win.

OCTOBER 3

We're winding up preparations for departure. Anne is doing most of the work. One thing on the list is to buy enough pills to control my epilepsy condition for the best part of two months. With that amount I could get stopped by Customs.

Tonight it's another meeting again with my 1960s flatmates from Busaco Road. We haven't been together since the night before the England test in June. It's pelting down outside, so hard that we adjourn to the Green Parrot for dinner at 5.30pm. The World Cup tops the discussion topics. There's also some talk of us going to the Wellington versus Otago NPC "game, but who would want to go in weather like this? Instead we nip around the corner to The Sports Cafe bar in Courtenay Place and watch it from the warmth there.

Otago win 26–8, which in the slushy rain is a thrashing. Grumbling heavily, we decide not to have one for the road and head home. We will meet as a gang before Christmas, where one of our number may be forced to eat humble pie – when the boys ask me who'll win the World Cup, I say: "England."

OCTOBER 4

More goodbyes and socialising. At lunchtime old friends Peter and Glenda Gallagher, of Cromwell, tell us of flying to Wellington last night and seeing John Mitchell board the plane in Christchurch. He must have been heading home at the end of the week-long Terrace Downs training camp.

The Gallagher's report that Mitchell had to sit in the middle of a row of three seats on the plane. He was verbally bombarded all the way to Wellington by a bloke on his left and a woman on his right. "He seemed to handle it well," says Glenda, "but I did feel sorry for him. The people never let up."

Tonight I meet my old friend, Warwick Burke, who is still the best newsreader on radio's National Programme. We meet at the Bellevue Hotel in Lower Hutt. Some other friends gather and one bloke proceeds to tell us that he's heard a story about a prominent very recent All Black player who admits to getting home at 5am before a test match he was playing that day. It's another of those stories where you listen but have to ask: "Can this possibly be true?" The fellow telling me the story insists that it is from an impeccable source.

OCTOBER 5

Quinn and McBeth appear on the morning children's TV show *What Now*. We are in a skit with Jason Fa'afoi, supposedly telling Jason how to behave on an overseas All Black reporting assignment. "You must be home early every night," is one of the lines. Some chance. Reporters are allowed to go out – it's the players who aren't supposed to.

The *Sunday News* is very kind today, publishing a lovely picture of granddaughter Maggie and me.

I've had more reporters and radio stations ringing this week. All this

*This **Sunday News** story sent me off to the World Cup in good spirits.*

attention is making me a tad nervous, as my return to the commentary box gets closer.

I spend the rest of today packing books and papers for Australia. There will be two suitcases packed with stuff.

Tomorrow is Departure Day. I can't wait. It is going to be some trip. I *hope* New Zealand win, but have that nagging feeling about the Poms.

This afternoon I write my weekly piece for *Rugby News*. In trying to find a suitable quote with which to send the All Blacks on their way, I delve into the writings of Paul J Meyer, a US motivational authority. He wrote: "Whatever it is in life that you vividly imagine, ardently desire, sincerely believe in and enthusiastically act upon, must inevitably come to pass." The quote should be tucked into the All Blacks' back pockets.

OCTOBER 6

World Cup travel day. The alarm rings at 4am. The journey for me begins on a cold Wellington morning after a weekend of storms and floods. I thank my dear wife Anne for a sensational job packing all of my stuff. I have two suitcases, one sportsbag and one laptop to carry. My three baggage pieces weigh 60 kilograms.

The ageing process of a rugby commentator is all too evident as I prepare for my fifth World Cup.

It is an uneventful flight over, apart from a man three rows back, cackling loudly at the movie. At this time of the morning his laughter is insufferable. I turn around to shoosh him and find it's trusty Peter Marriott, our TVNZ stats man.

I read yesterday's *Sunday Star-Times.* Ali Williams gets big space for his still-injured foot, and there is speculation as to who might replace him. I would plump for Norman Maxwell. The delay in confirming whether Williams will travel indicates his injury is serious. There are rumours of a pin in the broken bone.

Sydney's Monday papers are full of last night's NRL Grand Final, but it's pleasing to note the space dedicated to the World Cup. Most teams are now here. The All Blacks will come across mid-week. I expect that if

New Zealand win the tournament, their delayed arrival will be hailed as a "wise move to keep away from the Australian hype". If they don't win, the delay it'll be "slack planning; the team were not involved in the excitement until too late".

(I remember the 1999 World Cup All Blacks flying to France to rest for a few days. They continued to practise over there, of course. But after the team lost their World Cup semi-final, the break was derided as "a junket trip". We all have 20/20 vision in hindsight.)

The rest of my first day in Sydney is spent unpacking at the Kirribilli Village Apartments, where I'll be resident for seven weeks.

After being accredited, the crew has an informal meeting at the nearby Kirribilli Club, where my turn at a "shout" of three pints and a glass of Coca-Cola comes to A$10. Not bad, we all agree, and have another.

It's great to meet again Sean Glover and Fred Howard, two Englishmen who are joining us to work their brilliant package of television graphics into our coverage. I've worked with Sean many times, most recently at the World Sevens tournament and at the Manchester Commonwealth Games. Fred is the old "Fearless Fred" Howard, who was "capped" 26 times as a test referee. He officiated at the 1987 World Cup and recounts a great story about how he controlled the Australia versus Wales third-place match at Rotorua and sent off the Aussie flanker, David Codey: "You know, that night at the test dinner, the losing Australian team were pretty sore. Alan Jones [the Wallaby coach] glared at me for three hours. He never said a word, mind, just glared. That Codey, he had to go." Fred is called "Fearless" because he holds the world record for sending off more players in tests (four) than any other referee.

The Sydney Morning Herald has been wondering about the whereabouts of the trophy the Australians won for finishing fourth at the 1987 World Cup. It was handed to the Wallabies at the dinner in Rotorua. But such was their dark mood that they did not care to take the splendid carved Maori canoe from the function hall. I have seen this trophy in New Zealand several times over the years. The last time it was in the company of the great Christchurch memorabilia collector, Russell Vine. He put it on display in the International Rugby Hall of Fame building in Auckland. After Russell's sad death and the downfall of the hall of fame, the memorabilia went to the new Eden Park grandstand in Auckland. If anyone was to look, that might be a good place to begin.

We go to the TV studio for the morning. It's a check-up kind of day.

It's great at a time like this to meet old friends from other parts of the broadcasting world. Tex Texerais, from SuperSport in South Africa, is producing its coverage. With him is his boss, the affable Gert Roets. Their front man is Joel Stransky, the ex-Springbok, a very nice man. I tell Joel that in my book last year, *Outrageous Rugby Moments,* there's a chapter devoted to him. He gives a wry smile, perhaps not quite sure how we Kiwis feel about him, I suppose. He knows we cannot quite get over his soaring dropped goal at Ellis Park in the 1995 World Cup final. It really did us, that one.

We talk about recent racial problems within the Springbok team. Tex says he feels the players are okay, that it's part of the "changeover" South Africa is still going through. Joel talks about the new jerseys the Springboks will be wearing. "It looks odd to me to have rugby kit with no collars. Our players look like they're choking," he says.

The Australians announce their team for the tournament opener. It has six changes from that which played their last test, against the All Blacks eight weeks ago. Al Baxter, who played so well off the bench in Auckland, will make his test starting debut. He will be on the tighthead side of the front row, against Argentina's scrum monsters. Baxter may have one of the most difficult debuts of all time. The first scrum might tell us about Australia's chances of defending the Cup.

Phil Gifford, of Radio Sport, rings. "This Saturday, when New Zealand plays Italy, I'll be on a plane flying home from Auckland's Ranfurly Shield challenge against Canterbury. Will the All Blacks game be replayed later?" he asks. I want to reply: "No, Phil, because there are three other games to play back-to-back that night and the next day we have three more live games to show you. You might like to have the All Black game recorded at your place." But he cuts me off for the five o'clock news. It's clearly hard to please some people. There will be more than 160 hours of coverage of the World Cup on TV1 and *before it starts* people are complaining.

MONDAY	TUESDAY	WEDNESDAY	THURSDAY	FRIDAY	SATURDAY	SUNDAY
(6) FLY TO AUSSIE CHECK-IN APARTMENT COLLECT ACCREDITATION 0600-1700	**(7)** HL - 0900-1730 L - 0900-1730 CO- 0900-1730	**(8)** HL - RDO L - RDO CO - RDO PROD CREW 0930-1730	**(9)** HL - 0900-1800 L - 0900-1800 CO - 0900-1800 MNET 5min feed	**(10)** L - 1730-2230 **OPENING CEREMONY** 1930 **AUS V ARG** 2030 Sydney with Jeff W HL - 1330-2330 L - 1330-2330 CO - 1330-2330	**(11)** L - 1330-1615 1645-2400 with Jeff W **NZ V ITALY** 1430 Melbourne **IRE V ROMANIA** 1700 Gosford **FRANCE V FIJI** 1930 Brisbane **SA V URUGUAY** 2200 Perth HL - 1330-2200 L - 1200-0200 CO - 1200-0200 World Feed MNET - 1 hr show	**(12)** L - 1745-2400 **WALES V CAN** 1800 Melbourne **SCO V JAPAN** 2000 Townsville **ENG V GEORGIA** 2200 Perth with Jeff W HL - 0730-1730 L - 1430-0200 CO - 1615-0200 MNET - 1 hr show
(13) HL - 1300-1500 **ARG V NAMIBIA** 1930 Gosford HL - 0730-1730 L - RDO CO - 1130-1600 MNET 5min feed	**(14)** L - 1915-2130 HL - RDO L - 1530-2200 CO - 1745-2230 MNET 5min feed	**(15)** HL - 1400-1500 L - 1915-0200 **FIJI V USA** 1700 Brisbane **ITALY V TONGA** 1930 Canberra with Steve Bachop on World Feed **SAM V URUG** 2200 Perth HL - 1730-0300 (PA 1600) CO - 1230-1515 1815-0300	**(16)** HL - 1300-1500 HL - 0730-1730 L - RDO CO - 1130-1600 MNET 5min feed	**(17)** L - 1830-2130 **NZ V CANADA** 1930 Melbourne with Jeff W on World Feed HL - RDO L - 1400-2330 CO - 1700-2330	**(18)** HL - 1300-1500 L - 1540-2400 **AUS V ROMANIA** 1600 Brisbane **FRANCE V JPN** 1900 Townsville **SA V ENG** 2200 Perth with Jeff W HL - 0730-1730 L - 1300-0200 CO - 1130-0200 MNET - 1 hr show	**(19)** HL - 1300-1500 L - 1930-0200 with Jeff W. **WALES V TONGA** 1800 Canberra **IRE V NAMIBIA** 2000 Sydney **GEORGIA V SAM** 2200 Perth on World Feed HL - 0730-1730 L - 1730-0400 (PA 1700) CO - 1130-1515 1830-0400 MNET - 1 hr show
(20) HL - 1300-1500 L - 1915-2130 **SCOT V USA** 1930 Brisbane HL - 0730-1730 L - 1730-2230 CO - 1130-1515 1815-2230 MNET 5min feed	**(21)** HL - 1400-1500 L - 1915-2130 **ITALY V CANADA** 1930 Canberra with Willie Lose HL - 0730-1730 L - 1730-2230 CO - 1230-1515 1815-2230 MNET 5min feed	**(22)** HL - 1400-1500 L - 2000-2230 **ARG V ROMANIA** 2030 Sydney with Willie L HL - 0730-1730 L - 1530-2330 CO - 1230-1515 1900-2330	**(23)** HL - 1400-1500 L - 1930-2200 **FIJI V JAPAN** 2000 Townsville HL- 0730-1730 L - 1500-2300 CO - 1230-1515 1830-2300 MNET 5min feed	**(24)** HL - 1400-1500 L - 1630-2200 **NZ V TONGA** 1730 Brisbane with Willie L. **SA V GEORGIA** 2000 Sydney HL - 0730-1730 L - 1330-2300 CO - 1230-1515 1530-2300	**(25)** HL - 1300-1500 L - 1540-2230 **AUS V NAMIBIA** 1600 Adel **ITALY V WALES** 1830 Canberra **FRANCE V SCO** 2030 Sydney HL - 0730-1730 L - 1230-2430 CO - 1130-2430 on World Feed with Willie L MNET - 1 hr show	**(26)** HL - 1400-1600 L - 1800-2230 **ARG V IRE** 1830 Adel **ENG V SAMOA** 2030 Melbourne HL - 0730-1730 L - 1430-2430 CO - 1230-1615 1700-2430 with Willie L MNET - 1 hr show
(27) HL - 1400-1600 L - 2030-2230 **JAPAN V USA** 1930 Gosford HL - 1800-2330 (PA 1830) CO - 1230-1615 1930-2330 MNET 5min feed	**(28)** HL - 1500-1600 L - 2045-2245 **GEORGIA V URUGUAY** 1930 Sydney with Willie L. HL - 0730-1730 L - 1815-2345 (PA 1830) CO - 1330-1615 1945-2345 MNET 5min feed	**(29)** HL - 1500-1600 L - 2045-2245 DINNER **CANADA V TONGA** 1930 Wollong. HL - 0730-1730 L - 1815-2345 (PA 1830) CO - 1330-1615 1945-2345	**(30)** HL - 1500-1600 L - 2100-2300 **NAMIBIA V ROMANIA** 2000 Launce. HL- 0730-1730 L - 1730-2400 CO - 1330-1615 2000-2400 MNET 5min feed	**(31)** HL - 1500-1600 L - 1900-2130 **FRANCE V USA** 1930 Wollongong HL - 0730-1730 L - 1530-2230 CO - 1330-1615 1800-2230	— on-air times — RWC games — shift hrs -- MNET progs HL - H'lights Show L - Late Show CO - Cross-over shift (covers both shifts)	

The first three weeks of our World Cup schedule. A busy time awaits.

OCTOBER 8

I slog it out in my room all day. There are three matches in three days and an awful lot of prep work to do. Plus, there's the opening ceremony to think about. I put my head down and write notes to myself about players, stats, histories etc – all the stuff a commentator needs to have ready on the desk-top come commentary time.

I emerge into the fading daylight at 6pm to go to the TV studio at Epping to watch the rehearsal telecast of the opening ceremony. It looks okay but the show is far from slick and there's only 48 hours for them to get it right. The producers stop the action several times, music doesn't play and several "props" do not seem to work properly. Harish Bhana, our sound expert, comes in from his booth and says the sound is out of sync as well. We're not pleased.

The All Blacks have arrived in Melbourne. There are wild scenes of familiar faces pushing through wellwishers, many of whom are dressed in black. There must be thousands there. Joe Rokocoko blinks at the camera in apparent amazement. Get used to it Joe – this is your life from now on.

The All Blacks have brought Ali Williams with them. It's a gamble but they must be confident he'll play at some stage. The other injury concern is Aaron Mauger. He has a groin strain, described as "slight", but is here, which is good.

The New Zealand team for the opening game is named and it is as strong as they can run. Only Williams and Mauger are missing from the recent big victories. Brad Thorn and Dan Carter take their places.

OCTOBER 9

Robbie Deans is quoted in the paper today, saying: "We've come here to play an expansive game. We don't want to go home wondering." Nice, strong words about the All Black attitude.

The weather in Sydney is anything but nice. I go downstairs to meet ex-All Black and Manu Samoa international Steve Bachop, who has just flown in, and I take my coat to keep warm and keep the rain off. Steve is a really nice bloke. We've brought him over to be a studio guests for the World Cup, which is now just 36 hours away.

Steve has made huge personal sacrifices to be with us. His wife, Sue, a former New Zealand rugby international, has leukemia and only weeks ago had a bone marrow transplant. Steve says the signs are promising for a good recovery, but Sue is in considerable discomfort. Steve had had the invitation to join us for some time but had been reluctant to leave home. He told Sue he had turned down the job in Sydney with TVNZ. "She went crook at me," Steve says this morning. "She told me she'd be okay in the hospital with all the family around, and that if I didn't come to the Cup I'd be turning down a great opportunity. So here I am in Sydney, thanks to her."

Sue broadcast the World Cup women's final with me at the Avalon Studios in Wellington a few years ago and has also worked at touch commentaries.

The rest of today I stay in my room, collecting thoughts and notes.

Tonight the crew meet at the Kirribilli Club. The club is full. It's a noisy, smoky, boisterous place, with meat and chook raffles going all the time. We enter one of the trivia quizzes as a "Kiwi Sports" team. We don't do very well (Question: Name seven countries that end in the letter "E"). Steve Bachop earns us valuable points with the knowledge he has tucked away that the most predominant colour in a box of M and M chocolates is brown.

Another former All Black, Richard Loe, comes in quietly and sits down. He will be part of our studio team and will also be with the All Blacks team for a time, acting as their front row coach. He will be away from his North Canterbury farm for seven weeks. He talks about leaving his wife Felicity in charge of docking 5000 lambs. Aren't these wives great! Richard is a very nice man – yes, you read that correctly. He's far from the hard man he was on the rugby field. How often I recall, years ago, getting the grim Loe stare when I had criticised his style of play. Still, time passes and these old toughies eventually cool down.

OCTOBER 10

Pool A: Australia 24 – Argentina 8

At last. The World Cup opening match in Sydney, Australia, 2003. I pull back the curtains at 6am and the view takes my breath away: blue skies, no clouds, and 30 little boats bobbing gently on the waters of Lavender Bay. The Milson's Point Ferry crosses to Circular Quay, leaving a trail of gentle wash, which ripples all the way towards Darling Harbour.

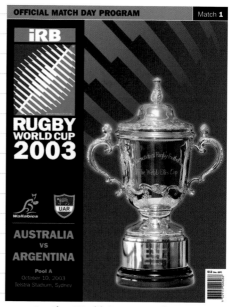

Another World Cup gets under way.

But there is work to do this morning. I have neglected thinking much about the opening ceremony commentary, so that has to be done first. Jeff Wilson will be arriving soon, so he and I should have to chat this morning. There are some good luck emails I should reply to, like those from the kids – Shelley in Korea, Rowan in Queenstown and Ben in Wellington (he has forwarded pictures of his two children, Maggie and James). Also John Hart, Blair Wingfield and Chas Toogood have emailed me. And Alan Trotter, from Durban. I thank them all. Blair says: "Just be yourself at the microphone tonight."

It's good to meet Jeff Wilson, who breezes in from New Zealand late this morning. He looks fit and keen and ready for his first "cap" as a TV commentator. We're driven to the ground mid-afternoon and are in position five hours before the opening ceremony, the equivalent of being in place at Eden Park or Jade Stadium at 9am for an afternoon kickoff. In other words, far too bloody early!

Jeff is to appear on the *Holmes* show direct from the ground at 4pm. Just as he makes his first statement to the New Zealand audience, John Williamson, the great Aussie balladeer, launches into his full-blast rehearsal for *Waltzing Matilda*. Jeff struggles to catch the studio questions over the cacophony of sound. Later we hear that he has done just fine.

I share the opening ceremony commentary with Bernadine Oliver-Kerby. Bernie is a pleasure to work with and is well prepared tonight. Our work together over the ceremony goes well, except for the part where a young lad steps up to kick a symbolic ball at some goalposts 80 metres away. The idea was that when the lad kicked the ball a rocket would fire off, travel between the posts and ignite a blast of pyrotechnics above the stadium. It had worked spectacularly at rehearsal two nights ago but tonight there was ... nothing. How sad for the lad, and how wild the producers must be when one of the best gimmicks of the night doesn't work.

Next the teams emerge. Australia are led by a grim-faced George Gregan, while Argentina favour their long-serving No 8 Gustavo Longo to lead them out. Their captain, Agustin Pichot, apparently prefers running out at the tail of the field. Soon the anthems have been sung, New Zealand referee Paul Honis blows his whistle and the World Cup 2003 is on.

The game is full of drama, though the action is never of the highest quality. Australia win but do not secure a bonus point. Everyone in the 81,350 crowd leaves the stadium only reasonably happy.

Jeff and I see the Aussies as being too keen to force the pace. It's as though they've been pent up training for too long and are bursting to play. They score only three tries. Wendell Sailor goes into the trivia books by scoring the first try of the fifth World Cup.

Argentina, on the other hand, come to the game with a big reputation for powerhouse scrummaging, which will hopefully be turned into attacking chances wide out. It doesn't happen for them. A strapping young lad named Al Baxter, with only a few games at first class level and playing his first run-on test for the Wallabies, does a superb job of holding out the seasoned props, Roberto Grau and Omar Hasan. And without forward dominance the Pumas offer nothing through their backs. The night becomes a disappointment for them.

After the game it's straight home to the apartment, as we are to be up early to fly to Melbourne tomorrow. As I sip my supper coffee tonight I reflect on a good day. That's all, just a *good* day, personally. My first commentary was a bit stuttery, with a few mistakes. I was only mildly satisfied. I felt though that my effort was not bad considering I had told no-one, including my always-concerned family, that in the depths of last night I woke from a deep sleep, made my way to the bathroom and vomited violently. Sheer nerves, I suspect. After all, I haven't done a major test for nearly four years. I have never been ill before in 30 years of broadcasting sport.

OCTOBER 11

Pool A: Ireland 45 – Romania 17
Pool B: France 61 – Fiji 18
Pool C: South Africa 72 – Uruguay 6
Pool D: New Zealand 70 – Italy 7

Taxi at 6.30am. The flight to Melbourne is early and uneventful. By 10am, Jeff Wilson and I, producer Stu Dennison and production manager Maree Simpson, are installed in the rather splendid downtown Grand Hotel. It's the hotel with surely the widest corridors in the world. We have arrived early because the All Blacks are kicking off against Italy in an afternoon game. However, before we get too excited about the team playing with the

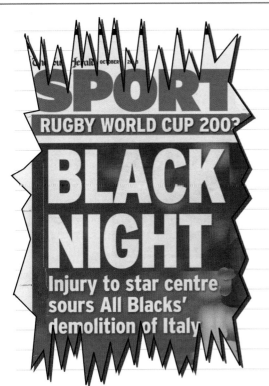

Concern over Umaga overshadowed the hammering of Italy, this is how **The Sydney Sun-Herald** *reported it.*

sun on their backs we arrive at the nearby Telstra Dome to find it has its roof closed. Today's game could have been played in the same conditions any time, day or night.

At 2.30pm, the teams come out into the superb arena and the game starts in front of 40,715 fans. One can sense early that New Zealand are going to be comfortable winners. That's because Reuben Thorne's men are playing keep-ball and Italy are reduced to being defenders only. It's a matter of time before New Zealand sort out how to score a swag of points.

A couple of early things are noted. One is that the All Blacks are so keen. They're running everywhere at a crazy pace, often forcing passes at far too high a velocity. More patience is needed. It's what the Aussies did yesterday. On the other hand, Italy have sent on to the field a hardy band of tacklers who are pulling down All Blacks at a high rate. There are no jokes about Italian soldiers here. These *Azzurri* are very committed.

Soon enough though the points come. Brad Thorn crashes over for a try, followed by Reuben Thorne a few minutes later. The other All Blacks rush forward to embrace Brad (his first try for his country), but there isn't a similar reaction when Reuben scores. Jeff Wilson notes this in an aside to me, and we wonder why there's no celebration when the captain scores. A return to the unsmiling giants of yesteryear, perhaps?

Then, disaster. Carlos Spencer has been playing well. But the Italian defenders force a collision between Spencer and Tana Umaga. Down go the two All Blacks. My first reaction is that Spencer's in trouble. But then it becomes obvious Tana is the one who's not at all well. He's lying back, clutching and indicating to team doctor John Mayhew that his left knee is the painful problem.

Tana tries to play on but there is a serious problem. TV replays show his leg being extended backwards in the collision. He limps off and is replaced by Ma'a Nonu.

More concerns follow. Spencer has a serious case of the "yips" in his goal-kicking. He misses three shots from a relatively easy range and, still limping from the crash with Umaga, leaves the field at halftime with a look of disappointment and confusion on his face. New Zealand lead 25–0.

In the second spell Joe Rokocoko is all speed and dash on one wing, but is seen stretching his hamstrings a number of times. He makes one of his characteristic bursting, twisting runs, which leads to a try by Carter. Then, while galloping in for one himself, he pulls up short and grimaces in his dive to score. Off he limps.

The game ends 70–7 to the All Blacks, only one point different from the 70–6 result when the two countries met in Auckland in 1987 in the first World Cup game. The Italians play a strong part in tonight's fixture. I'm most impressed with the tackling of several backs – Francesco Mazzariol and Andrea Masi in particular. The New Zealand-born players playing for Italy, Matthew Phillips and Scott Palmer, are both outstanding. Phillips crashes over for a deserved try. Having enjoyed a night in the Kaitaia RSA a few weeks ago, I can just imagine them all jumping about in delight. The Phillips name has been big in rugby up there for years.

Afterwards, I hear the two Kiwis talking in fluent Italian to their media. What a great opportunity their rugby experience in Italy has proven – from Kaitaia and Palmerston North to Italy and now the World Cup.

New Zealand's first match and already injury concerns about Tana Umaga.

Despite the impressive score, there is grave concern for Umaga's knee. And also for Spencer's confidence. Mind you, Ma'a Nonu, played the best I have seen him. He was a rampaging charger in midfield. And Daniel Carter, too, played a game with brilliant touches at second five-eighth. His goal-kicking was also excellent, totalling six conversions.

So that's two commentaries down. Today's was a lot better. Jeff Wilson and I were the "world feed" broadcasters today. All English-speaking countries took our commentary, an audience of millions. Jeff is going well as a commentator and Bernadine Oliver-Kerby did a good job with the end-of-match interviews.

At the press conferences afterwards, Italy coach John Kirwan looks much more relaxed than John Mitchell. Confidently cutting across two languages, Kirwan speaks of the next game, against Tonga, as being the target for his team. He talks proudly of his players and what they "achieved" against the All Blacks tonight.

Mitchell doesn't say much. He hadn't turned up for any world feed TV interview after the game. That is his perogative. In front of the media here, he looks blankly ahead as Robbie Deans takes up the first responses. Reuben Thorne is also there, as are Doug Howlett and Dan Carter.

Mitchell makes only brief replies to questions directed his way. I wonder if he is massively disappointed at losing one of his senior players to injury. But surely he has geared himself beforehand for the likelihood of losing key members. It'll happen to all teams here.

Little is said about Umaga's condition. "It's serious for him," says Deans. When asked if a replacement might be needed, Mitchell says emphatically: "I'll decide that."

Finally, after 40 minutes of questions, Radio New Zealand's Barry Guy pipes up from the back of the conference hall: "Can you *please* take us through, point-by-point, what happens in the case of a knee injury like Tana has, how it is fixed, what the processes are, whether hospitalisation might be needed?"

There's a moment's silence from the top table, and then Deans launches into a long, detailed reply. He covers waiting for the swelling to go down, scans being taken, x-rays if needed, visits to hospital, meetings with specialists, and so on. The reply is delivered in an open, honest way. I'm left thinking: "Please can we have more of this openness." I also wonder why has the coach not spoken more tonight.

We wander back to the hotel. By scoring 11 tries, New Zealand gained the first bonus point at a World Cup game. Yet there's much to talk about. Umaga may be out of the tournament, Ali Williams is still hurt, so is Aaron Mauger. What about Joe Rokocoko's hamstring, and Carlos's yips?

(I spare a thought for Umaga. Having been on the road over the past few weeks and seeing the All Blacks traipsing around to their training camps and seeing him putting in a huge training effort, it must be shattering for him to have had only 15 minutes in the tournament before being so badly crunched. Tana is a solid citizen and deserves better. It was touching to hear the Melbourne crowd chanting "Ooh Ah, Umaga" in the hope he would be able to play on tonight.)

At our studio base in Sydney John McBeth, fronting the show, asks for text comments on the game from New Zealand viewers. Most of the hundreds of responses are about sympathy for Umaga and the shortcomings of Spencer as a goal-kicker. "Bring in Mehrts," say many of the texts.

That's because at home today at Jade Stadium, the indomitable Andrew Mehrtens made a statement about goal-kicking. He kicked six penalties, two dropped-goals and one conversion, though he couldn't prevent Canterbury losing the Ranfurly Shield to Auckland. And he controlled the Canterbury effort superbly, we're told. Still, he has as much chance of being flown to Australia and joining the All Blacks as I have.

OCTOBER 12

Pool B: Scotland 32 – Japan 11
Pool C: England 84 – Georgia 6
Pool D: Wales 41 – Canada 10

We return to Sydney. Jeff and I do the England versus Georgia game as an off-tube call. This involves us sitting in a studio in Epping and commentating to the pictures coming in from Perth. It's fun, though it has pitfalls. Sometimes it's difficult to tell who's running with the ball or what's happening away from the action. The commentary can only be of the picture being offered by the TV director at the ground. A broadcaster has to be alert or big mistakes can be made.

I enjoy watching Georgia. They are only the ninth-ranked team in Europe and are probably the lowest-ranked team here. But they give plenty against mighty England. At halftime England have made just seven tackles against Georgia's 70. In the first 20 minutes Georgia hold out the English and only a Jonny Wilkinson penalty is scored. After that the floodgates open and England race to an 84–6 win. It's hard to make an assessment of England's talent. They run on players so regularly from the bench, and the conditions are so slippery, it's tough for them to look like World Cup winners.

Elsewhere, Fiji's Rupeni Caucaunibuca is suspended for two games after blotting his copybook by crudely thumping Olivier Magne on Saturday. A viewing of the videotape shows that Rupeni could have got a longer sentence.

In Melbourne, Umaga is confirmed as being out of the World Cup. Norm Maxwell arrives in Melbourne and is likely to replace him. This is a good move, because the All Blacks have plenty of cover in the midfield, but were always a player short at lock.

OCTOBER 13

We're told from home today of a *Listener* article in which always-grim All Black selector Mark Shaw has finally given an interview to someone in the media. All season Shaw has looked on stoically at press conferences. No-one in the media has bothered to ask him a question.

His comments are strong, ripping into the New Zealand media. He says they hang around like "fleas" and write "shit". As he has hardly spoken to me and I have been in his close company for decades, I conclude that he thinks I am a flea and talk and write shit.

There are no World Cup games today. So far France have made the most significant early running – their win over Fiji was impressive – followed by New Zealand, then England, and South Africa. Australia had the hardest game and so posted the most modest victory. There is nervousness around Aussie fans nevertheless.

OCTOBER 14

Pool A: Argentina 67 – Namibia 14

Another day off for me. I spend it in my room. Apart from a visit from Steve Bachop, and a few phone calls, I'm on my own for 24 hours. Steve and I discuss how we will do the Italy versus Tonga commentary tomorrow, his debut at the microphone. We check the pronunciations of both teams.

This evening in Gosford, the Pumas give the Namibians a right thumping. A couple of things that didn't go well for Argentina against Australia, like goal-kicking and lineout throwing, are much improved. On this form Argentina will have a cracking game in a couple of days against Ireland.

OCTOBER 15

Pool B: Fiji 19 – USA 18
Pool C: Samoa 60 – Uruguay 13
Pool D: Italy 36 – Tonga 12

There's a problem with our commentary tonight. After our good preparatory work, Steve Bachop and I go on air and do the "world feed" broadcast. We do well, I think, especially Steve in his debut, but circumstances work against us – Tongan locks Viliami Vaki and Milton Ngauamu come out wearing each other's numbers.

Apart from the obvious identification difficulties, this creates a more serious problem when, after repeated infringements, referee Steve Walsh of New Zealand yellow cards Viliami Vaki. But the computer graphic at the bottom of the TV screen says it is Ngauamu who has been ejected. The wrong man stands accused of foul play. There is even more confusion after the game, when No 4 is called to the drug-testing room.

The mix-up probably arose from a simple mistake, but I believe that no matter how poor Tongan rugby is, it should be fined. Not because of messing about the commentators, but because charges of tinkering with drug testing could be laid against the team.

The most intriguing aspect of the game tonight is the appearance of the fresh-faced Rima Wakarua at first five-eighth for Italy. He is everything that Frank Bunce had described. Smooth, balanced and a superb goal-kicker, Rima kicks three conversions and five penalties.

OCTOBER 16

We fly to Melbourne for tomorrow night's game against Canada. The All Blacks have had a rethink on the question of Umaga going home. He is staying with the team, because the swelling in his knee has gone down markedly, and he is feeling positive about playing later in the tournament. That is hard luck on Norm Maxwell, who is in town but, because of the rules, is not able to be in the company of the All Blacks, let alone train with them.

I was not present to see it, but Tana does the All Blacks' sagging PR image in Melbourne no end of good today. He pitches up at the daily press conference and speaks openly and honestly about his hopes for staying in the World Cup team.

Ric Salizzo comes to Sydney to film his *Sports Café* programme. He tells me Andrew Mehrtens was on the plane coming over. Just before I grab the phone to call our studio in Auckland with this astounding backpedal selection by John Mitchell, Ric tells me that Mehrts is here on holiday and has no tickets for any games.

Also from home, the NZRU apparently severed ties with Jonah Lomu today. It offered him a contract and Phil Kingsley Jones turned it down.

On a personal level, I rate a mention in *The Sydney Morning Herald* today. The paper is running a daily World Cup column called "Blindside", appraising the TV commentators' bloopers. A "Muzza Award" will be presented at the end, in honour of Murray Mexted, who is alleged to have made the odd broadcast fumble over the years. My contribution today, from the England versus Georgia game, was for saying: "The Georgians speak their own language. It is a language unlike any other." Oh well, when it's a live telecast, you can't get the words back. Unlike the editor of "Blindside", who has all day to correct his.

Pool D: New Zealand 68 – Canada 6

*Our commentary team before the Canada game – Keith Quinn,
Maree Simpson (production manager), Jeff Wilson, Bernadine Oliver-Kerby.*

A no-win situation for the All Blacks, who run on to the closed-in
Telstra Dome in Melbourne and score 10 tries and nine conversions against
Canada's second-string selection. They would have been hammered if
they had not won by such a margin and when they do, it's still a victory
many people will find fault with.

In many games so far, the favourites have weathered the early storm
of aggressive defence offered by the minnow teams. "After all, these little
teams here can all tackle," observes Jeff Wilson to me. When that early
defiance has been withstood, the good teams then apply their own
pressure and points come readily.

This is just what happens tonight. Canada's players (their coach, David
Clark, refuses to call them second-stringers) play very well, but only at their
level. In the end the New Zealanders' superior speed carries them away.

One of the stars is Mils Muliaina, who switches to the wing and scores
his first four tries for his country. A couple are beauties. Caleb Ralph scores

NEW ZEALAND 68 CANADA 6

Canada enjoy 15 minutes of fame before Kiwis steal show

A big win, but are the All Blacks really on fire?

two, one after a superb 80-metre swing downfield, Rodney So'oialo also snaffles two, and Ma'a Nonu gets one. Kees Meeuws also scores one, which has people in the commentary box rushing to hand me notes telling me Kees has equalled the world record for test tries scored by a prop.

Carlos Spencer plays but does not take the kicks at goal. Daniel Carter does the kicking and lands nine conversions. This raises issues. Can Carter hold down his test position at second five-eighth to do the goal-kicking in the big matches ahead? If he cannot, does the goal-kicking return to Carlos? The second question seems improbable, as Spencer should be taking the kicks now, shouldn't he? There were plenty on offer for him to cure his yips tonight.

Afterwards John Mitchell is his usual tight-lipped self about the kicking. There are more pressing matters concerning the team. Like more injuries. It is confirmed that Ben Blair has a prolapsed disc in his neck, the result of a collision at training, and might have to go home. Auckland's young outside back Ben Atiga is being put on stand-by. Tonight burly prop Greg Somerville was squeezed into jersey 22 as tiny Blair's replacement in the reserves.

It's also revealed that chirpy Byron Kelleher, the reserve halfback tonight, was warming up so vigorously during halftime that he pulled a hamstring. The list of injured backs now reads: Tana Umaga, Aaron Mauger, Joe Rokocoko, Ben Blair and Byron Kelleher. As of tonight, there are not enough able-bodied backs to fill a full complement of 10 for the next game.

The Ben Blair story bewilders me. I was sitting in my hotel room about 1pm today, compiling notes for tonight's game, and called the All Blacks' media liaison officer, Matt McIlraith, to ask a few questions. Questions like: "Anything I should know before the game tonight, Matt?", "Are the 'boys' all fit and well?"... stuff like that. Matt was his usual chirpy self and told me all was well. "Any changes?" I ask. "Not as far as I know," he replies.

When I get to the ground I hear Blair has sustained a neck injury at training and is going home. That gets me wondering: why didn't the media liaison officer know that, especially as it had happened at training the day before? Or, if he did know, was he told to keep it from the media for "strategic" reasons before the game? Are we media "fleas" that far removed from consideration now?

At the very least this is another example of a lack of communication from the All Black team. I hear also that all is not rosy between the bosses of the NZRU and the team. Has chief executive Chris Moller been on to John Mitchell about the team's supposed grim PR face in Melbourne? There was certainly an improvement when Tana Umaga turned up unexpectedly to speak to the news media about his knee injury. I also hear that one of the NZRU management feels so left out around the team here that he is thinking of returning to his desk in Wellington.

All this is being carried out in a kind of World Cup bubble. Melbourne's papers and electronic outlets are giving scant regard to the World Cup, while the New Zealand newspapermen here are complaining that there is no story around the team at the moment. That's because they are thrown only scraps at press conferences and there are few opportunities for individual interviews or angles.

OCTOBER 18

Pool A: Australia 90 – Romania 8
Pool B: France 51 – Japan 29
Pool C: England 25 – South Africa 6

It's back to Sydney today for Jeff Wilson, Stu Dennison, Maree Simpson and me. There's time for an afternoon of further note-gathering for tonight's call, and also a snooze before watching the trans-Tasman league test from Auckland. And it's bravo you Kiwis! A great 30–16 win over the Kangaroos.

Our friendly Aussie driver, Mary-Anne Morgan, takes our bragging in good spirit on the way to the studio for our commentary tonight on the first "biggie" of the tournament, England against South Africa from Perth.

What a fascinating game it is. England and South Africa have so much

rugby world cup 2003

Wilkinson's priceless boot settles humdrum affair

POOL C

Martin Johnson
IN PERTH

LET'S be brutally honest about this. If, in future, English rugby fans want to experience a brutal collision between two ancient and deadly enemies, where the result means everything and hang the fact that the game itself is almost guaranteed to be as skilful as *It's A Knockout* contestants exchanging custard pies, they do not have to fork out a small fortune and travel halfway round the world for the experience. They can stay at home and watch ... versus South ...
This was ... equivalent ...

The first real match of the tournament and England look ominously good.

at stake. To win means control of this "Pool of Death". The losers face the nightmare prospect of playing New Zealand in the knockout quarter-final.

South Africa play the first half with controlled aggression and composure. England withstand it with excellent poise and show how important is Jonny Wilkinson to their game plan. He thumps the ball off either boot, always looking calm and measured. He scores with two comfortable penalties. South Africa's ace kicker, Louis Koen, while not having a bad night, misses three from long-range but lands two and it's 6–6 at halftime.

The only try of the game comes from a Koen clearance that is charged down, allowing Will Greenwood to scamper away to score. With another couple of Wilkinson penalties and two late dropped goals, the score ends at 25–6. It looks like a yawning chasm for the Springboks but they have played hard and tough. They are not out of the tournament yet.

England look imposing tonight. When they score their try to lead 19–6, they "just came down and played for dropped goals", as skipper Martin Johnson says later. It's an ominous sight, as Wilkinson does just that, landing two from relatively close positions to stretch the winning margin. We New Zealanders can recall being on the end of South Africa's dropped goals in vital World Cup matches. So how do you like them apples?

Elsewhere tonight, Australia run all over Romania and France dispatch the willing and hugely popular Japanese.

It's a quiet TVNZ studio after the Perth game. Stephen Bachop and Richard Loe are most impressed by England. There had been talk of us heading out to have a late nightcap, but, possibly because of the sobering manner of the English dispatch, we all drift home. We knew about the problems of the All Blacks being in a weak pool before the Cup started, but now the action is upon us and there are the injuries we had not bargained on, *and* it looks like we might have to play South Africa, who will be battle-hardened, how well positioned are the All Blacks to cope?

OCTOBER 19

Pool A: Ireland 64 – Namibia 7
Pool C: Samoa 46 – Georgia 9
Pool D: Wales 27 – Tonga 20

Jeff Wilson is on his last day with us. He has first-class cricket commitments from this week. Today we do Wales versus Tonga, from Canberra. It's an excellent effort by the Tongans, but to no avail. They are out of contention, but give Wales a fright. Both these teams have still to play New Zealand. We hear from Melbourne that Leon MacDonald is being considered as a centre for New Zealand.

At fulltime Jeff and I consider heading to the Aussie Stadium to watch Namibia play Ireland, but the rain is so heavy we would be soaked in the run to the car. We decide to stay indoors and have a couple of beers. Working with Jeff these past few weeks has been a pleasure. He has shown a nice balance about life and prominence in New Zealand. I think he would be happy without the recognition factor that goes with being a

RECORD ALL BLACK TRY-SCORER CHRISTIAN CULLEN RELEASES A BIOGRAPHY CRITICAL OF COACH JOHN MITCHELL

SLAGGING PEOPLE IN PUBLIC, BEING DISLOYAL, REFUSING TO ADMIT MISTAKES, WHO THE HELL DOES CULLEN THINK HE IS, ME?

Another bullseye by Tom Scott.

famous All Black. Getting his house finished, enjoying his relationship with his special friend, star netballer Adine Harper, training his horses and playing cricket seem to be his priorities. He has told us he has enjoyed doing the commentaries, but he doubts whether he would like to have a higher profile on TV. Jeff is a very nice young man. I noted that he always stands to greet a woman who has entered our company. That shows good breeding, right ladies?

It is confirmed that Ben Blair is heading home. His prolapsed disc will not recover in time for him to play in this campaign.

The biggest news today is from New Zealand, where part of Christian Cullen's book, *Life on the Run,* has been serialised in *The Sunday Star-Times.* He apparently calls John Mitchell a "dick" and says he never trusted Mitchell after the latter became All Black coach. Such comments, released at World Cup time, will, if nothing else, assist sales.

Tonight we have four former All Blacks in our Epping studio – Messrs Wilson, Loe, Bachop and Zinzan Brooke (who was working the late-night shift for South African TV). The conversation between the four turns to Cullen's book. It is a sparky discussion. And, without breaking any confidences, as they were not "on the record", I would call the division of for-and-against John Mitchell as a person about two-each. It's intriguing to be around the edges of such a debate.

OCTOBER 20

Pool A: Scotland 39 – USA 15

John Mitchell's reluctance to speak to the media, and therefore the New Zealand public, is running heavily against the team. Here in Oz all we are hearing, via the news and Internet reading of papers from home, is that Mitchell's style of rare-speak is annoying the voracious fans at home, who are thirsting for information about the All Blacks.

To me this is also linked to increasing public nervousness about the All Blacks' performance. Even though two big wins have been posted, the average New Zealander is demanding more from the All Black management. More news is required about the tactical thinking around performances that are perceived to be only average, more information is wanted about the injuries to players, and more comment is needed on what Mitchell and co are thinking about the other teams in the competition.

This puts Mitchell in an invidious position. He could do as he has all year – offer little to the public, and just go on winning. That will silence the doubters. Or he could break away from his taciturn style and speak

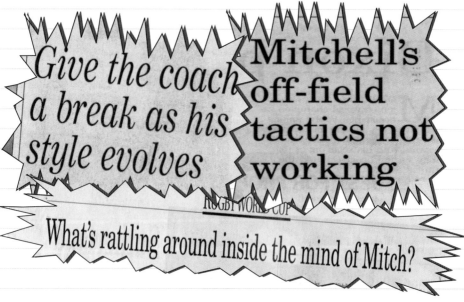

John Mitchell's off-field performance becomes one of the stories of the World Cup.

openly. Then he would no doubt be called a John Hart clone who speaks too much to the media.

Today the All Blacks team for the game against Tonga is named. It contains a number of strategic selections, designed to give some players time on the field, and to protect others from possible injury. For example, Justin Marshall comes in at halfback, but neither Steve Devine nor Byron Kelleher is in the reserves. Daniel Carter is apparently the cover for halfback, though Daniel Braid's name has been mentioned as a possible back-up. This is astounding, and every halfback in New Zealand must be squirming. No halfback reserve in an All Black team that has *three* in the squad. Carter was apparently a halfback in teenage rep games.

There are other intriguing placements: Leon MacDonald will be the third centre used in as many games, Mils Muliaina reverts to fullback (so why was he played on the wing against Canada?), Ali Williams is deemed fit enough to play, and the indestructible Kees Meeuws will switch to the loosehead side in the front row. Star players Chris Jack, Jerry Collins, Richie McCaw and Keven Mealamu are rested. MacDonald will do the goal-kicking.

OCTOBER 21

Pool D: Italy 19 – Canada 14

A curious day. I rise early at the behest of Radio Sport in Auckland. Morning producer Matt Gunn rang me last night to set up an early appearance on the Martin Devlin breakfast show. I agreed that, even though it is very early in Sydney, I would go on. I suppose it is loyalty to a show on which I have done a spot nearly every workday for six years.

But on checking the Internet version of *The New Zealand Herald* today I note that both Devlin, of Radio Sport, and Murray Deaker, of the sister station *Newstalk ZB*, have been very critical of the TVNZ World Cup coverage.

The *Herald* asked the two radio leaders about the coverage. From my reading of the piece, Deaker and Devlin want more coverage, but mostly they want replays of the New Zealand games and other significant fixtures. Are these two supposed sports nuts not watching those games when

The TVNZ studio in Sydney.

they come through live? The All Blacks-Italy game was on at 5.30pm and the Canada game at 10.30pm on a Friday night. Pretty relaxed hours, I'd have thought. The two also wonder why the England-South Africa game last weekend was not replayed the next day. What was wrong with their commitment to sit up till 1am to watch the game live, as hundreds of thousands of other New Zealanders did? Or, why not *record* the game and replay it themselves at their leisure?

I decide to decline to be on the breakfast show today. I know Devlin and I know myself. Such an interview today would descend into a shouting match. I would defend my employers, and Martin would rail against "State TV", as he loves to call us.

Martin would win such a "contest" because he can control the recording levels in his studio and therefore always be in the ascendancy. He also has the off-air button to cut me off when he wants, and after the interview is over can further promote his views.

In the end the expected call from Radio Sport does not come through at 7am. Perhaps Martin also thought it would not be conducive to good radio to interview me today, after his opinions were made public. He knows I would have shouted back at him.

Deaker added a twist to his responses to the *Herald*. He says he's taken calls declaring "Keith Quinn is past it [as a commentator]". You learn to take the good with the bad – in *The New Zealand Herald* yesterday, Stephen Jones, of the London *Sunday Times,* said I would lead his dream world TV commentary team.

With Jeff Wilson's departure from our team, the polished and friendly Willie Lose arrives to replace him for a fortnight. Willie is a former Auckland and North Harbour forward who played for Tonga in the 1995 World Cup. He spent several years in Japan and is fluent in Japanese, and also Italian.

He has called many games on radio and we worked together on the IRB World Sevens circuit one time in Japan. Tonight he goes very well as Italy slip and slide to a 19–14 win over fumbling Canada. I'm starting to wonder if we'll ever see any attractive football played at this tournament. Apart from the free-running All Blacks, that is.

We hear from Melbourne that Aaron Mauger is running at training, which is great news. Perhaps he will play against Wales next week. Mauger is quoted as saying: "At least they haven't shoved me on the plane yet." But Norm Maxwell, after waiting in Melbourne for nearly a fortnight to see if Ali Williams is okay, has flown home. Thanks for coming Norm.

OCTOBER 22

Pool A: Argentina 50 – Romania 3

It's a strange world. After the fuss yesterday about TV coverage at home, *The Sydney Morning Herald* today publishes a letter to the editor asking: "Why can't Keith Quinn and Jeff Wilson do all the TV commentaries (in Australia) from now on?"

I email Radio Sport, saying I will not be able to do any more interviews with them while the World Cup is on. It's for the best. My job for TVNZ here runs late in the day and is my first obligation. To get up at 6am to talk to radio is a burden I can do without.

The Romania versus Argentina game tonight is a tough one to call. It's not of a very high standard, many of the players are not easy to recognise and the names are difficult to pronounce. But hey, that's why we love it.

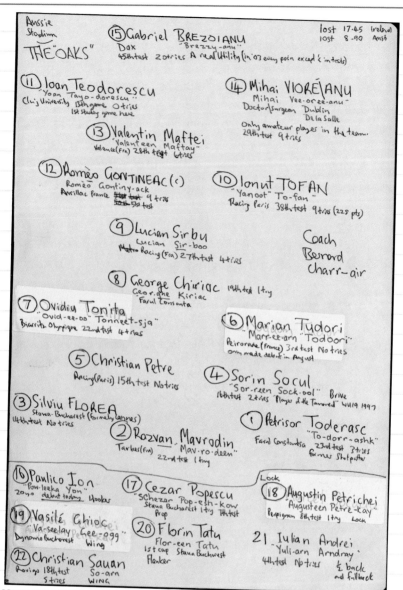

My pre-match information sheet on Romania before their game against Argentina. Note the phonetic spellings – pronunciation is always a challenge when commentating Romania.

OCTOBER 23

Pool B: Fiji 41 – Japan 13

We're up early and off to Brisbane for the All Blacks' third game, tomorrow night against Tonga. It will be an outdoor game at the superb new Suncorp stadium. The weather in "Brizzy" is hot and steamy, a contrast to the modest temperatures of Sydney and Melbourne.

Via the Internet I listen to Andrew Dewhurst on Radio Sport in Auckland talking to Murray Mexted. Concerning the placement of Leon MacDonald at centre, Kees Meeuws at loosehead prop and Daniel Carter as reserve halfback, Mex says: "A hallmark of this All Black selection panel is lateral thinking." A valid point. Mitchell, Deans and co don't mind making imaginative and tough decisions. They have been doing it all year. But when will they admit to naming a top All Black team?

I go on the Internet this afternoon to hear Martin Devlin talking to TVNZ sports boss Denis Harvey about the World Cup coverage. My spies tell me that in the interview, which played today, Devlin was way over the top in his utterances, and carried on strongly after Harvey had gone off the air. I wonder if Devlin continues this way, and feels so strongly, will he have the moral fibre to stop appearing on the *Game of Two Halves* show that plays on TV1 on Monday nights? After all, if TVNZ is that bad he would surely not want to have *any* association with it.

Jimmy Love, the Tongan coach, says today: "My team could pull off the biggest upset in the history of world rugby tomorrow. We are not going to lie down."

OCTOBER 24

Pool C: South Africa 46 – Georgia 19
Pool D: New Zealand 91 – Tonga 7

The game today is at 5.30pm. The TVNZ crew heads out to the ground hours early, because massive thunderstorms are predicted around Brisbane and none of us have appropriate coats. This is sunny Queensland, after all.

Bernadine Oliver-Kerby arrives from Melbourne. "Something has happened," she says. "The All Blacks have been so different this week. They have suddenly relaxed and become friendly. It's great. Such a change." This fits in with a rumour that John McBeth was telling me that someone high in the NZRU has given the team a burst about their indifferent public relations effort in Australia. Not all rumours can be discounted.

Phil Wilkins in Brisbane

New Zealand 91 Tonga 7

The Webb Ellis Trophy sat smugly like a golden dwarf on a dispay table before the Tonga vs New ...

gentleness of their souls, the better for their football. But so emotionally did the Tongans react as the All Blacks launched into their haka that they began their own war chant, advancing aggressively until Hea... Lavaka, the ... head Irish t...

off fullback Sila Va'enuku for the try near the left post. Strangely, Carlos Spencer took the kick from in front.

The Tongans' counselling became frayed at the edges as their captain, Benhur Kivalu led the... way ... one ...

as the Al... to one in... The se... rain and... th... Black...

Another World Cup mis-match.

The game against Tonga turns out to be a 91–7 thrashing. There's a steady downpour all game. Tonga have a number of brave personalities in their ranks, but are out-gunned all over the park. The All Blacks score 13 tries, and many are sweeping efforts from a long way out. It's a game of seasoned professionals against a team that has many New Zealand club players mixed in with Tonga's best-paid.

The win puts New Zealand through to the quarter-finals, with a pool game against Wales still to play. But again, being grim Kiwis, at the end of tonight's game we ask ourselves: "What does this win *really* tell us about the team?" Are Tonga that awful? Or are these All Blacks now firmly in control and heading for glory? They have scored 34 tries in three games.

A rare moment during the World Cup – John Mitchell fronting up to the media.

For New Zealand many good things come out of tonight. Leon MacDonald not only kicks 12 goals out of 12, but is a solid success as centre. With Tana Umaga wearing the smart team suit and sighted before kick-off walking somewhat gingerly, the MacDonald performance is intriguing. Might the solidity of his play tonight, and his goal-kicking, swing him into the No 13 jersey for big games ahead? In Sydney our production crew asks for a text response from viewers to the question: "Should Leon MacDonald now be our No 1 test centre?" The replies say yes, by 91 per cent. However, last week the same fans said Ma'a Nonu should be the top centre – and he secured a 91 per cent following, too!

Another heartening performance comes from Ali Williams. The big man secures a couple of early lineout takes and paces himself back into the action for the rest of the game. Apparently he has a pin in his injured foot. So it seems the risk of keeping him with the team has been justified. Ben Atiga comes on and plays the last few minutes at fullback. I don't think he touches the ball.

Another action of note is the substituting of Reuben Thorne with a quarter of the game remaining. This is the captain's first "rest" of the year. The quiet man has well and truly silenced his doubters today. Carlos Spencer takes over the captaincy for the last quarter and seems to do it well. But what a shame he is unnecessarily curt with a British reporter afterwards, when he is asked why he, and not MacDonald, had taken one of the 13 conversions. "If you'd followed the game at all," says Spencer with a derisory sniff, "you'd have noticed that Leon was slightly hurt while that particular try was being scored." It's a bit rude, as the try-scoring incident was about 100 metres away. Sometimes our Carlos doesn't promote himself very well to the world.

After that, no-one feels like asking more questions, so we troop away into the night.

OCTOBER 25

Pool A: Australia 142 – Namibia 0
Pool B: France 51 – Scotland 9
Pool D: Wales 27 – Italy 15

We fly to Sydney this morning. At the Brisbane airport lounge a man presents Christian Cullen's controversial new book for me to autograph.

"Me?" I ask. "Yes please," says the friendly stranger. So I sign with something like: "In acknowledgement of one of the great All Black fullbacks." I omit to mention that I don't regard Cullen as one of the best fullbacks in this World Cup year.

I also speak to NZRU chief executive Chris Moller, who is flying to Melbourne. We hold our coffee cups and chat away about this and that. I comment that the IRB should consider changing the World Cup format to stop all these thrashings. "Maybe make the top tier of 12 teams, split into two pools of six, then breaking into semis and a final." Chris is very nice about my mutterings. It isn't until I sit down that I realise Chris *is* part of the IRB these days, as one of the two New Zealand delegates on the executive board.

I also tell Chris that from what I have observed around Australia, I doubt whether New Zealand could have handled even being sub-host of the World Cup. "Would we have had the huge infrastructure needed to cope?" I ask. Chris's reply is non-committal, though I sense slight agreement. At this World Cup are thousands of volunteers working in media centres, security-accessed areas, player and team liaison places, medical rooms, administrative offices and so on. None will see one World Cup match.

John Mitchell pops by and says a friendly hello to everyone. There's a lot of smiling and handshaking. He seems in a good humour. Tony Johnson of Sky TV is there too, chatting away. So naturally the conversation soon turns to Marlborough, Blenheim or Picton. It always seems to when Tony passes by.

Back in Sydney, I decline to go to the studio to watch the NPC final, which is coming through from Wellington. I stay in the apartment, getting a few things together for later tonight.

The result of the final is not good for proud Wellington people. Auckland have won 41–29. Still, at least Wellington made the big game of the season, so things will be better next year. Mark my words.

When I get to the studio Zinzan Brooke is there. He is on a high and grabs my hand. He shakes it and keeps shaking. "What's happened?" I ask. "Auckland beat you bastards!" he yells with glee. I file away his taunts.

This afternoon Zinny and I, and others at the studio, watch Australia play Namibia in Adelaide. It's 142–0 to the Wallabies. It makes my idea of the top dozen countries playing in two pools of six seem even sounder. Under my plan Namibia and the others would still qualify to attend a World Cup, but in a second-level of competition. Maybe another 12 teams could be at that level, with a promotion-relegation system in place to go to the top group.

I make a note to myself. I have always considered "nil" to be an honourable score in rugby. I even wrote an entry for the score under "N" in my book *Encyclopedia of World Rugby* in the 1990s. So was Namibia's beautiful nil–142 the "highest" nil ever conceded? I wonder. What is also amazing is that 28,196 turn up in Adelaide, of all places, to see the game.

I think of Paul Henderson. Was the All Black test captain of 1995 sitting on the edge of his seat in Invercargill today? Paul was captain for the only time in a test when the All Blacks beat Japan 145–17 in Bloemfontein at the 1995 World Cup. In Sydney today we are all cheering that Paul's All Black team's World Cup record *total* for one match stays intact as a World Cup best score. Chris Whittaker, the ever-patient New South Wales halfback, led Australia today in George Gregan's absence. He might end up like Paul Henderson, a one-test leader who had a massive win.

Colin Hawke, the former test referee, arrives today to be in our coverage for the next fortnight. He makes a good start tonight. John McBeth and I, in particular, hope that with Colin on board the refereeing and the laws of rugby will be discussed in a dignified way, rather than shouted about in a disdainful way, as has occurred with some media in recent times.

Tonight at the main Telstra Stadium in Sydney, 78,974 people watch France beat Scotland 51–9. It's a right thrashing and the brilliance and solidity of the French make us look at each other and wonder: could they be the World Cup winners? They are very impressive, led by point-scoring machine Frederic Michalak. The brilliant young first-five notches 26 points and has 78 from three games.

Italy are eliminated tonight by Wales, 27–15 in Canberra. It's a clear-cut result but one can't help feeling sorry for the dignified John Kirwan. His team had to play four matches here in just 14 days and, like Tonga, are looking leg-weary by the end. Rima Wakarua kicks five penalties for their only points tonight.

[*Note*: though I wasn't there to hear it, Dave Waterston, the Namibia coach, tonight raises the subject of the food poisoning at the 1995 World Cup final in Johannesburg. He suggests the All Black management know what happened in those dramatic days, when a number of the New Zealand team suddenly became ill. What is Mr Waterston saying here? *The New Zealand Herald* suggests he is alluding to the recent report that a number of the New Zealand players ate bad prawns before that game and were sick.]

[*Further Note, to Laurie Mains, of Dunedin, New Zealand:* I, Keith Quinn, did *not* raise the subject today of the food poisoning at the 1995 Rugby World Cup. Dave Waterston, of Namibia, did. I am merely reporting his comments.]

OCTOBER 26

Pool A: Ireland 16 – Argentina 15
Pool C: England 35 – Samoa 22

There's a wave of expectancy in the air. Two absorbing games are scheduled today – Ireland against Argentina in Adelaide and Samoa against England in Melbourne. Willie and I are to commentate the latter game.

England relieved to get past a brave challenge by Samoa.

First we watch the Irish batter away against the Pumas. It's a contest of wills. Only one try is scored, by Irish flanker Alan Quinlan, who will become a hero at home. In his dive to score, his shoulder is shattered and he is led away, his face contorted in pain. They say he won't play for months. But he signals a commitment that inspires the rest of the team and they eke out a 16–15 win. I feel desperately sorry for the Pumas, but they are just a notch behind the Irish. With this loss they are eliminated. Why, oh why, did Marcelo Loffreda, the coach, not substitute Mario Ledesma a fortnight ago, when the hooker's poor throwing into the lineouts allowed Australia to gain control of the Pumas' opening game?

I try to ring my friend Frankie Deges, the best rugby writer in Argentina. I can't make a connection to his mobile phone. He must be taking other calls of sympathy.

There is little time for reflection, because soon follows Samoa versus England from Melbourne. And this is a *great* game. The Samoans have had a rough ride to get to this World Cup. Many stories have been written about British and European clubs not releasing their best players. The lack of funding means one cannot begin to compare their financial worth as a team to that of the English. Someone here said the Samoa Rugby Union would love its team to have the same budget to live on for a year as the salary of several of the poorest-paid England team members. Coach John Boe has spoken so passionately about his team and its dearth of opportunities to play this year – including criticism of New Zealand for not releasing players – that his on-loan contract from the NZRU to Samoa is terminated.

But tonight, when the teams come out in front of 50,647 at Melbourne's Telstra Dome, it's a case of "the bigger they are the harder they fall". Samoa begin at a zillion miles per minute. Their forwards rush at their vaunted England opposites and knock them sideways. The Samoans dominate the early possession like no team has against wonderful England for years. Earl Va'a, the pint-sized five-eighths, begins a super game, running and passing brilliantly, spinning the ball wide to the wings. In trying to cope, the big English forwards look sluggish and tired. Jonny Wilkinson, the great man, is seen to be shying away from many passes. He is obviously under instructions to avoid the hard-hitting Samoan tacklers. The early action thrills us Pacific watchers.

It crosses my mind that Willie and I are wildly in favour of "our" Samoan team. But the thought lasts only a second. The hell with it – this is great!

Soon the Samoans begin a driving charge in which the ball passes through 40 sets of hands. It's wonderful to see their forwards dashing forward and turning over possession for the wonderfully built and controlled backs. The passes eventually make it to the hands of Semo Sititi, the brilliant captain. He dashes to the line and scores. His team-mates run to embrace him. I can imagine the tears at home in the villages and hamlets of Samoa.

At halftime England have scored a grim drive-over try by Neil Back and the score is 16–13 to Samoa. That was the score by which Samoa (playing then as Western Samoa) announced their arrival on the world stage by beating Wales at Cardiff in the 1991 World Cup. That time it prompted a cruel joke: "If Wales can't beat Western Samoa, what might the score have been if they'd played the whole of Samoa?"

In the end there isn't similar success in Melbourne. Though Va'a keeps kicking penalties (he gets five and hits the post with another), England win 35–22. The English team's second try is a penalty try for a collapsed scrum on the goal line. Ian Balshaw, the wing, scores the third from a brilliant cross-kick by Wilkinson. Phil Vickery scores a fourth. Samoa can't score another try. They battle heroically but England make it through. Just.

Many issues are raised by Samoa's showing. From their point of view, they now face a crucial pool play-off game against South Africa next weekend. They will face it with growing confidence.

There are also questions about England. Based on their hesitancy under pressure tonight, are they the great team everyone (me included) has been wittering on about these past few months? Tonight at least two of their forwards, Lawrence Dallaglio and Joe Worsley, were hardly sighted. They were outplayed by the dynamic Sititi and the hard-tackling Maurie Fa'asa'valu.

In the centres, Mike Tindall looked out of his depth. And Jason Robinson at fullback was a skittery mishmash of nothingness. It's all very well to run tippy-toe this way and that at high speed, but if it's without purpose, then what is the point?

And there is the matter of persistent infringing. The referee, Jonathan Kaplan of South Africa, seemed to be on to England's tactic of slowing down the ball from ruck and maul by diving in and over it when it is on the ground. Skipper Martin Johnson was penalised repeatedly, though he was never cautioned. After a couple of similar offences by the Samoans, Sititi was called out and told to tell his men "to cut it out". I have felt for a long time that referees have a mindset against Samoan and other Pacific islands players, and tend to look for them first rather than speaking against famous opposing players. Why did Kaplan not warn Johnson?

And what of Wilkinson? He was hesitant to the point of being gun-shy. He even missed four shots at goal. At one attempt one of his feet twitched repeatedly before he ran in to kick. Signs to worry coach Clive Woodward?

Afterwards in our Sydney studio, there is agreement between Colin Hawke and Richard Loe casting doubt on the validity of the penalty try. "Certainly England were aggressively scrummaging towards the goal line," says Loe, "but the Samoan scrum had not broken up. They were just going backwards. It was England's prop who took the scrum down." Hawke has a long look at the replay and agrees with Loe.

In the last moments of the frenetic activity, England seemed to rush a 16th man on to the field. Dan Luger raced on as Mike Tindall was down being attended to. Luger made a tackle and was ready to be involved in more action when Kaplan ordered him off the field. Apparently the Englishman believed Tindall was out of the game and rushed on of his own accord. The law says he must be officially cleared by sideline officials, who must first establish whether the injured player can carry on. As that clearance hadn't been made, Luger was naughty.

The old joke of 1991 could be rewritten to say: "Fancy England, with 360,000 registered players, compared with a couple of hundred adult players in Samoa, having to put 16 men on to win!"

After today, I love this World Cup.

OCTOBER 27

Pool B: USA 39 – Japan 26

A day off for me. I do some washing in the apartment (Quinn family members – stop laughing) and mid-afternoon go for a walk to clear the head. I buy another book about John Lennon. It's a beautiful effort. That's three about The Beatles I've bought on this trip. My total is edging towards 385 books about them. I will definitely write a book about them one day. I've the research done already.

Tonight Willie Lose, Barbara Mitchell and I adjourn to the Kirribilli Club to watch the USA play Japan. The room is a bit smoky for us Kiwis. Afterwards we leave and meet the rest of our crew at the Kirribilli Hotel. There is only a slight difference in smokiness. I notice John McBeth has not come in. They tell me he is exhausted and has gone to bed. It's not just me feeling the pinch.

I miss eating a proper meal tonight, so supper is peanut butter and jam sandwiches, yet again.

Sport

16-MAN FURORE

How it happened

80th min: England replacement Dan Luger standing on sideline, touch judge tells him to wait for next break in play. England bench allegedly tell Luger to get on field which he does without a player coming off.

80min 50 sec: Penalty to Samoa – Luger makes tackle on Maurie Fa'asavalu in ensuing play.

81min 34 sec: Referee Jonathan Kaplan tells Luger to get off the field. Fulltime blown short time later England win 35-22.

What happens next Match commissioner Geoff Shaw passes on report to World Cup officials to be examined as early as today.

Referee Kaplan asks what is going on

Luger takes the field

Luger invloved in a tackle

Luger is ordered off by the referee

England to be investigated for rule breach

England's tweaking of rugby's replacement laws yesterday has caused an uproar. Sydney's **Daily Telegraph** *covered the story especially well.*

OCTOBER 28

Pool C: Uruguay 24 – Georgia 12

This is one of the more intriguing games I have covered. On one side we have to cope with Georgian names like Merab Kvirikashvili and Bessarion Khamashuridze, while on the other there are Uruguay's Marcelo Guttierrez and Joaquim Pastore. Plus there are about 40 other equally testing pronunciations from the two playing squads. I write their names down on my team sheets in crude phonetic form (K'viri-kash-vili, Kama-shir-rid-z, Goot-terr-ess and Path-tor-ray) It's fun to do, and though the game is a lower-level fixture, it is a dramatic contest as the two teams battle valiantly for their only win in Australia. Nearly 30,000 people turn up at Aussie Stadium as Uruguay get the victory, 24–12. On Channel 7 Gordon Bray calls it one of the great upsets of all time. I wouldn't go that far (Tonga beating Australia in a test in 1973 was a biggie), but certainly the Georgians were tipped to win.

When the final whistle goes you can see what the game means to the two teams – the Uruguayans do two laps of the field in delight, while many of the Georgians cry in disappointment.

We hear today from Auckland that Martin Devlin will be taken off the *Game of Two Halves* TV show. This is apparently payback for his trenchant radio criticism of TVNZ's World Cup coverage. What he said on air in one burst was too much for TVNZ's board to take. On hearing the disgusting nature of one of Devlin's on-air verbal eruptions, I have been hoping TVNZ would be strong in its response.

It's a person's right to give his or her view. But to air those views, then turn up and expect to appear on the same TV station that you have just criticised is not really on.

Back in my apartment, pondering Georgian and Uruguayan pronunciations.

OCTOBER **29**

Pool D: Canada 24 – Tonga 7

The big story is about that 16th England player at Melbourne the other night. More reports are being called for. It seems there were disagreements between team officials and sideline refereeing staff. One of these involved is New Zealander Steve Walsh. The IRB is investigating.

In today's *Daily Telegraph,* Sydney readers are being told in ex-Wallaby Toutai Kefu's column that he believes England should lose the pool points they won in the game. Kefu says the victory should be awarded to Samoa. I doubt it will happen – this must be the biggest "beat up" news angle of this Cup by a newspaper.

Tonight I have a delightful dinner with an old Wellington College school friend, Doug Lingard, his wife Margie and their children. Their apartment is just 60 metres from my Kirribilli apartment. Rugby is discussed all night and, though they have lived in Australia for years, there is a beaut Kiwi touch when the TV set showing tonight's World Cup game is wheeled close to the dining table. That's so we can follow the rugby action while we eat and talk. My wife Anne will recognise such "normal" behaviour.

Doug played hooker for University and Otago in the late 1960s and has recollections aplenty about the "good old days". Doug and Margie's two adult sons, Tom and Richard, tell us the fascinating story of a player in this World Cup who served time in a Sydney jail for armed robbery. At one point, say the boys, this player used to turn up for club games with a home identity bracelet on his ankle and security guards on each touchline, ready to take him away when the game was over.

We watch as Canada and Tonga play their last World Cup games, in Wollongong. I feel sad when Al Charron crashes out of the game, having been knocked out after a heavy collision with Pierre Hola. Charron is the oldest player at this Cup and this is his last game of rugby. He is carried off. Al has been a powerhouse figure in Canadian rugby in the past four World Cups. Late tonight a report comes through that he has recovered and has 17 stitches in his lip and head. Big Al quips: "It's just as well I'm married. No woman would want me, looking like this."

Pool A: Romania 37 – Namibia 7

The All Blacks team for Sunday's game against Wales is announced and we draw a breath and say: "Mitch, you beauty, thank you. At last a near full-strength team." Features of the lineup are the back three of Muliaina, Rokocoko and Howlett all in their rightful places, Leon MacDonald's retention at centre and Aaron Mauger's return at second five-eighth for his first World Cup game. With Carlos Spencer and Justin Marshall also there, the backline looks the best New Zealand can field. In the forwards only Chris Jack is absent from the top pack. They say his ankle is still not right, which is a worry.

Wales are saying that they must make 200 tackles to stay close to New Zealand. Their coach Steve Hansen won't announce his team until tomorrow. It's rumoured he'll give a few of his lesser lights a run. If so, I hope the All Blacks slaughter them.

There is another challenging game for Willie Lose and me to call today – Romania against Namibia. They run on to York Park in Launceston, Tasmania, looking ready to go at it big time. Again, despite the fact that the two teams are "small fry", the ground is packed. The Aussies are really doing a great job promoting these games.

Romania win 37–7 but I like the fact that, like last night in Sydney with Georgia and Uruguay, neither side fades out of the competition having been thrashed. Tonight you can say that, while Romania win the first half (32–0), the Namibians win the second (7–5), so have a victory of sorts to leave with.

Namibia can also take pride in the arrival on the scene of their second-half substitute, Rudi van Vuuren. He comes on looking tight and tense and plays the last few minutes at five-eighths. He has been out with injury but in his momentary appearance he becomes the first man to play in a cricket World Cup and a rugby World Cup in the same year.

Sean Glover stops me tonight and asks: "How many players from the four years of the IRB sevens circuit are playing in this World Cup?" I have no idea but Sean, whose English-based company, HgVision, is working the TVNZ graphics package here, does. "There are 127 players who have been on the sevens circuit," he says, puffing on his ever-present cigarette. I think of the prominent New Zealand radio man (hi Deaks, how are you mate?) who more than once over the past couple of seasons has loudly proclaimed that the sevens circuit is "no good for rugby".

OCTOBER **31**

Pool B: France 41 – USA 14

The focus today is the IRB report on England's 16th man indiscretion. I'm pleased at the outcome. Though England are found guilty and fined £10,000, they don't lose competition points.

New Zealand referee Steve Walsh cops a two-day ban for his part in the incident. His sideline verbals, directed at the England off-field staff, were apparently not in keeping with the dignity required of referees here, so Walsh misses out on a touch judge role in Wollongong tonight.

It seems a fair resolution, though the Sydney *Daily Telegraph* wants a more severe punishment for England.

The Wollongong game is a five tries to two win for France over USA. Again, the crowds roll up in style and there are thousands of painted faces and waving flags. The French team tonight features a number of players who might not make their top selection, but Brian Liebenberg's three tries will not hurt his chances. Gerald Merceron also shows he is fast approaching top form at first-five, but for me the 21-year-old Frederic Michalak is still their star player and should hold his place. Are France true contenders to win the World Cup? It would not surprise me.

Wales finally announce their team to play the All Blacks and it's called a "mix and match" selection. There are 11 changes from last week's team that looked so unconvincing. But who can say how bad the Welsh are? We know that the Welsh and the All Blacks have both qualified, so are playing only for the final placements in Pool D standings. Plus, of course, the honour of a winning in one of rugby's most enduring rivalries.

NOVEMBER

"Four years boys!
Four more years!"

NOVEMBER 1

Pool A: Australia 17 – Ireland 16
Pool B: Scotland 22 – Fiji 20
Pool C: South Africa 60 – Samoa 10

Three superb pool games to savour. Willie and I get the Scotland versus Fiji game.

Fiji start at a million miles an hour at Aussie Stadium. Rupeni Caucaunibuca, back from suspension, shows why many consider him the best wing in the world. His first try is great. With no room on the touchline and 30 metres out, he dashes past tacklers to crash over. Giant lock Api Naevo slips to his knees and polishes the gleaming white boots of his brilliant teammate. Minutes later Rupeni is weaving and ducking again, this time from 75 metres, to score.

Fiji lead 14–6 at halftime and the Scots look ponderous and beaten. But two changes come over the game. Greg Smith, the Fijian hooker and former captain, goes off injured and Fiji's lineout and scrum authority is lost. Then Rupeni is involved in a collision and takes virtually no further part in the game. Scotland creep back and snatch the win, 22–20.

Caucau has been talked about a lot at this tournament, but I believe he's a

Who'd have guessed it? Richard Loe and Keith Quinn,
Television New Zealand team-mates.

flawed genius at best. For a start, he has turned up overweight. And he seems to lose interest when play doesn't go his way. There remain questions over his temperament, too – he was suspended for punching earlier in the tournament, and today he came flying through and swung his arm across the face of his opposite, Simon Danielli. The Scot was led away to the blood bin.

Afterwards Richard Loe makes the clever quip that "Fiji were bad, Scotland were bloody awful, but Scotland won".

Then follows Samoa-South Africa from Brisbane. Sitting with Loe in the studio is Zinzan Brooke. As soon as the national anthems are played, Zinny remarks to the others sitting: "South Africa will win. I can tell by the looks on their faces. The Springboks are steeled to win; Samoa look slack and tired."

So it proves, as the Springboks storm to a 60–10 win.

One matter I did not care for was the sight of both teams linking arms and kneeling to pray in the middle of the field. Strong religious beliefs should be kept, at the very least, in the dressing rooms at rugby games. This is a rugby arena, not a church pulpit.

Then we tune in to Melbourne, where another packed house at the Telstra Dome sees Australia play Ireland. This is thriller, with the Wallabies winning 17–16. The Australians look far from composed and the Aussie commentators and reporters are almost unanimously pessimistic about their team's chances of winning the Cup.

NOVEMBER 2

Pool C: England 111 – Uruguay 13
Pool D: New Zealand 53 – Wales 37

Earlier this week All Black coach John Mitchell said: "I think this tournament is about to heat up. This is the weekend when a new phase begins." He's right. Today is the first crunch day for the All Blacks. From here there will be no "hit-and-giggle" scores like the 70–7, 68–6 and 91–7 they have notched so far.

Wales are an unknown quality tonight. I look at the names and see a mix-and-match selection from coach Steve Hansen, with 11 changes from

With Willie Lose in Sydney before the Wales game.

the team that beat Italy eight days ago. How can they possibly stand up to what New Zealand will throw at them?

When Willie Lose and I go to Telstra Stadium, my friends from the Welsh language TV commentary box, Wyn Gruffydd and Gerald Davies, come in to say hello. They are men of deep rugby knowledge and they say their hope is "that we just give you a game". Willie and I nod with sympathy – fancy the poor blokes having to broadcast a hiding to their viewers at home.

The next time I see them it is at halftime, when Wales have scored three great tries and, though New Zealand have scored four, the game is poised on a knife-edge at 28–24. Wyn and Gerald are punching the air in glee at the return of the old Welsh rugby fire. At halftime the Welsh team sprint for the dressing rooms. The All Blacks follow, looking stunned.

The second half is even more thrilling. A penalty and converted try give Wales a shock 34–28 lead. I don't dare peep into the commentary box next door.

I look for Reuben Thorne to be banging his fist and rallying his team, but I see nothing. The All Blacks finally regain control to win 53–37, but the score is deceptive. Too many defensive gaps were exposed, especially close to rucks and mauls.

At the press conference John Mitchell and Reuben Thorne act as if there is nothing untoward. "Though they really got stuck into us, we

iRB
RUGBY
WORLD CUP
2003

The World in Union

New Zealand v Wales
Sun 2 November 2003
8:35pm
Telstra Stadium
Sydney NSW

GATE: L

AISLE: 132
ROW: 38
SEAT: 34
TYPE: RWC

© Rugby World Cup Limited 1986 and TM

RUGBY

didn't really contemplate defeat," says Thorne. It's an odd statement considering the gaping holes everywhere on the field. Come to think of it Reuben – where were you today? Your name wasn't exactly rolling off the tongue every minute or so.

I wonder about Ali Williams. He plays one out of the box today, being everywhere and doing everything, but is far from universally admired, a number of reporters commenting on his apparent absence from " the tight".

So I ask Mitchell: "What did you think of Ali Williams today?" Mitchell's response hints that he might want his lock to stay closer to the ball next time they play. "Ali has good skills and enthusiasm. He took another step forward today. He's always trying to improve, but I think I will be sitting down and having a talk with him this week," Mitchell says.

Then one of the British press guys asks: "Tell me John, had you heard of Shane Williams, in the Welsh team?" "Is he the number 6?" replies Mitchell, obviously thinking of hard-driving young flanker Jonathan Thomas. "No, Williams was no 14, Thomas was number 6," replies the reporter. I wince. How embarrassing. Mitchell does not know two of the opposition players. One is left suspecting the All Blacks felt they didn't need to know who these Welsh were. Dare we whisper the word "arrogance"?

NEW ZEALAND 53 WALES 37

Red Dragons show there's fire in the belly

Gritty Welsh throw a scare into the All Blacks camp

A match that did justice to a century of rivalry.

NOVEMBER 3

Eight teams left. There have been no real surprises, though nearly every team left has had at least one moment of alarm: South Africa against England; England against Samoa; Scotland against Fiji (plus a thrashing from France); Australia against Ireland; Ireland against Australia and Argentina; Wales against Tonga; New Zealand against Wales. The only team not mentioned there are those crafty French, who have had a comfortable passage.

The quarter-finals pit New Zealand against South Africa, Australia against Scotland, France against Scotland, and England against Wales.

I see only France disrupting the chance of a New Zealand versus England final. But New Zealand will have to tighten their defence. And the Springboks did look awesome in dispatching Samoa.

NOVEMBER 4

Melbourne Cup day. The day a horse race stops the nation. It's also our daughter Shelley's birthday. With rugby tours in November having been almost an annual event, I've been in her company on only about eight of her 28 birthdays. I call her today and she signs off our conversation with a cheery "I love you Dad", sweet words to a guilty travelling father.

I scan the papers looking for an appropriate horse to back. There's one about the Welsh team's threat to the All Blacks a few days ago – "Frightening" is its name. And there's a starter that hints at the way the All Blacks have conducted their media relations here – "Distinctly Secret". Perhaps though, the best one is a hint of what an in-form All Black team might show in their matches ahead – "Ain't Seen Nothin". The race is eventually won by mare with a name like one of the Georgian players – Makybe Diva.

I read on the Internet a provocative day's writing by the staff and columnists of *The New Zealand Herald.* The strong words of Wynne Gray, Chris Rattue and John Drake are extremely condemnatory of John Mitchell and the All Blacks. Even Keith Quinn and TVNZ's coverage gets a burst from the paper's TV writer, Greg Dixon. Dixon says our crew "lack match fitness".

Gray pulls no punches: "After a month of freewheel cruising, the All Blacks' gearbox has developed a serious graunch." Gray says the All Blacks seriously underestimated the Welsh and ends with: "If the All Blacks were not awake to what was needed against Wales, after the pre-match spiel from the coaching staff ... then the surface rust has got into the chassis."

Rattue is scathing. "As there are only a couple of people in New Zealand who understand rugby, as All Black selector Mark Shaw kindly pointed out before the World Cup campaign, it is tempting to just accept the word here of John Mitchell and Robbie Deans that all is well. Then again, you might say their post-match utterances were rugby's answers to the Flat Earth Society ... The truth is the All Blacks succumbed to arrogance in their hearts. They didn't take the Welsh seriously. The All Blacks are not out of this World Cup hunt, but they are ripe for the plucking." Columnist Drake mentions the TV commentary team's praise of the around-the-field running of lock Ali Williams. "But really," writes Drake, "he didn't get stuck into the tight stuff at all."

The writing is the best and most barbed I've seen from the New Zealand reporters since the Cup started.

I wince when I see the headline about the TV coverage, but of course Mr Dixon is entitled to his opinion.

Tonight I make my first visit to the Sydney Opera House, with Frankie Deges of *The Buenos Aires Herald* and fellow-Argentinians, referee Pablo de Luca and World Cup refereeing selector Ricardo Bordcoch. We go to the Sydney re-opening of the rugby play *Alone it Stands*, by John Breen. It's the story of the day Munster beat the 1978 All Blacks 12–0. The six actors play 62 different parts and a rugby game is depicted on stage with all its excitement, glory and violence. Everyone seems to enjoy it.

Afterwards over supper I ask Pablo, who has not made the final cut of eight referees for the knock-out phase, who he thinks is the best referee here. He replies: "I theenk it is Paddy [O'Brien]." I'm pleased for our Kiwi whistle man from the deep south.

NOVEMBER 5

Willie Lose leaves us today to head back to work in Auckland. Thanks Willie, for aiding our TVNZ coverage.

Brendan Telfer rings from Auckland and reports that Martin Devlin and TVNZ management have had meetings to attempt to smooth things over after Martin's strong verbals on Radio Sport about the World Cup TV coverage. Apparently Devlin will not now be removed from *A Game of Two Halves*. So there has obviously been quite a deal of kissy-kissy going on between the two parties.

Tonight I make my first appearance on *Lion Red Sports Café*. Our normally sedate Sydney studio is transformed to include a bar and couches, a full rock band and dancing girls. Host Ric Salizzo tells me he has interviewed the Springbok captain, Corne Krige. "He and his team are *sooo* relaxed," says Ric. That news is worrying.

Out of the New Zealand camp tonight comes a rumour that Tana Umaga is going to be picked for Saturday's quarter-final. I hope not. In a game that will be played at a furious pace I could not support a player being chosen, no matter how great he is, who's not 100 per cent fit.

The Steve Walsh refereeing affair also seems to have been sorted out amicably and the likable New Zealander will whistle the Scotland versus Australia match in Brisbane on Saturday night.

NOVEMBER 6

All the teams are announced for the quarter-finals. The All Blacks name the same lineup that beat brave Wales, but with top lock Chris Jack back for Brad Thorn. There's no place for Tana Umaga, though at the team's release it is said he might be considered for the next game. There must be no concerns about the rib-injury that Jerry Collins suffered towards the end of the Wales game.

The Springboks have named Derick Hougaard at first-five and Danie Rossouw on the openside flank in place of injured Joe van Niekerk. Neither Hougaard nor Rossouw have been tried at this level.

I play my pre-match game of matching each player against his marker and making a judgment as to who is superior. By my reckoning, the Springboks have only four players who might be considered superior or equal to New Zealand's. I mark all New Zealand's outer backs as better than their opposites. I give Justin Marshall and Joost Van der Westhuizen a 50/50 share. In the forwards I give Corne Krige a higher mark than

Reuben Thorne and Victor Matfield I mark as better than Ali Williams, though that may be a tough call. I judge the hookers Keven Mealamu and John Smit as 50/50. In the rest of the pack positions I rate the All Blacks higher. That gives New Zealand a 12–3 advantage. On that basis the All Blacks should bolt in.

NOVEMBER 7

Travel day to Melbourne. At Sydney Airport I chat briefly to Paddy O'Brien. He says he thinks he's "in the frame" to do the final. "It might depend on the South Africa-New Zealand result," he says.

That means Andre Watson must be another main contender. The other refs being spoken highly of are Ireland's Alain Rolland and England's Chris White.

Tonight at the Grand Hotel in Melbourne I meet the "heavy-hitters", as I call them. Our new commentators, Grant Fox and John Hart, have flown in. They will be with me for the rest of the tournament. Both are confident about the All Blacks' quarter-final prospects. We have a drink together. Paul Holmes is also there with his crew. He has just done his nightly TV show, live from the city. We have a good session – friends talking in increasingly loud voices.

NOVEMBER 8

Quarter-finals:
New Zealand 29 – South Africa 9
Australia 33 – Scotland 16

In this morning's Saturday paper, *The Age,* Stu Wilson has an outrageously positive column about the game. He writes it (or, I suspect, someone writes it for him) almost as if he was one of today's players in the changing room, getting all fired up for the action ahead. His last words are: "Enjoy the flight tomorrow, Springboks – because you *are* going home!"

Yet we hear from home that the talkback lines are full of New Zealand rugby people, who, after the Welsh game, are worried. Grant Fox returns

The Quinn-Fox-Hart commentary team seemed to gel immediately.
Then again, we're old friends.

from his morning walk in Melbourne and says what should have taken him 30 minutes along the Yarra River has taken him more than an hour-and-a-half. He is stopped repeatedly by anxious Kiwi supporters and asked his views.

The game is amazing, especially when weighed against the history of clashes between our two great rugby powers. The final score is 29–9, more than most of us predicted. South Africa never really threatens the All Black line and New Zealand dominate possession.

While this team has been built on outstanding back play, tonight the forwards "front up". John McBeth tells me later that in the Sydney studios, after just two scrums, Richard Loe admired the effort of tighthead prop Greg Somerville against his opposite Christo Bezuidenhout and said: "We'll be all right tonight."

So it proves. There is soon an air of a black wild beast moving in for the kill. We wonder just when this All Black powerhouse will explode. It does eventually, first from a brilliant midfield run by Justin Marshall, which just fails to produce points. It becomes breathtaking, and is helped by wonderful tackling, especially from Jerry Collins, who thunders into Thinus Delport with such force that the Springbok winger hobbles out of the game. Delport says later that "being tackled by Collins was like running into a brick shithouse".

Carlos Spencer comes into his own. Beforehand, Grant Fox had said to

Spencer was magic against South Africa.

me: "You watch Carlos go tonight. I reckon he's been holding back at this Cup." Sure enough, Spencer shows us plenty of dash and flair, including a wonderful break that leads to the All Blacks' first try. At halftime the All Blacks lead just 13–6 but Fox and Hart agree they will win by 20.

The most telling aspect of the game isn't the final score, but the humiliation of the key aspect of Springbok rugby – forward strength. The New Zealand pack are all-powerful at scrum time, McCaw and Collins snap up any loose ball lying about and Chris Jack and Ali Williams do exceptionally well at lineouts. This is helped by Keven Mealamu's throwing, quite the best in a season when lineout throwing has been such a hot topic of discussion. Remember the demise of Anton Oliver? All is forgotten tonight anyway.

The only slight worry is the goal-kicking. Since the non-selection of Andrew Mehrtens, the erratic kicking form of Carlos Spencer and the injury to Tana Umaga, the arrival of Leon MacDonald as a goalkicker has been a blessing to the All Blacks. But will he be 100 per cent for what lies ahead? With the team so committed to scoring tries one has to hope that they won't be cast out of the competition because of this possible shortcoming. Didn't William Webb Ellis, whose name appears on the World Cup, want the game to be a running and passing one?

This is the first time New Zealand has beaten South Africa in a World Cup match. The All Blacks have now won the last seven games between the two countries. What was once an amazing rivalry – locked at 24 wins each as recently as 1998 – nows favours the All Blacks 34–26, with three drawn.

Reuben Thorne is interviewed after the game by Bernadine Oliver-Kerby. Apparently his nickname in the team is "The Freeze" (coolness under pressure). He says nothing earth-shattering, but at least he turns up. When coach John Mitchell is invited to appear, media man Matt McIlraith disappears for a few seconds into the team's dressing room, then returns with a firm "no" to our request. Very disappointing again. It reminds me of my abortive trips to Whangarei and New Plymouth this winter. Mitchell does speak to the media at the later press conference, but that is long after the TV coverage from Melbourne is over. Sometimes TVNZ's $25 million paid for three World Cup rights looks like very thin gruel indeed.

The All Blacks, spearheaded by a magic Carlos Spencer effort, handle their first real challenge of the Cup with authority.

Leon MacDonald, scorer of a try, three penalties and a conversion tonight, tells the world's press: "We're all living a dream at the moment." As the words drop from his lips we scribble them down. At last, *something* from inside this All Black camp that tells us there is some emotion behind the closed doors and media blackouts.

As we walk back to the Grand Hotel, Fox and Hart are cheered and surrounded by happy New Zealanders. This must have been pleasing for John – not at all like the last time he was at a World Cup.

We then watch Australia play Scotland on a hastily-arranged TV set in the Grand Hotel lounge. Soon drinks are being poured in abundance, and scorn is being poured on the Australian performance. The Wallabies are average, but beat Scotland 33–16 after being held to 9–9 at halftime. We trudge off to bed knowing it will be a trans-Tasman semi-final in Sydney next weekend.

NOVEMBER 9

Quarter-finals:
France 43 – Ireland 21
England 28 – Wales 17

Only 33,134 turn out to watch Ireland play France at the Telstra Dome. It's such a let-down after the excellent crowds at earlier games. The game is a bit of a let-down, too. Not because of the quality of play but because the French run away with it. Partway through the second half, they've jumped a 37–0 lead. Ireland come back with three excellent tries, but it's not enough.

When France are in full concentration mode they truly look the goods. They have forward might and backline speed. The loose forward trio of Olivier Magne, Serge Betsen and Olivier Harinordoquy leads the way, while Fabien Galthie, Frederic Michalak and Tony Marsh prove to be sharp and incisive backs.

However, John Hart questions whether they can play a full game with composure and clarity. They didn't tonight, which leaves a chink of hope for future opponents.

The sight of Tony Marsh, standing upright and proud as "La Marsellaise" played, was wonderful. I couldn't help but think of the boy, Tony, and his identical twin brother, Glen, coming through the ranks in modest Counties Manukau, then going different ways in their professional careers, one to France the other to Japan. Tony went to France where, in time, he made the French team. From the high of that experience, he was assailed with the most awful of masculine cancers, that of the testicles. The prognosis of him living a long life was bleak and the likelihood of him playing top rugby again was negligible. Yet here he was tonight, a lonely tear rolling down a cheek and his quivering lips shaping the words of the anthem of his adopted country. It was lump in the throat stuff.

After the game the cameras zoomed in on the heart and soul of recent Irish rugby, Keith Wood. With his team beaten he slumped to the ground, and when he rose there were tears in his eyes, too. Ireland had looked to him for inspiration for 58 tests spread over the past 10 years. And now he told us: "The heart and my head are willing, but the body says this is enough." And with that, this wonderful ambassador for rugby retired.

We also watch the fourth quarter-final from the Grand Hotel lobby bar. And when the Welsh score three tries against their mighty foes, the hint of the World Cup's biggest upset zooms into view. Alas, it doesn't work out that way.

Jonny Wilkinson kicks six penalties, a conversion and a dropped goal. That's 23 points for England (after Will Greenwood's solo try), the same total as young Michalak scored for France. Those two will be on opposite sides in the semi-finals next weekend. Somehow, we always knew it was going to be France versus England and New Zealand versus Australia. For the All Blacks it will be an epic trans-Tasman battle. Our team should win, shouldn't they?

NOVEMBER 10

The TV ratings come out for the weekend's viewing at home. On Saturday the highest rating was a 38 – about 1.6 million New Zealanders watched the All Blacks play South Africa. It's easily the biggest rugby audience on any station of the year. Even on Sunday night, the France versus Ireland game scored a 31. There'll be no stopping the interest from now on, especially as the kickoff times (10pm NZ time) for the last four games are so good.

Barbara Mitchell tells me that viewers of her weekday highlights show have caused a surprise. When asked to text whether "Tana Umaga should play in the semi-final versus Australia", 83 per cent said "yes". Does that mean 83 per cent want the goal-kicking duties to revert to Carlos Spencer? I don't think so.

I fly back to Sydney today and, armed with a large bunch of flowers, I welcome my dear wife Anne. She's here for the rest of the week. Her flight from New Zealand arrived before mine from Melbourne, so the curtains have been flung back in the apartment and the place is airing beautifully. I suppose I would have done that too, wouldn't I?

NOVEMBER 11

Anne and I walk across Sydney Harbour Bridge and head for Martin Place to visit the Australian War Memorial. Today is Remembrance Day, when Aussies honour those who have fallen in battle. There are a number of old diggers about, selling poppies. The weather is a scorcher. The World Cup suddenly seems a long way away.

But not for long. The All Blacks team to play the Wallabies in the semi-final is announced. It's the same starting 15 that dispatched the Springboks. Once again Tana is omitted. To me this is fair enough.

In Melbourne a swag of British reporters who wanted to speak to Carlos Spencer were angry that he was a "no show" at today's team release. It's said that media man Matt McIlraith was "forced up against a wall" by angry reporters demanding Spencer be delivered to them. Spencer has suddenly been thrust into the spotlight, because of his recent brilliant play, and because of comments made this morning by Wallaby coach Eddie Jones that Spencer might be the "weak link" in the All Blacks.

Then there is the quote from former Wallaby Sam Scott-Young. He tells Sydney's *Daily Telegraph* that the Wallaby forwards should "get a hold of that snotty little guy with the tattoos ... niggle him, smash him in defence, mess up his hair and he'll get cranky and start looking for who's coming at him next. Watch his game deteriorate under that sort of pressure."

On semi-finals form, dare we hope for a New Zealand-France final? To me that would be a perfect contest, even though I picked England to win the Cup weeks before we got here. It has to be said that England are starting to look their age. Just a bit. To me, the worst final would be Australia versus England. Now that would be awful!

NOVEMBER 12

The trans-Tasman taunting is building. Sean Fitzpatrick enters the fray with the view, after seeing the Wallaby team named for Saturday, that none would make a combined team chosen from both countries.

The former All Black captain is in Australia on a flying visit for Coca-Cola. He has spent most of the World Cup in Britain, where he has appeared regularly on the ITV coverage there. The money being talked about for Sean's contract in Britain is amazing. In fact, many former international stars continue to "coin it" big time at the World Cup, appearing on billboards, TV commercials and TV discussion panels, making breakfast, lunch and dinner speeches, and writing newspaper articles. John Eales, David Campese, Zinzan Brooke, Francois Pienaar, Phil Kearns, Peter FitzSimons, Gareth Chilcott, Stu Wilson and Chris "Buddha" Handy are leading the way.

The French name the same starting team for the semi-final as that which beat Ireland in Melbourne. All 15 players turn up at the media conference. Compare that to the sight of All Black media man Matt McIlraith (now cruelly called "Shrek" by the frustrated Kiwi journalists) seen on TV fending off demands for Carlos Spencer, Jerry Collins or Justin Marshall to be delivered to the media in Melbourne.

The problems between New Zealand rugby and the World Cup media may be forgotten should New Zealand win the Cup, but a serious re-think and repair job has to take place some time soon.

NOVEMBER 13

Today former Wallaby great Paul McLean has his turn. In today's *Sydney Morning Herald*, McLean says Spencer is susceptible to "cracking" under pressure. McLean says he doubts the mercurial Spencer will retain his new-found composure under the acid test of Saturday's semi-final. "The rest of the cream [of semi-final first five-eighths], Jonny Wilkinson,

Frederic Michalak and Stephen Larkham, will rise to the top while Spencer will crumble."

In the same paper is a story saying no-one is afraid of the All Blacks any more, while the *Daily Telegraph* yelps: "Eyeball them! [Brendan] Cannon issues haka challenge to the All Blacks!"

NOVEMBER 14

The word battles continue. *The Sydney Morning Herald* publishes a "recipe for success" for the game for Australia tomorrow night. It's based on the performance of Wales against New Zealand. There's mention of Scott Johnson, the ex-Aussie who is Wales' assistant coach, going to dinner several times this week with Eddie Jones, as well as having been seen at the Wallaby training camp at Coff's Harbour. So, the sneaky buggers have called in help from outside.

The five points listed as the Welsh recipe for success are:
- Forward dominance, fast, clean ball from the breakdowns, throw it wide early and test the outer defence.
- Restrict kicking, nullifying the New Zealand backline's ability to counter attack.
- Pinpoint the weaknesses in the All Black backline and run at them.
- Have nimble players go for holes near the big, slow All Black forwards.
- Backs, repeat after me: "Don't drop the ball."

Tonight the Quinns have a quiet dinner at a Chinese restaurant with TVNZ's statistician Peter Marriott and his wife Christine. Over coffee my fortune cookie reads: "Exciting adventures await you." It's a sign to me that whatever the Wallabies throw at the All Blacks tomorrow, all will be well.

NOVEMBER 15

Semi-final:
Australia 22 – New Zealand 10

Anne flies home and I spend the day preparing for the biggest commentary of my life. It will probably

One of the warming aspects of the World Cup was the rehabilitation of John Hart after his disgraceful treatment following the 1999 World cup. Here he is surrounded by the world's rugby media after the New Zealand-Australia semi-final.

be surpassed only by the one I will do *next* Saturday when New Zealand plays whoever in the final.

In our studio, the EA Cyberstrator system, which we have been using to predict results, has thrown up a score showing an Australian win, 20–17. Our production people decide not to play the short animated rugby video, their logic being we must show only positive things today.

At the ground in One Sport's buildup, Peter FitzSimons is interviewed by me. He has written a brilliant piece for today's *Sydney Morning Herald* about the final words used in Wallaby dressing rooms before big-match days, including the World Cup wins of 1991 and 1999. He says earnestly that he thinks the Wallabies will win by one point.

Our commentary team is split 2–1. With some reservations Grant Fox picks a win for New Zealand, as do I, but John Hart is less confident. He has concerns about some aspects of New Zealand's recent play. John is hoping for a win for the All Blacks, rather than being certain.

The teams march out proudly, led out by their captains George Gregan and Reuben Thorne, behind the flags of their two countries. When they are sighted by the 82,444 crowd, a massive roar erupts. The atmosphere of flags, faces, and fans is great to see, better than any Bledisloe Cup game.

During the national anthems, the Australians look grimly determined. Is it my imagination, or do about six of the All Blacks look distracted and detached while "God Defend New Zealand" is being sung? The haka follows. The Aussies do the respectful thing and stand upright and proud

The All Black hierarchy (left to right: manager Tony Thorpe, assistant coach Robbie Deans, coach John Mitchell, captain Reuben Thorne and winger Doug Howlett) – turn up for a press conference, but it's far too late for the New Zealand public.

while they face the New Zealand challenge.

In warm conditions referee Chris White blows for the game to start and another step on the All Blacks journey to winning the 2003 World Cup begins.

The pattern for the match is set in the first seconds after kickoff. The players leap for the Carlos Spencer kickoff, and, rather than New Zealand securing the ball to instigate their first attack, Australia win it. Then quite simply, they keep possession for most of the first half (and indeed most of the game).

They never kick it to the All Blacks' speeding back trio of Mils Muliaina, Joe Rokocoko and Doug Howlett. Instead, they hold possession by short, crisp passing among themselves.

Three times in the first five minutes we see big lock Nathan Sharpe in the midfield running hard at Leon MacDonald, who is forced to make grim tackles. The "Welsh recipe" is displayed from the start. It turns out to be the forerunner of a sweet taste of victory for Australia. New Zealand is not in this game from the early stages.

We cling to hopes that eventually the All Black hunters and gatherers of the ball will gain ascendancy and tries will follow. They do not.

There are a couple of early moments of encouragement. Muliaina crashes over in the corner from a back move, but the TV referee rightly rules no try. Soon there is another backline move near the Australian line and Carlos Spencer throws a long pass. The All Blacks might have scored had it gone to a New Zealand hand but Stirling Mortlock, wearing gold and green, swoops on it and bolts 80 metres to score. With Elton Flatley's conversion Australia lead 7–0. Later Flatley adds a penalty, then another, and Australia leads 13–0 after half an hour.

In the last minutes before halftime they finally let slip control of the ball. In a flash Justin Marshall flicks the ball to Spencer, who breaks into space and puts Reuben Thorne over to score wide out. The Leon MacDonald conversion (his first goal after missing two earlier penalty attempts) gives us hope at halftime, though Australia lead 13–7.

The second half is not much different from the first, with Australia

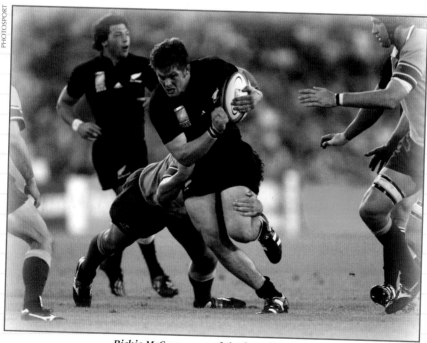

*Richie McCaw ... one of the few All Blacks
to emerge from the game with credit.*

Triumphant Wallaby skipper George Gregan commiserates with his All Black opposite, Reuben Thorne.

holding sway most of the time. Two more penalties by Flatley make it 19–7, before MacDonald kicks one for New Zealand.

There is enough time for the All Blacks to win but their deficiencies are being ruthlessly exposed. The lineouts are a shambles. The timing between Keven Mealamu and the jumpers is not at all like last week against South Africa. (Somewhere back in New Zealand Anton Oliver might have been thinking: "See? Keven is as human as me.")

The other area of concern is lack of leadership. When Flatley kicks his fifth penalty and the score leaps to 22–10, and the World Cup "journey" is nearing its end, yet again there is no sight of Reuben Thorne. He is not seen banging his fist into his hand. There are no shots of him exhorting the boys to a last laying down of body to the cause. Nothing. The captain's face is flat and lifeless. Worse, no plan B is unearthed.

The seconds tick down, referee White blows full time, and the crowd goes wild. Who can blame them? The result puts the Wallabies through to their World Cup final next week. It's a massive upset, but thoroughly deserved.

For the All Blacks there are scenes at the end not of despair, but mostly of numbness. Just blankness and disbelief. We see Joe Rokocoko warmly embracing Wendell Sailor but the rest of the New Zealand team seem to stand about before walking to the tunnels. They shake the hands of their opponents in an expressionless sort of way, looking as though they cannot believe what they have endured over the past 80 minutes.

None of us can believe it either. New Zealand had been expected to win comfortably. EA Cyberstrator was correct. Even Peter FitzSimons, just after he had finished our interview, had said as he left the room: "New Zealand to win by 20 points."

How did it happen that a New Zealand rugby team, bred to be the best in the game, and with more than 100 years of deep tradition, bowed out so toothlessly against opponents they had thrashed on the same ground only months before? Australia put into play perfectly a plan that squashed any hopes New Zealand had of imposing themselves.

Under the grandstand at Telstra Stadium after the final whistle, what occurs reveals all that is bad to the core about the public relations of the 2003 World Cup All Blacks. Immediately the teams come off the field, Bernadine Oliver-Kerby steps in with her microphone for the "world feed" one-minute interview. That's all it's allowed to be. Bernadine really has time for only two, maybe three questions, and the captains being interviewed know this.

So tonight Bernadine offers Reuben Thorne a chance to explain his feelings at the shock defeat. Reuben looks blank and shattered, but at least he has fronted up. George Gregan does the same length interview with his Aussie TV station interviewer, Tim Horan. That having been completed, all the TV stations around the world that are taking the full telecast, and therefore paying massive satellite fees, break away quickly to resume their own programming. Reuben Thorne moves away to the dressing rooms.

At that point TVNZ, which is still on air to feed a rugby-crazy nation, quite reasonably asks coach John Mitchell to come out and speak exclusively about what we have just seen on this sorrowful night. Media man Matt McIlraith disappears into the dressing room with our request.

He comes out and we are told Mitchell is not available. We ask again. This time our request goes via TWI (Trans World International), the British-based World Cup marketing people. Again, our request is declined. We know that behind the door there must be some devastated people, but we think we are entitled to some reaction from the team bosses. So we ask, again, for someone in authority from within the team to come

Pride of the Kiwis left Black and blue

Claire Harvey

NO excuses, no accusations: the All Blacks have apologised to a furious nation and admitted they simply did not deserve to win the World Cup.

Exhausted and miserable, the New Zealand coaches and players fled Sydney for their Melbourne training base yesterday morning, pausing only to congratulate the Wallabies.

to carry the southern hemisphere flag."

Captain Reuben Thorne said the team was "heartbroken".

"They didn't allow us to execute our game plan," Thorne said. "They forced us into errors and they took their chances.

"I can't fault the preparation for this campaign. The New Zealand Rugby Union, the coaches and players have put a huge amount into it. We came all this way and we head

The Australian *newspaper brilliantly captured the pathos in the Jerry Collins situation.*

out and speak to the nation about what has gone wrong.

I won't soon forget what happens next. A battered and scuffed Jerry Collins emerges from the dressing room and stands in front of the cameras. He is shirtless and shaking, his hand repeatedly plays across his face. He *might* be wiping sweat from his brow or are they tears he doesn't want us to see? I wonder why this young man has been sent to "front up" when Mitchell is behind the closed doors? Surely this is a day when someone of real clout from within the team has to emerge and look the massive home TV audience in the eye.

Instead we are offered one of the team's youngsters.

The interview, by John McBeth, from across town at the Epping studio, is agonising to watch. Collins can hardly raise his eyes off his feet. In the manner of so many of our delightful but shy Polynesian people, he looks ashamed. His replies are honest, of course, but who can expect this man, a mere cog in the wheel of the All Blacks, to answer hard questions? He cannot be expected to be qualified to do so. Instead, the fat cats of the team remain inside in their flash suits, sheltering from the storm.

When the interview is over, Collins doesn't go back inside the dressing room. He wanders back out on to the empty Telstra Stadium. Only the working media and a few of the crowd remain. Collins walks across the darkening field, wearing only a pair of All Black shorts. His barefooted track takes him across to the other side, where he embraces a woman. They speak for a few minutes before he trudges back. A truly sad sight, one that, from high in the stands, we commentators agree, should never have been allowed to happen.

Our live programming back to New Zealand ends. TVNZ, too, has other commitments on a Sunday night. We cannot wait endlessly, embarrassingly, for "no shows". Before our coverage ends, other players – Spencer, Marshall and McCaw – front up, but Mitchell chooses not to. And neither do Robbie Deans or manager Tony Thorpe, or All Black selector Mark "The Flea" Shaw, who's at the game somewhere.

This episode shows one last fatal flaw in the character of John Mitchell. While it may have been understandable that Mitchell preferred to maintain a low profile during the season – maybe he just doesn't like the media "lizards" – there comes a time when to ignore the fans back home is simply treating those people, many of whom have supported him through difficult days, like shit on his shoe. I mean it.

For me, the moments under the stand today are those of deep shame for this All Black team. It looks like the management didn't have the guts to offer opinions on the whys and wherefores of the defeat. And worse, when it was time to front up, they hid behind the kids and let them do the explaining.

[I thought back to what had happened in the past at times like these. I had an immediate memory of Alex Wyllie, John Hart and Gary Whetton speaking live on TV after the 1991 disappointments in Dublin. In 1995, Laurie Mains, Earle Kirton and Colin Meads did the same after the final at Johannesburg. And tonight in Sydney, I asked John Hart what happened at Twickenham in 1999 after the shock 43–31 semi-final loss to France. Said John: "Straight after the defeat, I came into the dressing room, and honestly, it was a sight to see. All the blokes were close to tears. They knew they had blown it. I looked at Taine Randell, our captain, and he *was* in tears. But, I thought, someone *has* to go outside and speak to the media. By agreement it was supposed to be the captain, but I did it myself. Someone had to front up."]

The Australian reaction ...

True, the 2003 All Blacks top brass do eventually go to the international media room and speak. I follow across and am tempted to grab the questioner's microphone and ask: "Mr Mitchell, why did you choose not

to speak to your All Black fans back home via TV, straight after the game."
But I don't raise the issue. Maybe I don't want the world's press to see
how this All Black management treats their most loyal people.

The top table looks awful, actually. Robbie Deans sits still and granite-
like, not at all like him. I don't think anyone of the hundreds in the room
asks him a single question. Mitchell looks pale and gaunt. Someone
whispers that if "Mitch has a racehorse, he'd better sell it now" – a
reference to the treatment that Hart's horse, Holmes D G, got from the
Addington crowd when it went to race there after the 1999 World Cup.

Reuben Thorne is courteous and short with his responses. His expression
has not really changed all year. He gives so little away. Doug Howlett is
also sitting there tonight, though I cannot understand why. He's had
only an average game tonight by his standards.

... and how New Zealanders saw it.

Our TV producer Stu Dennison storms into the press conference hall,
angry like never before. His language is not warm. He tells me he has just
given an NZRU official who was in the room a "right burst" about the

263

no-show interviews. "Good," say I, "I just gave him one, too." The response to us both from the NZRU official was not warm about Mr Mitchell. We think John might be in trouble with his bosses and his job shaky. It's sad that one loss can bring a year of festering to the surface.

One bloke I see in the press conference room is Phil Gifford. He approaches me looking grim. "I wonder, Keith," he says, "if this result will mean Robbie Deans will go down with the sinking ship?"

Is there no time during any day – or night – when Phil *doesn't* put Canterbury things first?

In the car home we talk about what tonight's result will mean. Australia may go on to win the final and be able to wave the Cup at the rest of the world for four years. Certainly Aussie people can have a "we beat you at the World Cup" brag over us in New Zealand for four long years. We've heard from one of the sideline photographers that during the last moments of tonight's game George Gregan was shouting to the struggling All Blacks: "Four years boys! Four more years!" The echo of that call will resonate louder than any Tri Nations or Bledisloe Cup wins the All Blacks might have before 2007. How depressing.

Back in Kirribilli, I trudge upstairs to the apartment, with a video of tonight's game in my hand. I watch the game over and over by myself. The journey is over. "Our" team is out.

I go to bed, sober and staring at the roof, at 3am.

NOVEMBER 16

Semi-final:
England 24 – France 7

Sunday morning and yes, the sun did come up today. But even after a night's rest and a wake-up coffee, the banner in *The Sun-Herald* newspaper, "It's Magic", doesn't help a weary head. "Against all odds, the courageous Wallabies win their place in the final," it reads. Suddenly, my head hurts again.

It seems Alan Jones and Nick Farr-Jones were correct in what they said months ago. Jones said the All Blacks were haunted by the failures of 1991, '95 and '99. Farr-Jones said New Zealand would crumble under pressure.

From home we hear that the All Blacks are headlined today as "World Chumps" and "Chokers" by one Sunday paper, while the other says, "The End of the World".

This afternoon we taxi to Telstra Stadium again. The ground is fresh and cleaned from last night. It's almost as if the ordeal 24 hours ago never took place.

By kick-off it's raining heavily and is only 16 degrees – perfect conditions for the ageing England forwards who are content to rumble the ball downfield into attacking positions, hoping for a penalty or dropped goal chance for Jonny Wilkinson. France, surprisingly, look dull and lifeless, happy to kick away possession. It ain't pretty – only a Pom could love this. It's the rugby equivalent of standing on an English beach in plastic sandals with a knotted handkerchief around one's head, calling life exhilarating.

The French hopes of first five-eighths Frederic Michalak being a powerful influence prove fruitless. Wilkinson, on the other hand, turns in a cracker. He scores all England's points, through three dropped goals, and five penalties. It's so calculated that even noted kicker Grant Fox laments the influence the dropped goal is having in rugby these days.

The England forwards are monstrous in their competence and organisation. Despite leading 7–3 at one stage, the French, like the All Blacks, head rather meekly to the third-place play-off game next Thursday. At the end there is no great celebration and arm-waving from the English, such as we saw from the Aussies last night. The grim Poms show that this is not the celebration night.

NOVEMBER 17

The papers today give more painful reminders of the All Blacks' effort. *The Sydney Morning Herald* opens with "Simply Brilliant, Now for England", *The Daily Telegraph* yelps "Embrace the Dream", while *The Australian* calls the Wallabies "The True Believers".

Writing for *The Dominion Post* in Wellington, Peter FitzSimons sums up some of his pre-match lack of confidence in Australia in his inimitable style: "Waiter! Some humble pie for me and my friends. The crow humble pie, please. And some serviettes, if you don't mind, to wipe away all this egg running down our faces. For after the Wallabies stunning 22–10 victory over the totally shocked All Blacks ... it is fair to say that rarely in the field of sporting endeavour have so many pundits and professional loudmouths – I specifically cite moi – been left looking so foolish." This is the same Fitzy who had called the Australians "road kill" for the All Blacks only days earlier.

And it's the same Fitzy who, when inviting me last week to a barbecue at his house, said: "It'll be a great show mate. I've invited Jock Hobbs and asked him to bring the World Cup with him!"

NOVEMBER 18

Andre Watson of South Africa is named to referee the final. The decision is a disappointment for Paddy O'Brien from Invercargill. He must have been close.

It's curious that the All Blacks are still in Melbourne this morning, with their play-off game only a day away. They travel to Sydney this afternoon. Since last Sunday morning they have flown back to Melbourne, announced their team, had one day's full training, then a light day of training, then packed everything and flown back to Sydney. After tomorrow night's game they'll be flying home.

I travel to Bondi to meet their French opposition at the final pre-game press conference. The French openness is refreshing. The retirement of their captain, Fabien Galthie, is announced. With a sad face Galthie says he will be leaving immediately for home, following the death of his uncle. It is a heartbreaking end for a charming man.

In the hotel foyer all the 22-man French squad chosen to play the All Blacks come out. I get to see how a professional team is relaxed and open with the media. Not like our suspicious mob.

The media time seems unlimited. I interview new halfback Dimitri Yachvili, new captain Yannick Bru, and of course Kiwi Frenchman Tony Marsh. Tony is now 31 and has a serene presence about him. Perhaps the battle through testicular cancer this year has given him a new vision of life. Certainly he is much more worldly than the shy lad we used to see, with his twin brother Glen, turning out at Pukekohe Stadium.

Tonight, at the International Rugby Players Association Awards dinner, the All Blacks win the Team of the Year title. Jonah Lomu and Andrew Mehrtens accept the trophy. Many of those present comment on Jonah's shuffle when he walks up on stage. He also accepts an award honouring him for his contribution to world rugby. Well done, Jonah.

NOVEMBER 19

There's a whisper – among a number from within the All Blacks camp – about Tana Umaga. This one says Tana has been recovered from his knee injury for weeks, but the coaches still won't pick him. It has got to the point where Tana has said "stuff it" to the men in charge and declared himself not interested in playing against France tomorrow. Surely it cannot be true.

NOVEMBER 20

Third place playoff:
New Zealand 40 – France 13

Unfortunately, there's more than a glimmer of truth in Jim Hubbard's fine cartoon in **The Dominion Post.**

Space is at a premium in our TVNZ commentary box.

France have put out a virtual new lineup after the semi-final loss, so a game dressed up to look like a full international winds up being well short of one.

There is a nice early touch, with Tony Marsh being handed the ball by Yannick Bru to lead out the French XV against his former mates. When the game kicks off though, there is little to enthuse about. Thank goodness for Mr Hart and Mr Fox in the commentary box – they dissect the game as though it is fair dinkum and somehow bring meaning to it with their expertise. I am battling tonight.

During the game there are several glimpses of the All Black reserves and squad members on the bench. It's noticeable that Tana Umaga is sitting there, looking grim and grey. Not enjoying it one bit?

When the blessed release finally comes, with New Zealand winning comfortably, neither side shows much emotion. Instead of being a glorious ride into a golden sunset for the All Blacks, the World Cup has instead been a journey to nowhere.

I don't bother attending the press conference. I'm told that John Mitchell fronted up to speak to the world, but again, despite our invitation, chose not to appear for our TV audience at home. Stuff him we say, heading for the car park.

Perhaps we should have stayed for the interviews – Mitchell tells the reporters that his team lost to Australia because of "immaturity". Just who was it, Mitch, who made that "immaturity" possible with the selections for this tournament?

"Mind you Keith," says my inner man, "*you* were one of those who believed in Mitchell until just a few days ago."

A lot of Kiwis were like me. We had faith, but that faith has not been rewarded.

NOVEMBER 21

At lunchtime I go to the French Rugby Federation's launch for the sixth World Cup, in 2007. The French have gone to great expense to fly in dozens of their old rugby stars, as well as a dozen or so former internationals from other nations. Up on stage go people like Serge Blanco, Gerald Davies, Hugo Porta, Graham Mourie, Simon Poidevin, Andy Ripley and Demi Sakata. My favourite is the slightly portly Irish flanker of the 1970s, the grey-haired Fergus Slattery. He is asked: "And how many tests did you play in your time, Fergus?" The Irishman quickly hitches his ample belt and replies: "Sixty-eight so far."

NOVEMBER 22

World Cup Final:
England 20 – Australia 17

The final. England are the favourites but Australia, after their impressive form last week, are bursting with confidence. I remember coach Eddie Jones' midweek quote: "I have a young side, but they hold no fear."

There might not be an All Black team in action tonight but the two best teams are here. No doubt about that.

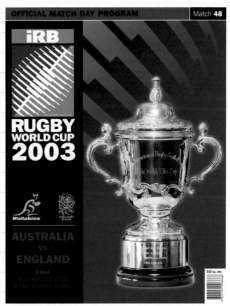

The World Cup final programme. How sad not to see New Zealand's name featured.

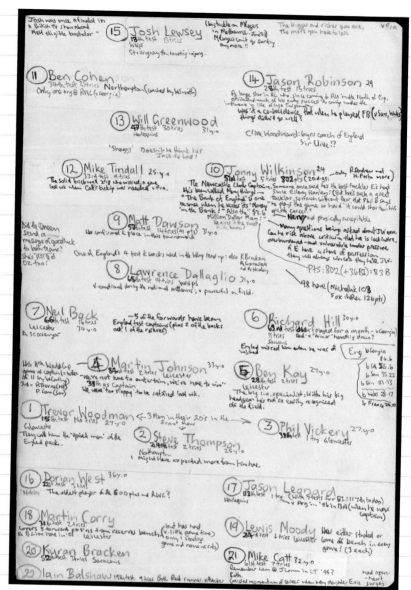

My preparation on England before the final.

One could write a book about the drama of this game. However, suffice to say that after a magnificent battle it was fittingly won by a Jonny Wilkinson dropped goal in the last seconds of extra time. And with his unfavoured right foot at that.

England have won the World Cup. The result marks an historic changing of the guard. World rugby power now belongs in the northern hemisphere.

270

The Aussies, true to their effort, congratulate the victors warmly and behave impeccably through the victory ceremony that follows. The English players are delighted, but their walk of triumph around the stadium has a heavy tread to its footfall – testimony to the closeness and hardness of the contest.

Our TV team, with nothing to celebrate except the excitement of the game, go back to the Duxton Hotel. The Pommy supporters soon arrive. One bloke, seeing Grant Fox, John Hart and Gary Whetton in our group, sends over two bottles of decent champagne, so we down a glass or three with them.

England and Australia line up before the final. What a match they turned on.

271

The maestro, Jonny Wilkinson, seals the World Cup for England with a last-minute drop goal.

England have waited a long time for this triumph. It's only right that Martin Johnson and his troops get the newspaper splash treatment.

NOVEMBER 23

It's all over. The fifth Rugby World Cup has been a resounding success in its organisation, planning, and presentation. The quality of the people playing and controlling the games has been of the highest standard. The Australian Sunday papers today salute England as worthy champions in a style you would not have thought you would see in this country. The Australian people, who I have always admired for their outlook on life, have risen even higher in my thoughts by their warm reaction to defeat.

Tonight I go to the IRB awards dinner, which doubles as the farewell function for the tournament. Our former TVNZ mate Greg Clark fronts a live telecast on *Fox Sports* and does a superb job. As expected, England win Team of the Year, Coach of the Year and Player of the Year (won by you-know-who), but New Zealand has its moments – a special award goes to the ex-All Black captain Bob Stuart for his service to the game, Ben Atiga is the Under-21 Player of the Year and those great men of the IRB sevens circuit, Gordon Tietjens and Eric Rush, receive the Sevens Team of the Year award.

The All Blacks do not feature tonight, but then again neither do the Wallabies.

NOVEMBER 24

There is a slight feeling of sorrow as I say goodbye to the Kirribilli Village Apartments to fly home. The streets, shops and restaurants of the neighbourhood have become home for our TV crew over the past seven weeks. But I'm looking forward to lying on my own couch for a spell. When I add the nearly four weeks of travel to film around Australia in July/August, plus countless nights away from home filming around New Zealand in August/September, I realise I've hardly drawn breath in the past six months.

Peeking out from under the bedclothes in my own bed after so long away feels great. And Wellington never looked better – bright and sunny. It's wonderful to be home.

However, the world of sport never seems to go away. Weeks ago I declined to appear each day on Radio Sport during the World Cup. Time differences made it difficult, and I was annoyed when I had heard and read from afar some of the comments made by Martin Devlin and Murray Deaker about TVNZ's Cup coverage.

Radio Sport is on the phone this morning, asking if I will speak to Martin on air. I'm wary – Devlin bright and cheery, Keith Quinn tired and off the pace. I decline. My position comes under the heading of "Give me a break!" I listen to Martin's show today and find he is making significant capital from a *faux pas* I made at the end of the World Cup final. In the last, summary sentence of the final game of 48 games, spread over seven long, tiring weeks, instead of calling the England captain Martin Johnson, I called him Martin Devlin.

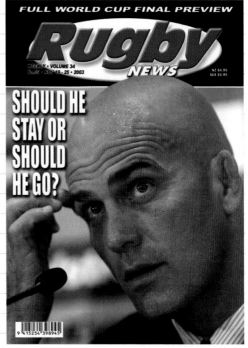

At the time I didn't even realise I'd made the mistake. It was only when I turned off the microphones and turned to thank my co-commentators, that I saw Mr Fox and Mr Hart killing themselves with laughter. Devlin will probably never let me forget my gaffe, given his daily replaying of my "widdle-meight" stumble from my first radio broadcast 36 years ago.

I go back under the blankets for a while.

Much more interesting to observe is the reaction throughout New Zealand to John Mitchell. From some quarters he is being

Rugby News *poses the question that now grips New Zealand rugby.*

given a right bollocking about all manner of things – his team's play, his selections, his attitudes to people around him, his relations with the NZRU bosses, the sponsors and the media.

Of course, I agree with some of the above, but it's amazing the weight of authority with which ordinary New Zealanders from the suburbs and cowsheds are now speaking. I note from the papers, which Anne has kept for me, and from today's radio and TV news, that the coach has few friends now in the media. This is a classic case of that old maxim: "You should be good to people on your way up the ladder of life, because you might need them on the way down."

NOVEMBER 26

Martin Devlin rings today from Auckland. He tells me with a laugh: "Yes, I'm still playing your little slip-up." I laugh too. But I tell him I need a break from Radio Sport for a while.

Someone has kept a video for me to watch of an excellent interview of Justin Marshall, done by Melanie Reid, of TV3's *20/20* programme. Marshall talks of the grudge he holds against the Wallaby flanker George Smith. Marshall claims he was the victim of foul play when Smith late-tackled him in the semi-final at the World Cup. Fair enough, perhaps, but other parts of the interview leave me with mouth agape. Here is an All Black who is *not* speaking in Mitch-Reuben-Robbie-rugby verbal nothingness. Marshall is speaking from deep in his heart. It's wonderful to hear.

There's anguish in Marshall's responses and they are not just about the serious rib injury that forced him out of the Australia game. There is also intense sadness expressed for the All Black team, which "went so close to winning the tournament", and there is support for Mitchell and Deans of a depth that we have not heard from any other member of the team (but we have not been allowed to hear, remember). Coming from a person of Marshall's seniority, it is impressive. At its conclusion I think of the weeks of platitudes and nonsense we heard from the All Black camp during the Cup. It need not have happened.

NOVEMBER 27

The Steinlager Rugby Awards are held in Auckland tonight. I'm invited but am too tired to go.

Richie McCaw wins the Kel Tremain Trophy as Player of the Year. No argument there. I reflect that I had Marty Holah as openside flanker when I scribbled my ideal XV for this diary on January 1. My view was that Holah had been outstanding on the short tour of Britain and France last year, while McCaw had been overworked during that season. Now, I hope McCaw becomes the All Black captain very soon.

And thanks to Grant Nisbett, of Sky TV. He calls today and we discuss the kind of slips of the tongue that only live broadcasters can truly understand. "When I heard you say Martin Devlin instead of Martin Johnson," says Nisbo, "it made me think back to several times I've said (broadcaster) Paddy O'Donnell's name during a live telecast instead of Paddy O'Brien's."

NOVEMBER 28

We now see evidence of a campaign in support of John Mitchell retaining his All Black coach's job. It may be needed – at a post-World Cup press conference in Sydney last Friday NZRU chief executive Chris Moller made a pointed comment, saying "we must raise the bar" in many areas concerning the All Blacks. That suggested Mitchell's shortcomings with the sponsors, media, and the NZRU were not just rumours. They're after him, I reckon. Big time.

Added to that was the announcement that the All Blacks coaching job is up for grabs. The position has already been advertised in the newspapers.

Today Robbie Deans goes in to bat for Mitchell on Radio Sport. Deans spends half an hour with Martin Devlin and says Mitchell is an expert coach, a top planner and an all-round good bloke. The other main candidate for the job is rumoured to be Graham Henry, of Auckland, who has been silent so far.

John Mitchell is interviewed tonight by Mark Crysell on the *Sunday* programme on TV1. Crysell travelled to Sydney a fortnight before the end of the World Cup, but failed to attract Mitchell's interest over there. Now home, and apparently launching an all-out bid to regain public support, Mitchell is suddenly available to the media. The interview was recorded at Mitchell's home in Hamilton. In it he stares wide-eyed at the camera and gives an air of innocence. He says things like: "I'm not arrogant and if I'm rude, I apologise. But I just have a passion for this team. In hindsight maybe I underestimated the level of communication which is necessary."

Mitchell also says the comments Chris Moller made at the press conference in Sydney had been hard to swallow.

I have some regard for Mitchell here. While it may seem hypocritical for me to say this, given my criticism of him for his reluctance to front for TVNZ at the World Cup, just because he didn't give the media dearies their interviews does not mean he should be written off as a coach. The next All Black coach should be judged on his ability to *coach* the team, not chat to reporters. He should be made to be better qualified to cope with the media scramble, but that should not be top of the credentials he needs to do the job.

It's the souring of relations with the sponsors and his NZRU bosses that will probably bring down Mitchell.

DECEMBER

"I've been dreaming for 30 years about this job."

DECEMBER 1

It is *Lord of the Rings* day in Wellington. More than 100,000 people cram Courtenay Place to see the stars of the world premiere. It's the biggest crowd I've ever seen in my beautiful home city.

The Quinns and McBeths, among others, descend on Peter and Chris Marriott's place for cocktails and canapés. They have an apartment overlooking the streets in front of the plush Embassy Theatre. From our vantage point on the sixth floor we see the stars go in. We note that All Blacks Jerry Collins, Ma'a Nonu and Tana Umaga are among them. Those three hometown boys get a wonderful reception as they walk down the red carpet.

DECEMBER 3

The plot thickens today, as the NZRU outlines changes to the All Blacks' management structure. Chairman Jock Hobbs says that from 2004 the manager's role will be significantly upgraded.

The all-powerful grasp that John Mitchell held over this year's team will now shift to the manager. Hobbs says: "The manager will have overall responsibility for leadership, strategy and planning of the All Blacks and will report to the board and NZRU chief executive officer. From next year the coach of the All Blacks will (only) be responsible for selection, training and coaching of the team."

This in effect confirms the rumours of division between Mitchell and his NZRU bosses that were heard first well before the World Cup. The two groups grew apart because the NZRU felt that Mitchell had total control of its team. The new system looks better to me. And who cares if it is an admission that the 2002–03 system has not panned out? The Hobbs executive did not put that system in place. This is a new body, and, may I say, a better one.

The question now is: who can fill the big shoes the new position of All

278

Blacks manager will demand? My thoughts flit immediately to a person with true Kiwi rugby *mana* and credibility, like Sean Fitzpatrick. Or John Hart? Ian Kirkpatrick? The position will have to go to a man of deep understanding of the All Black and New Zealand rugby traditions.

DECEMBER 4

Lying on the couch this afternoon I decide to watch a replay on Sky TV's *Rugby Channel* of the second test between New Zealand and Australia in 1982. I do this to confirm whether an incident took place in that match that has been mentioned to me several times over the years. Mark Shaw, of the "media are fleas" fame, was playing as a loose forward for New Zealand, and in the Australian pack was a lock named Duncan Hall.

A couple of years ago a friend told me that in that game Hall was so badly injured by one of the All Blacks that he had had to leave the field. The impact smashed vertebrae in his spine and he could not play for months. I was told that 20 years later Hall still suffers pain from that injury. Duncan Hall is married to Ann Oliver, Anton's aunt, though I have never talked of this to Anton.

Sure enough, in the telecast, in an incident that the commentators of the day, Keith Quinn and Grahame Thorne, did not see, Hall is seen to be kneed badly in the back. He falls back and lies for some moments on the ground in distress. He is then assisted away and takes no further part in the game, or the tour.

I see that the person responsible for kneeing Hall in the back is the All Black No 6, Mark Shaw. It is a foul of the worst kind – the ball in the ruck is nowhere near Hall.

Watching the game today I wonder if, 21 years ago, had I seen the incident, I would have had the courage of a flea to mention it as a foul by the famous and tough Mark Shaw. I hope I would have.

DECEMBER 6

Is there no end to the lengths John Mitchell will go to regain his lost status among New Zealand rugby fans? Today a new group, calling themselves *Friends of Mitch* and based in Hamilton, Mitchell's home town, release the results of an opinion poll that shows 67 per cent of New Zealanders want Mitchell reinstated as coach. I reckon this poll will probably harm Mitchell more than help him. All week, since his appearance on the TV1 *Sunday* show, he has been everywhere in the media. Peddling his backside, you might say.

I don't think it's wise for Mitchell to be doing this. The decision as to who will coach the All Blacks next year will be made by the NZRU board and not by public vote. Given the personalities on the NZRU executive, I know they will not be swayed by outside factors, so why do it Mitch?

Maybe Mitchell will get the job again. With the new management structure in place, perhaps Mr Hobbs is just saying to him: "We just want to claim back some of your previous power Mitch. You just coach them diligently."

That is eminently sensible.

Meanwhile, the other main suggested candidate, Graham Henry, of Auckland, is not saying a peep. To me, that's the smart course of action.

Let me spare a thought here for the beleaguered All Blacks media man, Matt McIlraith. I note from emails and press releases that Matt is back at his desk after the World Cup. What pressure he was under during those six weeks.

At times in this diary I have questioned whether McIlraith was doing a competent media liaison job. We wondered at times whether he was passing on our messages and requests to Mitchell. Now, when we hear admissions from Mitchell that he had difficulty facing up to his media responsibilities, perhaps we can ease back on the tough stance we took on McIlraith. To put it bluntly, the lad had a shit of a job. On one side of the closed door he had the flea-ridden rats of the media, scratching away repeatedly. On the other side there was a coach who, by his own admission, was saying "no" to most interview requests. Tough job Matt. I hope you get paid well.

Applications for the All Black coaching job close today. Chris Moller confirms what we all suspected – only two candidates out of 50 applicants meet the criteria. "The others are just poking fun at themselves," he says. I would have liked Colin Cooper to throw his hat into the ring. He's the kind of bloke who might need help with the media, but he might also be an inspirational choice to coach the All Blacks.

I hope they give Mitch another year in the job, to see how he goes under the new structure. However, I suspect the board will kick him out with as big a boot as it can find.

DECEMBER 10

The England rugby team have been having a whale of a time on their arrival home. Today a large bus drives the team through the streets, while 750,000 flag-waving Poms are going loopy at the sight of them.

John McBeth tells me today that last week, when he was flying home from a South Island function, he stopped in Christchurch to talk to Robbie Deans and John Mitchell about improving their media skills. The three had a 45-minute chat at a cafe. I would like to have been a fly on the wall at that one.

Mitchell is going on Radio Sport tomorrow for an hour of talkback. Why does he feel he has to do that? The board won't be listening. Mitchell says if he retains the job he will need help with the media.

Meanwhile, Graham Henry still has not been sighted by anyone, anywhere. We know that Henry does not have a perfect record with the media either, but he's playing the game better at the moment. It is a case of just keeping your head below the parapet – we all know what happens in New Zealand when one sticks one's head boldly over the top.

Mitch, I think "Ka-boom" is how it is written!

DECEMBER 11

On Radio Sport with Brendan Telfer today John Mitchell gives the same accomplished performance as on other occasions in recent weeks. The callers are mostly deferential to his position as one of the most recognisable people in the land. But what is the point of all this, Mitch?

DECEMBER 14

I am MC at a Christmas fun night in our suburb tonight. Father Christmas arrives and the kids flock to him. Standing in the crowd, I get asked more than once who I'm for: Mitchell or Henry? It is the question of the moment throughout the country. I reply that with the new management structure in place I think Mitch should get another year at least, but that I reckon Henry will get it.

On radio today Murray Deaker is pitching heavily for Graham Henry to get the job, but then we know that is just part of a deep mateship built from their school teaching days. Both are also close friends of John Graham, who just happens to be on the NZRU interview panel.

DECEMBER 15

I fly to Auckland today for a TVNZ Sports end-of-year get-together, combined with a look ahead to next year. Everyone is still talking about the World Cup. Flying home, John McBeth and I run into Wellington business executive Kerry McDonald. He was a fine Wellington and New Zealand Universities forward in his younger days and knows his stuff.

"I have a theory about the All Blacks in the World Cup semi-final," says Kerry. "In the stadium that night against Australia, did you notice how stiflingly hot it was?" I reply that I didn't, because I was in the luxury of an air-conditioned broadcast box. McDonald goes on: "You know what you're like when you get in a very hot place, and you get sluggish and feel tired. And sometimes your reactions reflect that you're not used to the heat. Who knows, maybe the heat got to the boys?"

It's a fair point, especially when you recall that the All Blacks had played four of their previous five World Cup games under the regulated temperature of the Telstra Dome in Melbourne. The only outdoor game they'd had was against Tonga, and that was in rain at Brisbane. The Aussies, meanwhile, had been training at Colundra, a Queensland beach resort, for weeks.

DECEMBER **16**

Still more comment and good sporting logic tonight, this time from the Busaco Road boys. The boys ask some pointed questions: why wasn't Tana picked to play those last few games? Why didn't we see hard captaincy in those last minutes against Australia? Who's going to get the coaching job? Shouldn't John Graham, as one of the interview panel, have stood aside during Graham Henry's interview, because they're mates?

I can't answer most of these questions adequately, but then neither can the rest of the country. We lads agree, as we adjourn to Wellington's famous Green Parrot restaurant for a great end-of-year dinner, that a pro-active NZRU could have looked beyond the only two applicants who met "the criteria". Why not headhunt offshore for a coach? Steve Hansen, Wayne Smith or Warren Gatland might have been interested in at least hearing the job specifications. Their departure from New Zealand had nothing to do with the current NZRU board. Or why not try for Colin Cooper? The Hurricanes coach has obviously got something as a quietly-spoken but follow-me type of leader. Cooper might have declared himself not ready for the job but the NZRU could have made him an offer he couldn't refuse. To have only two candidates who meet the criteria is a sad situation.

DECEMBER **18**

Radio talkback is going hell-for-leather about the coach today. Newspapers have pages smothered with pictures and profiles of Mitchell and Henry, and the TV news has repeated shots of the two leaving NZRU headquarters in Wellington carrying bundles of papers under their arms. The union is saying a decision will be made before Christmas.

Goodbye Mr Mitchell - hello Mr Henry?

WHAT a sad end to the journey.

Just as the All Blacks needed to go up a notch to secure World Cup glory, they went down several and gave a bumbling, thoughtless display against a magnificently prepared Australian team.

The conclusion was inevitably be that the All Blacks couldn't ...

was never assured from the current pack, attack was probably the better option, certainly the more entertaining.

But now that has failed and the coach has to go.

Also counting against Mitchell the damage was perceived ... done to All Blacks ...

D-DAY

World Cup failure is not tolerated in New Zealand. Alex Wyllie, Laurie Mains and John Hart all eventually paid the ultimate price. Today, John Mitchell tries to buck that trend. Graham Henry will ...

The verdict may have been reached

Despite his nationwide charm offensive, there aren't many in the media tipping John Mitchell to hold on to his job.

DECEMBER 19

While at home baby-sitting, an email arrives from the Rugby Union, saying a media conference to announce the All Blacks coach will be held at midday. This leads to a mad scramble of shower, shave and shampoo, plus a rearranged baby-sitting schedule, to make it on time. But I am in place at the Centre Port Offices of the New Zealand Rugby Union at high noon.

TV3 is taking a live telecast of the momentous event, interrupting a scheduled Oprah Winfrey show. Four nights earlier the same station had not interrupted programming to take live coverage of the capture of Saddam Hussein in Iraq. Clearly the announcing of an All Black coach ranks ahead of the capture of an evil dictator.

We are in the same media room where, in late May, John Mitchell had walked in to proudly announce his first test squad of 2003, to take the first tentative steps on this year's All Black journey.

Soon enough the moment arrives and in walks Jock Hobbs, followed by the new coach, Graham Henry. Chairman Jock reads from a prepared statement that says, in essence: "The old king is dead, long live the new one." At Hobbs' elbow, "Ted" Henry listens intently, pretending to scowl in the best "Unsmiling Giant" tradition of New Zealand rugby. But every time a satisfied smirk crosses his lips the cameras clatter away.

The short statement includes the phrase "this appointment comes after a comprehensive and robust process" and I immediately think: "Cripes, that bit could have been written by Mitch himself."

Henry is asked first, not about his reaction to getting the job, but about his age – he is 57. He replies that his age will be a huge advantage, saying experience is a vital factor in a job like this. I take an immediate liking to the man, he being the same age as myself.

"I have been dreaming for 30 years about this job," he says. "I am a better coach now than when I left to go to Wales. Over there I was more of a cup-winning coach, now I am much more of a people coach. I am so excited about what lies ahead. I feel privileged, I feel very excited, and I'll give it 100 per cent. I know it's a job with huge responsibility."

It is an impressive performance. Henry even uses the sponsors' names when he makes mention of the tournaments he will need to watch in 2004 to assess his potential All Black talent. At that I turn my head and whisper to Chris Moller, who is standing nearby: "He's been well briefed." Moller nods in reply. He looks very pleased.

So Mitch is gone as the All Black coach. Just like that. He is brusquely mentioned in the statement read by Hobbs. "John has a very good record as a coach and still has a lot to offer New Zealand rugby. The board thanks John for his significant contribution as All Blacks coach."

That's it – two lines for two years in the job. It's a tough world.

With the 15-minute interview over, Henry stands and moves forward, smiling and offering his hand to all the reporters and photographers present. I simply say good luck to him. The handover day to a new All Black coach is always exciting. I might be something of a fatalist, but I can't get the nagging feeling out of my head that the job will end in tears down the track. Ask Alex Wyllie, John Hart, Wayne Smith and now Mitchell. Only Laurie Mains, in recent times, was able to "retire" as All Black coach with some dignity.

Tonight on the TV news we see the other side of the day's story. A tight-lipped Mitchell, staunchly wearing an adidas T-shirt, is shown at his press conference in Hamilton. He looks grim and rigid and speaks carefully. I feel sorry for him. His words echo a feeling of being let down by the NZRU. He will be seeking a meeting with the union to find out the reasons he has been passed over. He wants to clear his name of all of the rumours that have been gathering around him in recent weeks.

KEITH QUINN COLLECTION

Is there just the hint of a curious smile in the way Graham Henry is regarding All Black media man Matt McIlraith? I wonder how they'll work as a team.

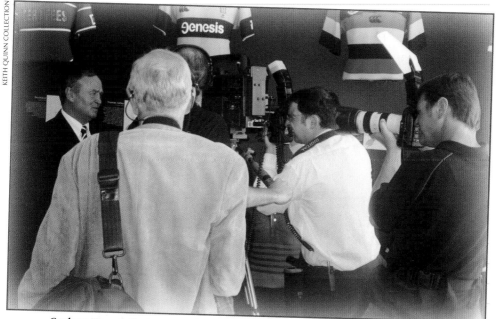

Graham Henry's first press conference as All Black coach. The unmistakable figure of legendary photographer Peter Bush is in the foreground. Bushy has been watching and photographing All Black coaches arriving and departing since the 1950s.

DECEMBER 20

The Graham Henry announcement as the new coach goes down pretty well with a section of the public, and most of the media. This is only to be expected of the latter group, despite Mitchell's frantic efforts in recent weeks to butter them up. Those reporters who stood in grim frustration outside the closed doors of the All Blacks in Melbourne have not felt inclined to endorse Mitchell staying on.

Even so, judging by the amount of calls on Radio Sport today, Mitchell still has his supporters.

A poll of 750 people by UMR Research endorsed this feeling. When asked for their preferred coach, 54 per cent opted for Mitchell and 32 per cent for Henry, with 14 per cent unsure. When asked if the World Cup semi-final loss was just one bad game or stemmed from deep-seated weaknesses in the team, 57 per cent said one bad game, 38 per cent said bigger problems and 5 per cent were unsure.

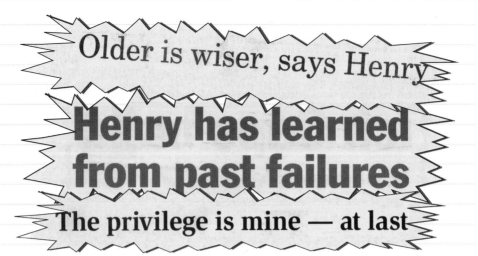

A new era dawns as Graham Henry takes over.

DECEMBER 21

In the early hours of this morning I watch the New Zealand Barbarians lose 42–17 to England in front of 75,000 at Twickenham. Only four or five of the England World Cup-winning squad play. It is a bit of a hit-and-giggle affair, although former All Black Troy Flavell spoils it with a forearm jolt across the face of the England flanker Richard Hill. He breaks Hill's nose and opens a cut above his eye that needs 13 stitches. Flavell demonstrates again that, while he has come a long way in rugby, he has no regard for its decency.

There is another turn in the John Mitchell saga today. He announces from Hamilton that he is to return to the NZRU offices in Wellington tomorrow to meet his employer to sort out "things" further. Mitchell wants to know officially why he was not reappointed, and is demanding he be cleared of rumours of misconduct in Australia. Mitchell wants to know if the gossip played a part in his downfall. He is taking his lawyer to the meeting.

DECEMBER 22

Mitchell meets Chris Moller at NZRU headquarters in Wellington. We also find out that Mitchell is in talks with the Waikato Rugby Union, which has yet to appoint its NPC coach for next season.

John Mitchell still searching for answers.

DECEMBER 23

A New Zealand Press Association report tells us that Graham Henry wants Steve Hansen, of Wales, and Wayne Smith, of Northampton, as his All Blacks coaching assistants. I would be surprised if he gets both.

DECEMBER 24

Mitchell is confirmed as Waikato's NPC coach for three years, and possibly for up to five. Two other poor buggers who were on the short list were seemingly shoved aside to accommodate the dumped All Black coach. Mitchell is also announced as an NZRU "high performance coaching advisor" for two years.

Moller's announcement has tones of a handshake and a hush-up. He says Mitchell delivered an outstanding on-field performance at the World Cup with a young and exciting All Blacks team, offset only by the disappointing loss to the Australians. Given that the NZRU implied at a Sydney press conference on November 21 that Mitchell's performance had shortcomings, to the point where it later sacked him as coach, this is a bit rich. It reminds me of political party leaders who organise a successful coup then go out of their way to praise the person they've just rolled.

The union also clears Mitchell of any "unsubstantiated and hurtful gossip and innuendo". Of course, no-one is spelling out just what the gossip and innuendo is that he's being cleared of, so it's all rather woolly and feel-good. Everything is so nice between Mitchell and the NZRU today that there is, for me, a strange aroma wafting in the air. Why has a new job been gifted to a man to whom many in the Rugby Union, from the bottom to the top, had developed such an obvious aversion?

DECEMBER 25

Christmas Day – and what a very nice family day it is, with grandkids (plural) at home for the first time, and a full card of our own kids in attendance, including daughter Shelley, now back permanently from Korea.

From All Black coach to Waikato coach. The year hasn't turned out as John Mitchell had hoped. As he so often does, Tom Scott sums up the situation expertly.

DECEMBER 26

Today Anne and I attend the official luncheon on the first day of the Boxing Day cricket test between New Zealand and Pakistan at the Basin Reserve. New Zealand Cricket chief executive Martin Snedden is kind enough to place us at his table, with luminaries such as Chris Laidlaw and Sir Robert Jones. While we dine, the conversation is not about cricket but mainly about the Rugby World Cup and the decisions made in recent days. The views of these men are intriguing. Bob Jones warms my heart by saying he enjoyed hearing me back in doing the TV commentaries. "It made me feel like none of us had aged," said Bob.

Martin Snedden wonders if the Rugby Union has announced its recent appointments in the correct order. He would have preferred the new All Black manager to be chosen first and then the coach added. That would ensure the union got its man, rather than the coach getting his preference. Chris Laidlaw recounts a quote doing the rounds from a high-ranking Rugby Union official who, when asked whether the NZRU would have sacked John Mitchell even if the All Blacks had won the World Cup, said something like: "...Er, um, it would have made it harder."

DECEMBER 27

The New Zealand Herald reports today that Graham Henry is trying to talk Troy Flavell out of signing with a Japanese club next year, to keep him in the All Black frame. That's fine by me – I encourage any attempts to keep top players from heading offshore – but in this case I support it only if Flavell can be persuaded to play within the laws of the game.

DECEMBER 29

A number of newspapers are publishing their 2003 sports quotes of the year. One from Anton Oliver has popped up. When asked to reflect on John Mitchell's demise, Oliver said: "From a selfish perspective, it offers me at least some hope of regaining All Black honours next year."

DECEMBER 31

We're all geniuses in hindsight, but as I sit here basking in Wellington's sun, I can't help reflecting on what has been a tumultuous year for New Zealand rugby, and for the All Blacks in particular.

Some key questions need addressing, and as someone who followed things closely all year, I'll do my best to answer them.

Did the All Blacks have the talent to win the World Cup?

I don't think so. As I said throughout this diary, I always felt England were the best team. They were the No 1 team at the start of 2003, they played like champions all year and they produced the goods when it counted – at the World Cup.

I thought John Mitchell and his fellow selectors did a pretty good job of picking their World Cup combination. There was a lot of fuss about a few big-name omissions, but overall, I agreed with the selectors. I wouldn't have picked Christian Cullen – he was a couple of years past his best. Andrew Mehrtens left his run too late. He didn't have the focus, commitment or fitness during the first half of the year, when the selectors were doing their work. By the time Mehrtens started to play with conviction and look more like the player of old, it was too late. The die was cast and he had been excluded.

Taine Randell could have been chosen, but it would have been a line-ball decision and I certainly wouldn't classify his omission as a mistake. Having Randell in Australia wouldn't have won us the World Cup.

The only selection with which I am at issue was the choice of Corey Flynn ahead of Anton Oliver. That was cruelly unfair on Oliver (and, I suspect, Flynn). Oliver might have made a significant difference at the World Cup. I can only surmise that Oliver was disregarded for matters other than rugby because his performances on the paddock certainly merited his selection.

The All Blacks simply weren't the best team at the World Cup, no matter what players were chosen.

Did Mitchell coach the All Blacks well?

He did some good things and some not so good, as with most coaches. I loved the sort of rugby he tried to get the All Blacks to play. He developed an exciting, potent backline full of flair and try-scoring potential. That made the All Blacks a terrific team to watch. He introduced some talented players to the big-time, players like Joe Rokocoko and Mils Muliaina.

On the other hand, he got it wrong with the forwards. Not his selections – he chose the best players around. But the All Black forwards under Mitchell failed to establish dominance. There was talk that Mitchell discouraged rucking, possibly to avoid conceding penalties. He wanted the All Blacks to win matches in the backs, but disregarded the importance of doing the spadework up front first, to set the platform.

It was revealing that the World Cup winners were the team that played in the old style, making sure they won the forward battle. Rugby is evolving quickly, but we went too far too fast and didn't emphasise forward dominance enough. In that respect, you'd have to say the All Black forwards were not as well coached as the backs.

What about some of Mitchell's selection decisions at the World Cup?

There were two critical aspects – the injury to Tana Umaga and the loss of confidence in Carlos Spencer's goal-kicking. The impact of those two factors hurt New Zealand.

Umaga's injury was unfortunate, but it would have been somewhat overcome if a top-class centre like Ma'a Nonu or Muliaina had taken his place. Instead the selectors were desperate to have MacDonald in the side because they wanted his goal-kicking. I felt the All Black management should have had more faith in Spencer. He'd been their kicker all season and he wasn't inferior in that regard to MacDonald. Once they decided Spencer wouldn't do the goal-kicking, there was a bit of chaos in the ranks.

The decision to play MacDonald at centre, of all places, was questionable. If he had to play, surely it would have been preferable to play him in his best position – fullback – and put Muliaina at centre, where he has played so much of his rugby. The Aussies targeted MacDonald and ran through him from the opening minutes. It was a chink in the All Black armour in the semi-final.

I was surprised there wasn't more faith shown in Nonu, who is a brilliant attacking player. Mitchell and his assistant, Robbie Deans, clearly didn't have confidence in Nonu's defence, but had had him in the All Black squad all season and work should have been done to tidy up his deficiencies in that area.

Ben Atiga was drafted into the All Black squad during the World Cup when Ben Blair went home. But Atiga was only ever going to be a back-up player. There was a suggestion that Mehrtens should have been called in at that point, but people saying that were not being realistic.

Mitchell made the decision that he wasn't going to select either Cullen or Mehrtens for the World Cup. It was an important and significant call and to expect him to back down midway through the tournament was silly. I don't go along with the theory that Mehrtens would have kicked the goals to win us the World Cup. He has been a very good goal-kicker, but not infallible. To assume he would have landed every goal from anywhere on the park, no matter what the pressure, is naive. I recall him missing the vital drop kick during the 1995 World Cup final and I can remember a succession of mistakes he made for the All Blacks in 2002. Mehrtens has been a great player, but he has always been as fallible as anyone else.

Was Mitchell out-coached during the World Cup?

Yes, without doubt – especially in the game New Zealand lost. Perhaps we All Black supporters were lulled into a false sense of security because of some early big wins. The draw did the New Zealand team no favours because we won our early pool games so comfortably.

When things came to the crunch, Wallaby coach Eddie Jones out-thought Mitchell. The Aussies targeted the weak links in the All Black side, like MacDonald at centre. They denied the All Blacks possession. And we had no counter, no plan B. We went into the game hoping and expecting to win because of the brilliance of our backline, but had no alternate plan when it because obvious the backline was not going to get the chance to rip the game apart.

Over the year, did Mitchell do a good job?

While there were aspects of Mitchell's performance that were sub-standard, I thought that overall he was good. There was much to be admired in his attitude. He decided to choose a young team and to play with speed and commit to attack. Mitchell is only 39 and relatively new to coaching, so I imagine he is still learning and improving.

As a person and in his capacity as All Black coach off the field, Mitchell let himself down. I've known him for a long time and he is a good bloke, very genial. But he put up a wall to the public and the media and came across as uncommunicative and gruff and arrogant. That's not the Mitchell I've known. During 2003 I saw glimpses of the real Mitchell, but it seemed he was going to take the All Blacks out of the public domain. Would it not have been great to see our All Blacks as open and free with their public as were the Wallabies this year? As the home team, Australia were under enormous pressure, yet Eddie Jones and George Gregan were always available and smiling. Our chaps were not. That was sad to see. And at the end of the World Cup final, when disappointment must have been shattering, the Aussie team and their supporters brought honour and esteem to themselves and their country by the manner in which they accepted their disappointment. Did our team do the same? No, they did not. To their everlasting discredit, the All Black bosses sent out kids to talk to their waiting home public after the semi-final loss.

The All Blacks were far too introspective. We had various secret training sessions, a lack of inter-action with the media and, in the end, quite an unpopular team because of its aloofness.

Mitchell must take most of the blame for this. It was his show and he was shaping the team as he wanted it. He had the management structure he wanted and punted that it would return from Australia with the World Cup. It didn't.

Mitchell lost his job as All Blacks coach because he lost touch with his greatest allies, the New Zealand rugby public. The confused Mitch-speak was contrived to confuse when he should explained in as simple terms as possible. His qualities as a coach were good enough for him to be employed by England a few years ago and to be welcomed as All Black coach in 2001. However, those qualities became submerged this year as the pressures of the post weighed down on him and he adopted a siege mentality.

Did Reuben Thorne deserve his place in the All Black team and should he have been the captain?

Thorne was a figure of controversy all year. My feeling was that he deserved his place in the team, but that making him captain did not work.

The position of blindside flanker is probably the most unspectacular in modern rugby. It is the responsibility of this player to police the rucks and mauls and to prevent breakouts by the opposition. It's a stopping role, "guard dog duty", as Grant Fox so colourfully described it. I cannot name one blindside flanker from the World Cup who shone in that position.

Australia used two openside flankers, George Smith and Phil Waugh, to good effect. That was also an option for Mitchell, who could have gone with Marty Holah and Richie McCaw, as Fred Allen used Waka Nathan and Kel Tremain in the 1960s, while in the late 1970s Graham Mourie packed down with such other openside flankers as Ken Stewart and Leicester Rutledge. But Mitchell decided to go the more conservative

Reuben Thorne ... good player, but not the most inspirational of captains.

way, with specialist openside and blindside flankers. England did the same, and Richard Hill was as unspectacular for them as Thorne was for the All Blacks.

People who criticised Thorne were perhaps looking for a blindside flanker more in the mould of Alan Whetton, who in the 1980s shone with his driving running. But the position has evolved and we don't see blindside specialists in that role much now. I thought Thorne had a reasonably good season as a player and merited his selection. Don't forget that Mitchell is the third All Black coach, following John Hart and Wayne Smith, to pick Thorne, who is closing in on 50 test matches, so he must be doing something right.

If Mitchell had wanted to look elsewhere he could have tried Jerry Collins as No 6, but I don't think he would have been as efficient as Thorne in the guard dog role, though he might have stood out more because of the odd bullocking run.

Thorne the captain is a different story, however. I have mentioned a number of times in this diary that when the going got tough for the All Blacks, I looked for leadership signs from Thorne and didn't see them. I like a captain in the George Gregan-Martin Johnson mould, imploring his troops to greater efforts at times of crisis. But I saw none of this from Thorne. Where was the cajoling, the urging? Graham Mourie and Sean Fitzpatrick were terrific when the game got close and a special effort was needed. They could lift their troops. Wayne Shelford was a lead-from-the-front skipper who inspired by his actions.

Thorne was the ultimate strong, silent type. But he was too silent. Going back to the 1960s, Brian Lochore was a quiet, almost reticent personality, especially in his early days as All Black captain. But there was always a certain steel about him. Even though he came from a minor union and was leading players of the stature of Ken Gray, Colin Meads and Kel Tremain, he would have his say when he thought it was required. He was always the captain, and at times of urgency he made sure his men knew what he wanted. I never saw enough of that from Thorne.

As a bloke, Thorne is a very nice person, not driven in any way by ego. But he didn't quite do it for me as a captain, and during that torrid World Cup semi-final against Australia we really needed a captain. Mitchell might deny this but I think he chose as his captain, perhaps subconsciously, a person and a player in his own mould, someone he'd be compatible with.

It didn't work. Reuben Thorne simply didn't have the colour and dash of an outstanding captain. His after-match comments lacked breadth of expression. Sean Fitzpatrick cultivated the after-match interview and some of his expressions have become catchphrases. Graham Mourie was always intelligent and interesting. Wilson Whineray was a wonderful speaker. As for Thorne ... well, it's difficult to imagine him making a living on the speaking circuit.

My captain, once Mitchell had ruled out Oliver, would have been McCaw, despite his relative youth. He was a genuinely world-class player, and being on the openside flank was always in the thick of it, and therefore able to lead by example. He has proved a good thinker and I noticed that when things got close he took on quite a leadership role within the team anyway.

Did the All Blacks have a successful year?

No, the harsh reality is that the All Blacks failed in 2003. They might have won the Tri-Nations and the Bledisloe Cups and scored brilliant tries and beaten Australia and South Africa by record margins, but they lost in the semi-finals of the World Cup. In a World Cup year, that's all that matters.

John Hart's 1999 All Blacks won the Tri-Nations, but no-one says they had a triumphant year because they lost in the World Cup semi-finals. It was the same with Mitchell's team.

Would I have retained Mitchell as coach?

Yes, I would have. I'd have given him a one-year contract and seen how he operated under a different management structure. It would have been interesting to see a chastened Mitchell operating with a strong manager, someone like Sean Fitzpatrick, running the show. Maybe Mitchell would have adjusted and we'd have seen him flower as a coach.

Is Graham Henry a good replacement?

I'm definitely not unhappy with Henry's promotion. If Mitchell was to be sacked, as it seemed from about September that he was going to be, Henry was a good choice to replace him.

Henry has a proven track record at NPC and Super 12 level. He has coached at international level and he is extremely experienced. There has been criticism of him in the past that he has been too dour and a bit prickly, but, being optimistic, I like to think he has matured in this area.

He's 57, and he seems to have learnt a lot along the way. I was very impressed with how he handled things in the last weeks of 2003. He didn't get caught up in the publicity campaign before the election of the All Black coach. He stayed out of that, which was a sensible decision.

When he was named coach he showed humility and pride in his appointment. He did all the right things, like mentioning the sponsors and shaking hands with the media people at the press conference. Of course, it's a honeymoon period and it may all be different in the middle of 2004 at the height of the battle, but I liked what I saw at the end of this year.

What about the role of Robbie Deans?

Deans hitched his star to the Mitchell wagon. In December, he stood only as Mitchell's assistant when he obviously had the credentials to have a crack at the top job himself. But I wouldn't rule him out as a future All Black coach and not that far in the future, either.

I think Deans should be exempt from much of the criticism of this year's All Blacks. Mitchell was the boss, the gaffer. Deans was merely his assistant and, as such, it was important he fell in with his boss and didn't rock the boat. I've heard a number of assistant coaches say it's a thankless job because in that position you are morally obliged to follow the boss. If there is criticism of the image of the All Blacks, or the selections, that criticism should be directed at Mitchell, not Deans. Deans was a loyal deputy.

Can Mitchell be All Black coach again?

Absolutely. He's 18 years younger than Henry, so has many years ahead and it's logical to think he will improve as a coach.

I can see a line of succession something like this: Henry, then Colin Cooper or Wayne Smith or Steve Hansen, then Robbie Deans, then perhaps Mitchell. That's a timeline of only about 10 or 12 years.

It's incredible how quickly things change in New Zealand rugby. The turnover is amazing. I doubt that Graham Henry would have been appointed All Black coach if David Moffet and Rob Fisher were still in charge. But they've gone, and so have their successors, David Rutherford and Murray McCaw. A new regime, headed by Jock Hobbs and Chris Moller, had no compunction about going with Henry. There was no loss of faith for them, whereas Moffet and Fisher might have still regarded Henry as the bloke who walked out on them in 1998.

In a decade's time, with new people in charge, I can't see why those making the decision would have any problem in picking Mitchell as All Black coach if he was the best person for the job at that time.

Besides the Rugby Union and the coaches and players, I hope the New Zealand rugby public learns something from 2003. We as a rugby nation have to realise that we are not the greatest as of right, and learn from those who are, for the moment, our betters in the game. Their systems, their planning, their leadership and their ability to take defeat as well as one should take victory.

By doing two dozen or so test commentaries this year, I was gloriously reminded again of the risks every broadcaster takes. There was the usual broad assessment of my trade by viewers and reviewers – from being voted the best at TV rugby commentary in New Zealand in one paper (*The New Zealand Herald*) to being called "too old" and "the most boring" by the same newspaper only weeks later. Life is still fun. And it's still baffling.

In the end one rugby memory stands out in 2003. It was that moment on a rainy November night in Sydney when a handsome young Englishman, born to be great at such a time, grabbed one last pass in extra time in the World Cup final and sent a trademark dropkick towards the posts. The spinning kick by 24-year-old Jonny Wilkinson was a classic example of grace under pressure. When it went over it signalled not just the winning of the World Cup, but that the most appropriate player had sealed his place in history.

And it signalled that the best team had won the Cup. England's courage, planning and professionalism bred in them a confidence to stick to their game plan throughout. I felt privileged to be there to watch their journey end in triumph. What a shame it wasn't our team that brought home the big prize.

I pay tribute to the England rugby team by hoisting their flag outside my house. In rugby terms, it's been their year.

MITCH-SPEAK

Throughout the year, and especially at the World Cup, many New Zealanders were confused by the way John Mitchell expressed himself. His utterances became known as "Mitch-speak", but the curious way the All Black coach used the Queen's English might also have been called "rugby non-speak", "rugby babble", "Stengelese", gobbledegook, or "speaking in tongues".

However, as *The New Zealand Herald* said late in the year, "his manner of speaking was nothing a good interpreter couldn't fix". Here is a glossary of terms from the John Mitchell dictionary:

A

Absorb – "We showed we can absorb a lot under pressure today" – JM after New Zealand versus Wales, Sydney, November11, 2003.

Accuracy – "We intend to make the team strong in accuracy" – JM, at the announcement of the first All Black team, Wellington, May 26, 2003.

Accountability – "The accountability is back with the team now" – at the announcement of JM's All Black team to play France, Melbourne, November 18, 2003.

B

Barometer – "Ali Williams' barometer is his enthusiasm" – JM after Williams' comeback game versus Tonga, Brisbane, November 2003.

Block-building – "This team is in a block-building process" – JM in June 2003 after the All Blacks played England.

Breached – "We breached a lot today, which is really encouraging" – JM after the All Blacks versus Italy game, Melbourne, October 2003.

C

Channel – "His channel can't afford to leak"– JM's job description of a first five-eighth to Phil Gifford on Radio Sport, July 8, 2003.

Chemistry – "The team's chemistry is phenomenal" – JM during an interview with Bernadine Oliver-Kerby, Melbourne, October 2003.

Cut the cake – "We must cut the cake with this All Black team and good players will miss out" – JM after the announcement of the All Blacks to play France in Christchurch, June 2003.

D

De-clutter – "When I get the team from Super 12 play, I have to de-clutter their team cultures" – JM after the announcement of the first All Black team, May 26, 2003.

Defence compliance – "Defence compliance is going to be important to us this year" – JM after the first All Black team was announced for the year, Wellington, May 26, 2003.

Dominant tackler – "Corey Flynn is a very dominant tackler" – JM at the World Cup team announcement, August 2003.

Drivers – "On the field today we had discussions with our drivers" – JM after the Tonga game, Brisbane 2003.

E

Executed – "We executed quite well today" – JM after All Blacks versus Tonga game, Brisbane 2003.

Execution – "Our execution was poor today. We did not deserve to win." – JM after the loss to Australia, November 2003.

Evolvement – "[With Corey Flynn] we see the evolvement of a different type of hooker" – JM when the All Black World Cup team was announced, August 2003.

F

Faith – as in "I have faith in the whole squad." JM's way of saying: "I will have a policy of rotation in team selection."

Fleas – to be fair this was actually a description of the news media given by JM's co-selector Mark Shaw, October 2003, but it deserves a place here. (See also lizards)

Fulfilment and growth – "I saw fulfilment and growth after the hiccup [of losing]" at Sydney last year – JM, quoted in *Australian Rugby Review,* preview edition, 2002.

G

Graduated – "We've graduated Aaron's foot injury" – JM at a press conference in Melbourne, October 2003.

Grinds – "We have to be able to win our grinds" – JM talks about tough games after All Blacks versus Australia, Auckland, August 2003.

Grouping – "Reuben is strong in his grouping on the field" – JM describing the play of his captain.

H

Hill – JM at Brisbane after All Blacks v Tonga, Brisbane, November, 2003. As in: "Richie McCaw is the Richard Hill of our team."

Hemisphere (southern) – as in "[the All Blacks team] now has the opportunity to carry the southern hemisphere flag [in the third place game].

I

Inches – "We didn't win the inches on the tackle line" – JM after All Blacks versus Australia, Sydney, November 2003.

Immaturity – "Immaturity cost us the Cup" – JM after the All Blacks beat France for third place, November 20, 2003.

Irrelevant – as in: "That is irrelevant to us". JM, when asked on the team's arrival in Australia why the All Blacks had maintained such a low profile before arriving?

J

June-work – "We've been looking at our June-work" – JM summarising the first tests played by his 2003 All Blacks.

Journey – the word JM used most constantly to describe the games ahead to the World Cup, and the passing of the months leading up to it. It became his trademark description of the season.

K

Keith – as in: "That's a good question, Keith." Heard several times on the Sky TV live telecast at the press conference after the announcement of the first All

Black squad in Wellington, May 26, thus making Quinn endure countless barbs from his media colleagues about being "up Mitchell's bum!".

L

Line of detail – "No differential lies between the line of detail" – JM in June 2003, to a mystified press group.

Lizards – reporters, writers, men and women of the media. A common expression used around JM's All Blacks this year. (see also fleas)

Loyalty – "Loyalty is a great word, but it does not exist in professional sport. It is what the players offer now and what we want now" – JM after his second squad selection, July 6, 2003.

M

Mix – "We're happy with the mix" – JM on the blend of players in his team at the announcement of the World Cup squad, Ponsonby Rugby Club, Auckland, August 2003.

N

Number six – "Is he the number six? I've never heard of him" – JM after the Wales versus New Zealand match when asked, "Have you ever heard of Shane Williams?" Williams actually was the exhilarating number 14, while number six was the outstanding Jonathan Thomas. JM apparently didn't know who either of those blokes was.

O

Outcome – "If the preparation is right the outcome will take care of itself" – a quote repeated often by JM in 2002–2003.

P

Predictable – "Anton's become too predictable in his lines this season" – JM after dropping Anton Oliver, in July 2003.

Process – "We're focused on the process, not the outcome" – JM at the All Blacks game versus Tonga, Brisbane, 2003.

Productive – "We have 28 productive players in this team at the moment" (Two were injured) – JM after the All Blacks game versus Tonga, Brisbane, 2003.

Q

Quantity – "The quantity of work offered by Anton hasn't been good so far" – JM to Phil Gifford, on Radio Sport, July 8, 2003.

Quality youth – "We have quality youth in our team" – JM interview with Keith Quinn, Terrace Downs, September 2003.

R

Rest and rehabilitation – JM's description of those left out of the touring team for the tour to Europe at the end of 2002.

Reload – "We are here to reload the fitness of the team" – JM interview with Keith Quinn, Terrace Downs, September 2003.

S

Skill habits – "We think [Andrew] Mehrtens should work on his skill habits" (Also "skill shifts" and "skill sets", uttered about other players at times during the year.)

Salvage – "The game against France is important because there's now something to salvage for" – JM at press conference, Melbourne, November 18, 2003.

Shared – "I've shared about [this topic] before" – JM talking about rucking the night after the All Blacks test with Wales, Melbourne, November 2, 2003 (Published in *Daily Telegraph* November 6 and described as "one of the most incomprehensible examples of coach-speak at the tournament".)

Slow-ball – "There was a lot of slow-ball, which ends up as being no-ball" – JM after All Blacks versus Australia, Sydney, November 15, 2003.

T

Tackle lines – "We've been disappointed with Anton's tackle lines this season" – JM after dropping Anton Oliver, August 2003.

Tier of talent – "There is a tier of talent who we want to grow" – JM before the 2002 end-of-year tour.

Triangle – "It's hard when you lose a triangle of experience like that" – JM at Sky TV Steinlager Awards, November 27, 2003. (He was possibly referring to Tana Umaga, Chris Jack and Justin Marshall.)

Unknown quantity – "An unknown quantity is a dangerous animal" – JM after the announcement of his first squad for the 2003 season.

Vision – "Clearly we have a vision" – JM interview with Keith Quinn, Terrace Downs, September 2003.

Wider group – "He has not been included in the All Blacks squad but instead he's gone into our wider group" – JM's description of those players he has dropped from his All Black team.

X-factor – "I think Reuben's got it" – JM's response to a question at a press conference, Auckland, 2003.

Youthful vigour aplenty – "This year's All Blacks will have youthful vigour aplenty" – JM in interview with Keith Quinn, Terrance Downs, September 2003.

Z

Zzzzzzzzzz – the sound of rugby reporters from all over the world falling asleep while trying to untangle "Mitch speak" specials during the year.

THE ALL BLACK YEAR IN STATISTICS BY PETER MARRIOTT

2003 WORLD CUP IN AUSTRALIA

Pool A: *Argentina, Australia, Ireland, Namibia, Romania* **Pool B:** *Fiji, France, Japan, Scotland, United States*
Pool C: *England, Georgia, Samoa, South Africa, Uruguay* **Pool D:** *Canada, Italy, New Zealand, Tonga, Wales*

POOL MATCHES

Date	Pool	Teams	City	Won by	Score
10/10	A	Argentina v Australia	Sydney	Australia	24–8
11/10	D	Italy v New Zealand	Melbourne	New Zealand	70–7
11/10	A	Ireland v Romania	Gosford	Ireland	45–17
11/10	B	Fiji v France	Brisbane	France	61–18
11/10	C	South Africa v Uruguay	Perth	South Africa	72–6
12/10	D	Canada v Wales	Melbourne	Wales	41–10
12/10	B	Japan v Scotland	Townsville	Scotland	32–11
12/10	C	England v Georgia	Perth	England	84–6
14/10	A	Argentina v Namibia	Gosford	Argentina	67–14
15/10	B	Fiji v United States	Brisbane	Fiji	19–18
15/10	D	Italy v Tonga	Canberra	Italy	36–12
15/10	C	Samoa v Uruguay	Perth	Samoa	60–13
17/10	D	Canada v New Zealand	Melbourne	New Zealand	68–6
18/10	A	Australia v Romania	Brisbane	Australia	90–8
18/10	B	France v Japan	Townsville	France	51–29
18/10	C	England v South Africa	Perth	England	25–6
19/10	D	Tonga v Wales	Canberra	Wales	27–20
19/10	A	Ireland v Namibia	Sydney	Ireland	64–7
19/10	C	Georgia v Samoa	Perth	Samoa	46–9
20/10	B	Scotland v United States	Brisbane	Scotland	39–15
21/10	D	Canada v Italy	Canberra	Italy	19–14
22/10	A	Argentina v Romania	Sydney	Argentina	50–3
23/10	B	Fiji v Japan	Townsville	Fiji	41–13
24/10	D	New Zealand v Tonga	Brisbane	New Zealand	91–7
24/10	C	Georgia v South Africa	Sydney	South Africa	46–19
25/10	A	Australia v Namibia	Adelaide	Australia	142–0
25/10	D	Italy v Wales	Canberra	Wales	27–15
25/10	B	France v Scotland	Sydney	France	51–9
26/10	A	Argentina v Ireland	Adelaide	Ireland	16–15
26/10	C	England v Samoa	Melbourne	England	35–22

Pool Matches continued over ...

Date	Pool	Teams	City	Won by	Score
27/10	B	Japan v United States	Gosford	United States	39–26
28/10	C	Georgia v Uruguay	Sydney	Uruguay	24–12
29/10	D	Canada v Tonga	Wollongong	Canada	24–7
30/10	A	Namibia v Romania	Launceston	Romania	37–7
31/10	B	France v United States	Wollongong	France	41–14
01/11	B	Fiji v Scotland	Sydney	Scotland	22–20
01/11	C	Samoa v South Africa	Brisbane	South Africa	60–10
01/11	A	Australia v Ireland	Melbourne	Australia	17–16
02/11	C	England v Uruguay	Brisbane	England	111–13
02/11	D	New Zealand v Wales	Sydney	New Zealand	53–37

FINAL POOL STANDINGS

POOL A	P	W	L	D	For	Agst	Pts
Australia	4	4	–	–	273	32	18
Ireland	4	3	1	–	141	56	15
Argentina	4	2	2	–	140	57	11
Romania	4	1	3	–	65	192	5
Namibia	4	–	4	–	28	310	–

POOL C	P	W	L	D	For	Agst	Pts
England	4	4	–	–	255	47	19
Sth Africa	4	3	1	–	184	60	15
Samoa	4	2	2	–	138	117	10
Uruguay	4	1	3	–	56	255	4
Georgia	4	–	4	–	46	200	–

POOL B	P	W	L	D	For	Agst	Pts
France	4	4	–	–	204	70	20
Scotland	4	3	1	–	102	97	14
Fiji	4	2	2	–	98	114	10
USA	4	1	3	–	86	125	6
Japan	4	–	4	–	79	163	–

POOL D	P	W	L	D	For	Agst	Pts
NZ	4	4	–	–	282	57	20
Wales	4	3	1	–	132	98	14
Italy	4	2	2	–	77	123	8
Canada	4	1	3	–	54	135	5
Tonga	4	–	4	–	46	178	1

QUARTER-FINALS

Date	Teams	City	Won by	Score
08/11	New Zealand v South Africa	Melbourne	New Zealand	29–9
08/11	Australia v Scotland	Brisbane	Australia	33–16
09/11	France v Ireland	Melbourne	France	43–21
09/11	England v Wales	Brisbane	England	28–17

SEMI-FINALS

15/11	Australia v New Zealand	Sydney	Australia	22–10
16/11	England v France	Sydney	England	24–7

THIRD/FOURTH PLACE PLAY-OFF

20/11	France v New Zealand	Sydney	New Zealand	40–13

FINAL

22/11	Australia v England	Sydney	England	20–17

NEW ZEALAND TEAM RECORD 2003

Played 14   Won 12   Lost 2   Drawn 0   Points for 602   Points against 207

Date	Versus	City	Result	Tries	Cons	Pens	Drops
14/06	England	Wellington	L 13–15	D Howlett	C Spencer	C Spencer (2)	
21/06	Wales	Hamilton	W 55–3	J Rokocoko (2), T Umaga, D Howlett, C Spencer, D Carter, K Mealamu, K Meeuws	D Carter (6)	D Carter	
28/06	France	Christchurch	W 31–23	J Rokocoko (3)	D Carter (2)	D Carter (4)	
19/07	South Africa (T-N)	Pretoria	W 52–16	D Howlett (2), J Rokocoko (2), C Spencer, K Meeuws, A Mauger	C Spencer (4)	C Spencer (3)	
26/07	Australia (T-N)	Sydney	W 50–21	J Rokocoko (3), D Howlett, T Umaga, A Mauger, D Carter	C Spencer (2), D Carter	C Spencer (3)	
09/08	South Africa (T-N)	Dunedin	W 19–11	J Rokocoko	C Spencer	C Spencer (4)	
16/08	Australia (T-N)	Auckland	W 21–17	D Howlett (2)	C Spencer	C Spencer (3)	
11/10	Italy (WC)	Melbourne	W 70–7	D Howlett (2), J Rokocoko (2), C Spencer (2), J Marshall, B Thorn, R Thorne, D Carter, L MacDonald	D Carter (6)	C Spencer	
17/10	Canada (WC)	Melbourne	W 68–6	M Muliaina (4), R So'oialo (2), C Ralph (2), M Nonu, K Meeuws	D Carter (9)		
24/10	Tonga (WC)	Brisbane	W 91–7	M Muliaina (2), D Howlett (2), C Ralph (2), D Carter, C Spencer, D Braid, C Flynn, K Meeuws, L MacDonald, penalty try	L MacDonald (12), C Spencer		
02/11	Wales (WC)	Sydney	W 53–37	J Rokocoko (2), D Howlett (2), L MacDonald, A Williams, A Mauger, C Spencer	L MacDonald (5)	L MacDonald	
08/11	South Africa (WCQF)	Melbourne	W 29–9	L MacDonald, K Mealamu, J Rokocoko	L MacDonald	L MacDonald (3)	A Mauger
15/11	Australia (WCSF)	Sydney	L 10–22	R Thorne	L MacDonald	L MacDonald	
20/11	France (WCPO)	Sydney	W 40–13	C Jack, D Howlett, J Rokocoko, B Thorn, M Muliaina, M Holah	D Carter (4), L MacDonald		

NEW ZEALAND TESTS 2003

PLAYER	TESTS BEFORE 2003	ENGLAND at Wellington	WALES at Hamilton	FRANCE at Christchurch	SOUTH AFRICA (T-N) at Pretoria	AUSTRALIA (T-N) at Sydney	SOUTH AFRICA (T-N) at Dunedin	AUSTRALIA (T-N) at Auckland	ITALY (WC) at Melbourne	CANADA (WC) at Melbourne	TONGA (WC) at Brisbane	WALES (WC) at Sydney	SOUTH AFRICA (QF) at Melbourne	AUSTRALIA (SF) at Sydney	FRANCE (PO) at Sydney
Doug Howlett	24	FB	W	W	W	W	W	W	W	r	W	W	W	W	W
Mils Muliaina	–	r	FB	FB	FB	FB	FB	FB	FB	W	FB	FB	FB	FB	FB
Ben Atiga	–	–	–	–	–	–	–	–	–	–	r	–	–	–	–
Ben Blair +	4	–	–	–	–	–	–	–	–	–	–	–	–	–	–
Leon MacDonald	18	–	–	–	–	–	–	r	r	FB	C	C	C	C	C
Joe Rokocoko	–	W	W	W	W	W	W	W	W	–	–	W	W	W	W
Caleb Ralph	8	W	–	–	–	–	–	–	–	W	W	–	r	–	r
Ma'a Nonu	–	C	–	–	–	–	–	–	r	C	r	–	–	–	–
Tana Umaga	45	2	C	C	C	C	C	C	C	–	–	–	–	–	–
Daniel Carter	–	–	2	2	–	r	–	–	2	2	2	–	r	–	r
Aaron Mauger	11	–	–	–	2	2	2	2	–	–	–	2	2	2	2
Carlos Spencer	15	1	1	1	1	1	1	1	1	1	1	1	1	1	1
Justin Marshall	60	½	–	–	r	½	½	½	½	–	½	½	½	½	–
Steve Devine	2	r	½	½	½	r	–	–	–	½	–	–	r	–	½
Byron Kelleher	23	–	–	r	–	–	–	–	–	–	–	–	–	r	–
Rodney So'oialo	1	8	–	–	r	–	–	–	r	8	8	r	–	–	–
Jerry Collins	1	r	8	8	8	8	8	8	8	–	–	8	8	8	8
Reuben Thorne	27	F	F	F	F	F	F	F	F	F	F	F	F	F	F
Richie McCaw	9	F	–	F	F	F	–	F	F	r	r	F	F	F	F
Marty Holah	13	–	F	r	–	r	F	–	r	F	r	r	r	r	r
Daniel Braid	1	–	–	–	–	–	–	–	–	r	F	–	–	–	–
Ali Williams	3	L	L	L	L	L	L	L	–	–	L	L	L	L	L
Chris Jack	13	L	L	L	L	L	r	L	L	L	–	–	L	L	L
Brad Thorn	–	–	–	r	r	r	r	L	–	L	L	L	L	r	r
Greg Somerville	22	P	–	P	P	P	r	P	P	–	P	P	P	P	P
Dave Hewett	10	P	–	P	P	P	P	P	P	–	r	P	P	P	P
Kees Meeuws	24	–	P	r	r	r	P	–	r	P	P	r	r	r	r
Carl Hoeft	27	–	P	–	–	–	–	–	–	–	P	–	–	–	r
Anton Oliver	39	H	–	H	–	–	–	–	–	–	–	–	–	–	–
Keven Mealamu	1	r	H	r	H	H	r	H	H	–	–	H	H	H	H
Mark Hammett	21	–	–	–	r	r	H	–	r	H	–	r	r	–	r
Corey Flynn	–	–	–	–	–	–	–	–	–	r	H	–	–	–	–

Note: + Ben Blair travelled to the World Cup as a member of the New Zealand team but did not appear in any matches. He returned home due to "injury" and was replaced by Ben Atiga.

NEW ZEALAND APPEARANCES AND POINTS IN 2003

	Player	Tests	T	C	P	DG	Pts
1	Ben Atiga	1 [1]	–	–	–	–	–
2	Daniel Braid	2 [1]	1	–	–	–	5
3	Daniel Carter	8 [3]	4	28	5	–	91
4	Jerry Collins	12 [1]	–	–	–	–	–
5	Steve Devine	8 [3]	–	–	–	–	–
6	Corey Flynn	2 [1]	1	–	–	–	5
7	Mark Hammett	8 [6]	–	–	–	–	–
8	Dave Hewett	12 [1]	–	–	–	–	–
9	Carl Hoeft	3 [1]	–	–	–	–	–
10	Marty Holah	11 [8]	1	–	–	–	5
11	Doug Howlett	14 [1]	14	–	–	–	70
12	Chris Jack	12 [1]	1	–	–	–	5
13	Byron Kelleher	2 [2]	–	–	–	–	–
14	Leon MacDonald	8 [2]	4	20	5	–	75
15	Justin Marshall	10 [1]	1	–	–	–	5
16	Aaron Mauger	8	3	–	–	1	18
17	Richie McCaw	12 [2]	–	–	–	–	–
18	Keven Mealamu	12 [3]	2	–	–	–	10
19	Kees Meeuws	11 [7]	4	–	–	–	20
20	Mils Muliaina	14 [1]	7	–	–	–	35
21	Ma'a Nonu	4 [2]	1	–	–	–	5
22	Anton Oliver	2	–	–	–	–	–
23	Caleb Ralph	5 [2]	4	–	–	–	20
24	Joe Rokocoko	12	17	–	–	–	85
25	Greg Somerville	12 [1]	–	–	–	–	–
26	Rodney So'oialo	6 [3]	2	–	–	–	10
27	Carlos Spencer	14	6	10	16	–	98
28	Brad Thorn	12 [7]	2	–	–	–	10
29	Reuben Thorne (capt)	14	2	–	–	–	10
30	Tana Umaga	8	2	–	–	–	10
31	Ali Williams	12	1	–	–	–	5
	penalty try		1				5
		271 [61]	81	58	26	1	602

Note: The figure on the right-hand side of the Tests column indicates the number of occasions a player appeared as a substitute and/or a replacement in a match. This figure is included in the total test appearances for that player.

NEW ZEALAND
CAREER RECORDS OF 2003 TEST PLAYERS
Records to 1 January 2004

Player	Debut	Tests	T	C	P	DG	Pts
Ben Atiga	2003	1	–	–	–	–	–
Daniel Braid	2002	3	1	–	–	–	5
Daniel Carter	2003	8	4	28	5	–	91
Jerry Collins	2001	13	–	–	–	–	–
Steve Devine	2002	10	–	–	–	–	–
Corey Flynn	2003	2	1	–	–	–	5
Mark Hammett	1999	29	3	–	–	–	15
Dave Hewett	2001	22	2	–	–	–	10
Carl Hoeft	1998	30	–	–	–	–	–
Marty Holah	2001	24	3	–	–	–	15
Doug Howlett	2000	38	31	–	–	–	155
Chris Jack	2001	25	3	–	–	–	15
Byron Kelleher	1999	25	4	–	–	–	20
Leon MacDonald	2000	26	11*	20	5	–	110
Justin Marshall	1995	70	23	–	–	–	115
Aaron Mauger	2001	19	6	5	1	1	46
Richie McCaw	2001	21	1	–	–	–	5
Keven Mealamu	2002	13	2	–	–	–	10
Kees Meeuws	1998	35	9	–	–	–	45
Mils Muliaina	2003	14	7	–	–	–	35
Ma'a Nonu	2003	4	1	–	–	–	5
Anton Oliver	1997	41	2	–	–	–	10
Caleb Ralph	1998	13	8	–	–	–	40
Joe Rokocoko	2003	12	17	–	–	–	85
Greg Somerville	2000	34	–	–	–	–	–
Rodney So'oialo	2002	7	2	–	–	–	10
Carlos Spencer	1997	29	12	49	39	–	275
Brad Thorn	2003	12	2	–	–	–	10
Reuben Thorne	1999	41	5	–	–	–	25
Tana Umaga	1997	53	27*	–	–	–	135
Ali Williams	2002	15	1	–	–	–	5

* Includes a penalty try.